Protecting Life

Protecting Life

The Ethics of Police Deadly Force

BEN JONES

OXFORD
UNIVERSITY PRESS

Oxford University Press is a department of the University of Oxford.
It furthers the University's objective of excellence in research, scholarship,
and education by publishing worldwide. Oxford is a registered trade mark of
Oxford University Press in the UK and in certain other countries.

Published in the United States of America by Oxford University Press
198 Madison Avenue, New York, NY 10016, United States of America.

Library of Congress Cataloging-in-Publication Data
Names: Jones, Ben, 1985– author
Title: Protecting life : the ethics of police deadly force / Ben Jones.
Description: New York, NY : Oxford University Press, [2026] |
Includes bibliographical references and index. |
Identifiers: LCCN 2025047858 (print) | LCCN 2025047859 (ebook) |
ISBN 9780197823286 paperback | ISBN 9780197823279 hardback |
ISBN 9780197823316 | ISBN 9780197823293 epub
Subjects: LCSH: Police brutality | Police shootings |
Police-community relations
Classification: LCC HV7936.P725 J66 2026 (print) |
LCC HV7936.P725 (ebook)
LC record available at https://lccn.loc.gov/2025047858
LC ebook record available at https://lccn.loc.gov/2025047859

DOI: 10.1093/9780197823316.001.0001

Paperback printed by Marquis Book Printing, Canada
Hardback printed by Lightning Source, Inc., United States of America

The manufacturer's authorized representative in the EU for product safety is
Oxford University Press España S.A. of Parque Empresarial San Fernando de Henares,
Avenida de Castilla, 2 – 28830 Madrid (www.oup.es/en or product.safety@oup.com).
OUP España S.A. also acts as importer into Spain of products made by the manufacturer.

Contents

Introduction   1

PART I. ETHICAL FRAMEWORK FOR DEADLY FORCE

1. Self-Defense, Policing, and War   21

2. The Priority of Protecting Life   41

3. Distributive Justice and Deadly Force   63

PART II. CONTEMPORARY CHALLENGES

4. Aggressors with Mental Illness   85

5. Racial Disparities in Police Deadly Force   112

6. Police-Generated Killings   133

7. Fleeing "Dangerous" Suspects   155

Conclusion   182

Appendix: Model Deadly Force Policy   187
Acknowledgments   191
References   195
Index   217

Introduction

As I began research for this book, police killed someone in my college town. For State College, Pennsylvania, it was a rare event—in fact, the first fatal shooting in the hundred-year history of the town's police department (Pallotto 2021). The shooting occurred the same day that Bryan Stevenson, the civil rights icon celebrated for defending the poor and marginalized facing harsh sentences, visited Penn State. The contrast was stark. Just miles from where many gathered to hear Stevenson's message of racial justice, police were at the scene where one of their officers had fatally shot a young Black resident, Osaze Osagie (Brown and Jones 2020).

Despite being rare for State College, the killing of Osagie included features that have become all too familiar. Osagie was a young Black man with mental illness, at the intersection of two groups especially vulnerable to police violence (Saleh et al. 2018; Edwards, Lee, and Esposito 2019). There was no video of the incident and, outside of local media, the case received little attention. Like most police killings, which never make national headlines, the community was largely on its own in figuring out how to grapple with it.

The details that eventually came out were heartbreaking. Osagie's parents worried that their son, who had schizophrenia and autism, had stopped taking his medication after he had begun living on his own. They called police hoping to get help for their son. But rather than help Osagie, the officers who went to his apartment killed him. According to the police account, Osagie had a knife and charged officers shortly after they arrived to serve him a mental health warrant. Officers first tried to incapacitate Osagie with a Taser. When that failed, an officer fired multiple shots and killed him (Pallotto 2021).

Despite disagreement over exactly what went wrong in this case, most agreed that *something* went wrong. The killing of Osagie raised concerns at multiple levels. Most directly, there were questions about whether police should have acted differently in this specific encounter. Did the officers have other options that could have reduced the risk of loss of life? Did the department have in place training and equipment to ensure that their officers were in the best position

Protecting Life. Ben Jones, Oxford University Press. © Ben Jones 2026.
DOI: 10.1093/9780197823316.003.0001

to de-escalate conflicts and avoid grave harm? Should the department have had a specialized team to respond to mental health crises? The case also prompted broader questions, especially since it epitomized well-established patterns of police violence. Why does such violence fall disproportionately on already disadvantaged groups? What aspects of policing make these groups vulnerable? What societal failures beyond policing are to blame?

The emergence of Black Lives Matter pushed the public to consider these broader questions, and rightly so. If we evaluate police killings in isolation without considering background conditions of injustice, we end up with an incomplete and potentially misleading picture. When police killed Osagie, it wasn't just an individual who killed him. *The state killed him.* The state and its institutions have obligations to protect its residents, which include special obligations to protect the vulnerable like Osagie. Police killings often are a sign that those obligations are not being met.

In cases like the police killing of Osagie, many have the conviction that an injustice occurred in their community. The moral issues at stake sometimes get short shrift, however. The media and the public understandably turn their attention to law and policy, which constrain how prosecutors, judges, police chiefs, and other officials respond. Debates over the particulars of law and policy have a critical role to play. But when they crowd out attention to the moral concerns raised by deadly force incidents, we risk overlooking more fundamental questions—ones we must confront in determining what values should guide policing.

Part of the frustration today over laws and policies governing the police is that they appear at odds with certain deeply held values. When we encounter that disconnect, it is important to step back and get a clearer sense of what moral values matter most. Such reflection puts us in a better position to design law and policy.

This book is about what moral principles, at the individual and institutional level, should guide and restrain police deadly force. Beyond just identifying those principles, it looks to translate them into law and policy. The most compelling reason to use deadly force is to protect life. In an imperfect world marred by violence, deadly force is sometimes needed to protect against life-threatening and other grave threats. Yet in too many instances, police use deadly force beyond the narrow confines of when it is necessary to protect individuals from grave harm like death and serious injury. The problem goes deeper than just a few cops who are bad apples. Law, policy, and training entrench police practices at odds with what should be our goal—prioritizing the protection of life. As protests in recent years highlight, the status quo is morally untenable. It needlessly takes too many lives while undermining the legitimacy of the police. We must demand more of both the police and democratic institutions charged with overseeing them.

The Scope of the Problem

Though there is still much to learn, we have better data today on police killings than in the 2000s and early 2010s due to the efforts of journalists, researchers, and activists. Each year in the US, police kill over a thousand people (Edwards, Esposito, and Lee 2018, 1243; GBD 2019 Police Violence US Subnational Collaborators 2021, 1243–44; *Washington Post* 2024). Individuals killed are disproportionately Black, Native American, and Hispanic. Black men in particular face a heightened risk of being killed by police—well over twice as high as the risk for White men. One out of every thousand Black men are killed by police, making police violence one of the leading causes of death for young Black men (Edwards, Lee, and Esposito 2019). Data on nonfatal police shootings show even more pronounced racial disparities (Nix and Shjarback 2021). Along with Black men, persons with serious mental illness face a high risk of police violence. One study estimates they are seven times more likely to be killed by police than those without mental illness (Saleh et al. 2018, 114).

There are also notable age disparities. Those killed by police tend to be young adults, which translates into more years of life lost than if the victims were older on average. Police killings result in over fifty thousand years of life lost each year in the US, around the same number of years lost annually due to maternal deaths (Bui, Coates, and Matthay 2018, 716).

Police killings have further consequences that go beyond those directly impacted. A study of high school students in Los Angeles found that Black and Hispanic students living in close proximity to a police killing were more likely afterward to miss classes, experience a drop in grades, and be diagnosed with a chronic learning disability associated with post-traumatic stress disorder and depression (Ang 2021, 117–18). Similarly, a study of the effects of the 2014 police killing of Michael Brown and subsequent unrest found higher absenteeism and lower test scores for elementary students in Ferguson, Missouri, where the killing occurred (Gershenson and Hayes 2018). These findings are consistent with research showing that violence has profound and negative effects on student achievement (Sharkey 2018, 76–95).

As this research indicates, police violence has ripple effects throughout communities. High-profile police killings can affect people's emotional and mental health, while also undermining trust in police, especially among those most harmed by policing. After the brutal murder of George Floyd by a Minneapolis officer in 2020, the US population reported higher rates of anger, sadness, anxiety, and depression, with Black Americans experiencing the most dramatic increases (Eichstaedt et al. 2021). Other high-profile incidents of Black life lost to police violence likewise have had negative mental health impacts for Black Americans (Curtis et al. 2021). The share of Black Americans expressing confidence in the police dropped to its lowest level ever recorded by Gallup after Floyd's murder—less than 20 percent (Jones 2020). Past police brutality has had similar effects on public opinion (Weitzer 2002, 398–99, 401–3).

In many cases, this anger and distrust extend to government institutions responsible for overseeing the police. That was clear in the summer of 2020 when millions poured into the streets to protest the police killings of George Floyd, Breonna Taylor, and other Black lives. Estimates suggest that the 2020 Black Lives Matter protests may have been the largest social movement in US history (Buchanan, Bui, and Patel 2020). These protests condemned the status quo and government's failures to rein in racial bias, brutality, and other abuses by police. Research finds that protests and voting tend to increase in areas that experience police killings (Williamson, Trump, and Einstein 2018; Morris and Shoub 2024; Ang and Tebes 2024). In addition to galvanizing democratic action, police killings and brutality can cause violence and social unrest. Many of the largest urban uprisings in US history have one feature in common: police violence sparked them (DiPasquale and Glaeser 1998; Hinton 2021).

All this research suggests that the harms from police killings are substantial. Loss of life is perhaps the gravest harm one can suffer. Police who wrongfully take a person's life abuse their power by violating a fundamental right—the right to life—they are charged to protect. It should not surprise us that repeated violations of this right and the public trust have broad-ranging effects, inflicting a psychological toll beyond just those directly impacted.

Obviously, some already see police killings as a serious problem, evident from the mass protests in response to them. But concerns over police killings strike others as overblown. A common objection from skeptics is that statistics on police killings, when placed in context, turn out to be less troubling than they initially appear. For instance, police in the US come in contact with civilians millions of times each year and only a tiny percentage of these encounters prove fatal. In fact, more people die in falls, traffic accidents, accidental poisonings, or suicides than from police violence. From this perspective, the current level of police killings in the US hardly constitutes a national crisis demanding urgent action. Though regrettable, police killings should be understood as rare events (Johnson 2016).

This line of argument fails in other contexts, and there is reason to conclude that it fails here, too. Imagine after a deadly plane crash if the airline involved dismissed concerns about what went wrong by pointing to all its flights that arrived safely without incident. That response would come across as incredibly tone deaf. It displays a troubling lack of urgency to better protect life. All the flights that landed safely do not minimize the importance of learning from the crash, identifying mistakes made, developing strategies to correct those mistakes, and implementing changes to make future flights safer. Just because a particular disaster occurs infrequently doesn't mean that those responsible are morally off the hook. The number of people in the US killed by police is equivalent to several plane crashes each year. On its own, this substantial loss of life demands action. When we account for the considerable indirect harms of police killings, there is an even stronger case for addressing the problem.

Another reason given to temper worries about police killings is that the bulk of them involve armed suspects. The implication is that, when police use deadly force, most of the time it is for good reason (Johnson 2016). Popular narratives about police killings sometimes miss this point since many high-profile incidents involve unarmed victims like George Floyd and Tyre Nichols, who were both defenseless when they died at the hands of police. According to the *Washington Post*'s (2024) database of fatal police shootings in the US, over 80 percent of those killed were armed, with weapons ranging from guns to knives to bats.

The high percentage of armed individuals killed by police serves as a reminder that these incidents pose thorny challenges, often without obvious fixes. If police never again used deadly force against an unarmed and defenseless individual, it would be a welcome development, marking an end to the most egregious uses of force by police. Such a change, though, would bring only a small reduction to the overall number of police killings in the US.

It is important to recognize these nuances and grapple with the realities reflected in the data, but it does not follow that worries over police killings are unfounded. Some killings of armed suspects stem from questionable decisions by police and could have been avoided (Zimring 2017, 56–59, 100–2). Too often, officers use tactics that unnecessarily raise the risk of lethal outcomes. Moreover, lack of services and support for vulnerable groups create conditions where deadly encounters with police become more likely. Permissive gun laws also contribute to these conditions (Kivisto, Ray, and Phalen 2017; Rogna and Nguyen 2022). The fact that many police killings involve armed victims hardly means we lack policy tools to address the problem.

Common Ground in a Polarized Debate

As high-profile killings and protests have put heightened attention on policing, the public debate has become increasingly polarized. Black Lives Matter protests prompted Blue Lives Matter counterprotests, which defended the police against criticism. Like many issues in politics today, people have broken into separate camps at odds with one another. In this environment, the prospects for finding common ground seem bleak.

But common ground may not be entirely out of reach. The fundamental principle guiding this study is that police should prioritize the protection of life when making decisions about deadly force. This principle does not wholly preclude deadly force. As unpacked in greater detail in Chapter 2, the principle still allows deadly force when necessary to prevent life-threatening and other grave harm. But the principle sets a high bar for justifying deadly force by police.

One reason to see this principle as potential common ground is that many in law enforcement already endorse it. In fact, statements expressing a commitment to prioritizing the protection of life frequently appear in use-of-force policies (e.g., Association of State Criminal Investigative Agencies et al. 2020, 2). This basic principle also aligns with the expectations that many outside policing have for officers. Most people do not want to entirely take away from police the power to use deadly force. If there is an active shooter and deadly force is needed to stop the threat, we want professionals well trained in the use of deadly force to respond and minimize the loss of life. At the same time, we don't want police to shoot someone fleeing from a gas station robbery where no one was harmed simply to prevent the suspect from getting away. In this instance, deadly force likely does more to endanger life than protect it.

Identifying common ground is important but only a first step. There is the additional work of tracing out the implications of prioritizing the protection of life, which are not always obvious. Despite espousing a commitment to prioritizing the protection of life, police continue to rely on tactics at odds with the principle. For instance, no-knock raids and high-speed pursuits in response to small infractions put suspects, bystanders, and officers in greater danger. By posing greater risks to all parties involved, these tactics undermine the protection of life.

This book highlights such conflicts in policing and considers policy tools for bridging the gap between ethics and practice. It agrees with many in policing that protecting life should be a priority. It then takes seriously the task of figuring out what it means to make this principle a reality. A true commitment to prioritizing the protection of life demands, in many cases, rethinking the legal status quo and current police training and policy.

Policing and Distributive Justice

Even if there is broad agreement that police should prioritize the protection of life, the guidance offered by this principle is less straightforward when protecting one life conflicts with, or is in tension with, protecting another life. In an ideal world, police would be able to carry out their responsibilities without ever needing to resort to deadly force. But sometimes circumstances arise that make it impossible to protect everyone's life in an encounter. Ethics and law recognize various factors as relevant when determining which lives to prioritize and whether deadly force is justified, permitted, or prohibited. For instance, innocent life takes priority over the life of someone culpable for threatening unjust harm. In an active shooter scenario, where an innocent child will be killed by a school shooter unless police kill the shooter, it is better to prioritize the life of the child by killing the shooter. Who should bear harm when it is unavoidable can be understood as a matter of distributive justice (Montague 1981, 2010; Draper 1993; McMahan 2005a, 2005b). In its most basic sense, distributive justice concerns the just or fair way to distribute harms and benefits among individuals and groups.

On the question of which lives to prioritize in decisions regarding deadly force, the standard response from the ethics of policing literature is that officers should prioritize the lives of innocent civilians, then their own lives, and finally the lives of suspects (Klinger 2021, 131; del Pozo 2023, 45). This simple rule, though plausible on its face, can prove misleading. If police should prioritize their lives over suspects, does that mean they should always avoid tactics that involve taking on extra risk to save a suspect's life? That conclusion is questionable, especially when alternatives to deadly force—like de-escalation tactics—have a real chance of success but in some cases require officers to take on slightly more risk than just shooting a suspect. And it is not clear that officers always are required to prioritize the lives of innocent civilians over their own, particularly when it involves an officer effectively sacrificing themself in exchange for exceedingly low prospects of saving a civilian. Such action may be laudatory but not obligatory or even recommended. In short, we need a morally richer account of how to weight different lives during encounters than what the ethics of policing currently offers.

The conditions in which police work complicate questions of distributive justice. In the US and across the world, police carry out their jobs against background conditions of injustice. Policing often has the effect of reproducing injustice. Groups most vulnerable to police violence, such as persons with mental illness and Black Americans, also find themselves disadvantaged in other areas of life. Indeed, this aspect of police killings makes them especially controversial.

What responsibilities do police have to combat societal injustice, and what implications do these responsibilities have for the use of deadly force? On the one hand, police are not responsible for or capable of solving all of society's ills. While Chief of the Dallas Police Department, David Brown expressed frustration with the demands on his officers: "We're asking cops to do too much in this country . . . . Every societal failure, we put it off on the cops to solve. Not enough mental health funding, let the cops handle it . . . . Schools fail, let's give it to the cops . . . . Policing was never meant to solve all those problems" (Dennis, Berman, and Izadi 2016). On the other hand, it is implausible that police have *no* role in addressing persistent and systemic injustice. The police are a core institution of the state. As such, they should contribute to, rather than undermine, the state's efforts to advance distributive justice. Laws, policies, and practices related to deadly force prove relevant for distributive justice because they impact how policing's harms and benefits are distributed among individuals and groups.

If police should be a partner in efforts to advance distributive justice, that raises the question of what principles should guide those efforts. Political philosophy offers no shortage of theories of distributive justice, from libertarian to egalitarian varieties. Finding a theory with universal support is a fool's errand. No theory satisfies everyone. Still, some distributive justice principles have broader appeal and resonate more with people's intuitions than do others.

To understand police obligations or duties (terms used here interchangeably), I turn to a principle consistent with several theories of distributive justice: prioritizing the vulnerable. This principle says that the state has a special responsibility to protect vulnerable groups—those who, due to factors beyond their control, are more susceptible to suffering harm and as a result are worse off. To fulfill that responsibility and reduce the risks facing vulnerable groups, the state should give them some priority in how it distributes resources and goods in society.

The idea of prioritizing the vulnerable aligns with basic notions of fairness. It is fundamentally unfair that some, due to no fault of their own, are born into circumstances that render them more vulnerable to suffering harm. Everyone should have a fair shot in life, but that is not the case when certain groups exist under conditions of persistent vulnerability.

Some already endorse that police should advance distributive justice by prioritizing the vulnerable (del Pozo 2023, 213–15). My point is that this principle needs to carry over to the use of deadly force. Police and other institutions can advance distributive justice through developing policies and practices that reduce the risk of deadly force, especially to vulnerable groups.

Prioritizing the vulnerable does not exhaust all that can be said about distributive justice. In fact, it is common to find the principle within broader theories of justice. Many theories of justice, like what is proposed in the influential work of John Rawls (1999), make more extensive prescriptions for the structure of societal institutions and distribution of goods, as well as more extensive assumptions about morality and justice. With additional assumptions come additional sources of controversy and greater uncertainty about the claims made. So there is reason to be less confident in such a theory than an ecumenical principle, like prioritizing the vulnerable, compatible with various conceptions of justice. Starting from an ecumenical principle also proves valuable in a democratic society where people with different beliefs and values have to find ways to live together, coordinate action, and structure society. Under such conditions of pluralism, a principle that can appeal across different systems of belief has a better shot of being accepted as a point of common ground for guiding policy.

These considerations structure the book's approach to distributive justice. It starts from principles with generally broad appeal. As we will see, basic intuitions about vulnerability and culpability can take us a long way in guiding police deadly force.

If culpability and vulnerability are both relevant distributive justice considerations for police deadly force, we need to figure out how they fit together. I suggest that we can understand distributive justice as existing at two different levels. At the level of the individual encounter or micro-level, the consideration of culpability has a strong influence on how we think about the just distribution of harm (or risk of harm) among individuals. If someone has done nothing wrong or is barely culpable, it seems unfair for them to suffer grave harm. Rules on deadly force should reflect that point and give extra (though not absolute) protections to those with diminished culpability, mitigating their risk of suffering grave harm. At the societal or macro-level, the consideration of vulnerability plays a more prominent role in conceptions of justice. Certain groups are more vulnerable to police deadly force due to factors beyond their control. It is unfair for individuals in these groups to live under greater risk of being killed by police. Police and other partners, as part of their role advancing distributive justice, have institutional obligations to reduce the risk of deadly force facing vulnerable groups.

This account highlights a point sometimes overlooked in the ethical literature on force: unjust, nonideal conditions in society can affect individual and institutional obligations regarding force. For this reason, the ethics of police deadly force must grapple with questions of distributive justice. When police and democratic institutions ignore distributive justice's relationship to deadly force, they risk entrenching police's role in exacerbating societal injustice.

Should Different Rules Apply to Police?

Criminal statutes reveal different rules on deadly force for police and civilians. Such differences have long been in place, going back hundreds of years to the common law. Though laws on deadly force have changed and evolved over time, one constant has persisted: police enjoy more extensive legal rights than civilians to use deadly force. In many jurisdictions, the law imposes on civilians a duty to retreat when they can safely do so and limits their use of deadly force to only imminent threats, while these same restrictions do not apply to police.

From one perspective, it makes sense for police to have more extensive rights to use deadly force. While retaining certain rights to self-defense, civilians cede to the state the responsibility for ensuring public safety. To fulfill that responsibility and fend off threats, police need broader permissions to use deadly force.

But even if different rules for police are sometimes justified given their professional responsibilities, legal exceptions for police merit scrutiny. A bedrock legal and ethical principle is equality before the law, the presumption that the law should treat everyone equally. A law that gives police more expansive permissions to use deadly force treats police and civilians differently and goes against that presumption. Such a law is not necessarily morally suspect, but there must be a compelling reason to override the presumption in favor of equal treatment.

Countervailing forces, though, push against a critical lens. When rules have long been a part of law, policy, and practice, the fact that they have endured creates barriers to questioning them. Why mess with rules that have served their purpose for so long? But there is good reason to guard against status quo bias in this context. Especially in countries with a high per capita rate of police killings, like the US, the status quo takes life with alarming frequency (Hirschfield 2023, 472). The moral costs associated with the status quo undermine the case for deferring to it.

The question that matters is not how long a rule on police force has been around but whether it prioritizes the protection of life. Rules in conflict with that principle should be abandoned in favor of alternatives more consistent with it. This analysis sometimes reveals that more expansive permissions for police to use deadly force rest on shaky moral ground and that more stringent rules, like those on civilians, could save lives. If a rule minimizes harm in other contexts, it is worth considering whether the rule would have the same effect on policing.

Ending questionable distinctions in how the law governs deadly force by police and civilians touches on a broader debate. One worry with policing today is that the law is fundamentally unfair in how it treats officers who engage in questionable conduct. A different set of rules applies to them, allowing them to get away with rights violations that others cannot get away with. We see this frustration in debates over the judicial doctrine of qualified immunity, which shields police from legal accountability even if they violate someone's constitutional rights (Schwartz 2017). Uneven rules and lack of accountability are a dangerous combination to guard against. Together, they open the door to police abusing their power to use deadly force.

Some Remarks on Methodology

One challenge for ethical analysis that aims to inform policy is determining which features of institutions, law, and practice to hold constant and which to treat as having a real potential to change. On the one hand, if we treat all existing structures as mutable and formulate sweeping policy prescriptions to bring about a utopian future, we run the risk of offering proposals that prove infeasible and ill-suited to address the immediate challenges at hand. On the other hand, if we are too complacent and treat present imperfections as largely fixed, we risk suggesting proposals that further entrench injustice.

Given future uncertainty, we cannot escape this dilemma, but there are better and worse ways to navigate it. My strategy is to start from plausible assumptions about the present and near future, without precluding the possibility of more dramatic change in the distant future. I understand the police as a core institution of the state, whose responsibilities include protecting the rights of those within it. Some argue that we rely too heavily on the police to carry out functions that professionals with different skillsets are better positioned to handle in ways that minimize harm (e.g., Friedman 2021). Though sympathetic to that argument (see Jones and Lim forthcoming; Jones and Martin forthcoming), I don't think it makes thinking through the ethics of police deadly force any less urgent. Even in public safety systems that take certain tasks off the plates of police, there are some calls police must handle. The adoption of civilian crisis response programs across various cities in the US bears out this point. Civilian crisis responders handle calls for service related to mental illness, substance use, or homelessness that previously fell to police. For understandable safety reasons, civilian crisis response programs instruct their workers not to handle calls involving someone who has a weapon or is violent, which instead requires a police response (Midgette and Reuter 2024, 784–85). If systems of public safety move toward greater specialization, so that police no longer are the default response to calls for service, we end up with police forces *more* focused on dealing with threats that require skills in de-escalation and use of force. Under that scenario, it remains a pressing question which principles should guide how police use force—including deadly force.

In exploring those principles, the book contributes to an area of philosophy known as the ethics of defensive force. This scholarship seeks to understand what moral considerations matter when evaluating force in defense of oneself or others. It makes distinctions between when force is justified, permitted, or prohibited. The bulk of this scholarship focuses on force in war and individual self-defense (e.g., Coons and Weber 2016). Though there are examples from this scholarship on policing (e.g., Miller 2016; Bolinger 2017; Page 2019, 2023; Ford 2022; Jones 2022, 2023a, 2024; Ferzan and Harmon 2023), the body of ethical thought on police force is less extensive than what exists for war or individual self-defense. This book engages with the ethics of defensive force, drawing insights from it and taking it in new directions by thinking through its implications for a context sometimes overlooked.

Though indebted to the ethics of defensive force literature, I depart at times from approaches that have come to dominate this literature. The ethics of defensive force is known for close analysis of thought experiments and our moral intuitions in response to them. Many thought experiments are admittedly "fantastic" (Frowe 2014, 4), designed to isolate variables impacting our moral judgments and less concerned with constructing scenarios resembling our world. Thought experiments can veer into the bizarre, involving guns with a thousand chambers (Ferzan 2005, 744–45) and detached limbs used to beat others—then reattached after the beating (Quong 2020, 63)! Heavy reliance on thought experiments can come at the expense of engaging with social science research (e.g., Frowe 2014; Quong 2020), reflecting a lack of attention to whether the causal relations in the scenarios imagined approximate those in our world. I opt for a different approach. Though in some places the book's ethical analysis appeals to thought experiments—particularly when confronting arguments reliant on them—it dedicates more space to actual cases of police killings and related social science research.

Thought experiments certainly have a role in moral reasoning. Some prove valuable in illuminating the moral issues at stake and challenging our assumptions in constructive ways (Brownlee and Stemplowska 2017). But relying almost exclusively on thought experiments comes with drawbacks. Due to their artificial nature, there is little guarantee that the moral issues raised by thought experiments track the most pressing issues for a profession like policing. Jumping from one thought experiment to another can yield fine distinctions of interest to philosophers without necessarily offering concrete guidance for action and policy under real-world conditions. This limitation raises little worry for ethical analysis not concerned with informing law and policy (e.g., Frowe 2014, 2; Quong 2020, 12). But it is a problem for ethical analysis with policy aims. If our goal is to offer ethical guidance to the police and democratic institutions, we need to study incidents representative of the ethical challenges that police face (see Burri 2020b). Staying in close touch with the moral realities of policing puts us in a better position to develop strategies to navigate them.

These commitments inform my approach to a method of moral analysis known as reflective equilibrium, which involves considering general principles and testing their appeal in specific cases. A principle like "never lie" might seem appealing in the abstract but less so after realizing its implications for those who hid Jewish children during the Holocaust. Morally repugnant conclusions in concrete cases suggest the need to revise a principle. Alternating between judgments about general principles and specific cases helps refine our views. We achieve reflective equilibrium when the principles proposed, along with their prescriptions, match our intuitions across cases and levels of analysis (Rawls 1999, 40–46; Quong 2020, 15).

Actual incidents from policing and social science data serve as guardrails for this method of analysis. Starting from recent cases where police used or considered deadly force keeps the focus on dilemmas that officers confront in real life. Thought experiments, particularly ones resembling features of our world, supplement the analysis by altering key variables to better understand their moral relevance. Social science research serves as a check to ensure that the challenges considered are not aberrations but persistent issues worthy of policymakers' attention.

The reflective equilibrium strategy helps identify ethical principles to guide policy, but we need to adjust our approach when translating those principles into policy. Under the reflective equilibrium strategy, the standard way of challenging a moral principle is to point to an example in which the principle yields implausible conclusions. Counterexamples push moral theorists to refine their principles, leading to more complex and nuanced principles that aim to capture our intuitions across all relevant cases. A principle that realizes that goal has strong theoretical appeal. But just because a principle is good in theory doesn't mean it will be good in practice. A theoretically compelling principle could be a disaster as a practical guide to action due to difficulties in interpreting it, ambiguity over how to apply it, and noncompliance in upholding it. These factors complicate the task of implementing principles into policy, making for a messy process that almost always involves tradeoffs. Indeed, a feature of policy that helps it perform well on one metric can be the same reason it performs poorly on another. Rarely is a policy ideal in *every* scenario. Counterexamples can be constructive for identifying tradeoffs—in particular, areas where a policy fares poorly and may need refinement. But given the nature of policymaking, we should be cautious about treating counterexamples as decisive in this context. Pointing out a policy's downsides is not the same as showing that its downsides morally outweigh its advantages, and that we should reject it as a result.

Consider an example from criminal justice. A high burden of proof advances the goal of protecting the innocent from wrongful conviction. Yet that same policy makes it more difficult to achieve another goal, convicting the guilty. Pointing to an example of a guilty person going free due to the high burden of proof required for conviction is, by itself, not a knockdown argument against the policy. Even if imperfect in some cases, a policy may do a better job overall of realizing the moral values we care about than do alternatives, which have their own tradeoffs.

Empirical data on a policy's outcomes offer insight into how well it advances certain moral goals. So translating ethics into policy requires close engagement with social science research. There is sometimes a tendency for ethicists to see that work as outside their purview. That is understandable—most ethicists aren't trained as social scientists. But it's also the case that most social scientists aren't trained as ethicists. If ethicists don't engage with social science research and social scientists don't engage with ethics, everyone remains stuck in their silos.

We shouldn't let disciplinary boundaries get in the way of translating ethics into policy. When ethical analysis is informed by social science and vice versa, we gain a morally richer understanding of our policy goals along with evidence-based approaches to realizing them. The responsibility for translational work falls to both ethicists and social scientists. My book contributes to that work, fully aware that it is an ongoing project. At points, I note policies with ethical promise, but whose impacts require closer study. My hope is to speak not just to fellow ethicists, but also to police practitioners and social scientists interested in experimenting with strategies to bring policing closer in line with our moral commitments.

The social science I engage with primarily concerns the US. Part of the reason is practical: the bulk of the research on police deadly force looks at the US (Oramas Mora, Terrill, and Foster 2023, 12). My interdisciplinary approach lends itself to a focus on the US since it is the context with the most research on police deadly force. But there are other reasons, too. The US has been ground zero for protests of police killings, which spread throughout the world. It is not a coincidence that US policing sparked this response. Among developed democracies, the US has the highest rate of residents who die from police violence (Hirschfield 2023, 472).

This choice of focus does not mean we should downplay problems of police violence elsewhere. Other countries also deserve attention. Though some ethicists take up police deadly force in non-US contexts (e.g., Coady et al. 2000), more work is needed, especially for areas with high rates of police killings like South America (González 2021; Hirschfield 2023).

Since the book's policy recommendations primarily have the US in mind, it is important to be cautious about applying them to dramatically different contexts. That said, police around the world face common challenges. Wherever police operate, there should be a high justificatory bar for resorting to deadly force. Police and governments have an obligation to ensure that this high bar holds up in practice, not just in theory. By taking up that challenge and offering principles to navigate it, the book's suggestions have potential relevance beyond just the US.

Key Terms

The ethics of defensive force has specialized terminology to highlight and distinguish between different morally relevant factors for evaluating force. When using terms from this scholarship, I try my best to avoid needless confusion by sticking with definitions that reflect standard understandings of the concepts in question. That said, terms and definitions are not always used consistently, so inevitably there will be some incongruities in how I use terms and how others do.

For the sake of clarity, this section offers a short glossary of key terms from the ethics of defensive force used frequently throughout the book.

In many cases, I repeat and expand on the definitions below when reintroducing and looking more closely at specific concepts. The brief definitions here are not always sufficient for dealing with some of the nuances that arise with police deadly force. So throughout the book, there are further explanations of the terms. This section is by no means readers' only chance to familiarize themselves with them. The following glossary is meant as a concise reference, especially for those interested in policing but perhaps less familiar with scholarship on the ethics of defensive force (terms separated by a slash are used interchangeably).

- *Aggressor*: someone who intentionally threatens to violate another's right against being harmed
- *Culpable*: to be morally blameworthy for wrongful action—fully culpable means to lack moral justification, permission, or excuse for one's action
- *Deadly/lethal force*: force involving significant risk of death or serious bodily injury (e.g., gunfire or a knife attack)—it has the real potential to kill but does not in all cases
- *Duty/obligation*: something that one is required to do (typically, for moral or legal reasons)
- *Excuse*: mitigating circumstances that lessen or eliminate the moral blame normally associated with a wrongful action
- *Grave harm*: a harm significant enough that deadly force represents a proportionate response to avert it; specifically—death, serious bodily injury, being raped, or being kidnapped
- *Imminent/immediate threat*: danger clearly at hand that will cause harm at once absent intervention; someone posing such danger has the present (1) ability, (2) opportunity, and (3) intent to cause harm (or whose reckless, negligent, or blameless action is about to cause harm)
- *Impermissible/wrong/unjust*: refers to action that violates or threatens to violate another's rights without moral justification
- *Innocent*: not culpable, meaning that one's actions merit no moral blame because they are justified, permitted, or fully excused
- *Justified*: refers to permissible action for which there is also positive moral reason to do it
- *Liable*: to have lost moral rights—which individuals normally possess—against being harmed by others
- *Necessary*: refers to force that does not inflict harm beyond what is required to avert a threat
- *Permissible*: refers to action that is not wrong

- *Proportionate*: refers to force whose harm does not greatly exceed the harm that it seeks to prevent
- *Vulnerable*: to be susceptible to harm due to factors outside one's control (Definitions draw from Goodin 1985; McMahan 2009; Dubber 2015; Delmas 2018; Quong 2020; Association of State Criminal Investigative Agencies et al. 2020.)

Overview of What's to Come

Three central claims sum up the book's argument:

(1) Current law and policy on policing too often fail to prioritize the protection of life.

(2) Applying principles from the ethics of defensive force more consistently to policing reveals neglected obligations at the individual and institutional levels.

(3) The ethics of police deadly force must grapple with questions of distributive justice, which suggest greater protections for groups vulnerable to police violence.

I defend these claims over two parts. Part I outlines a framework for evaluating police deadly force. Part II applies that framework to contemporary challenges that face police today.

Chapter 1 opens Part I by examining how defensive force in policing compares to other contexts, specifically individual self-defense and war. In each context, three core principles—just aim, proportionality, and necessity—constitute a framework for determining when defensive force is justified. This analysis brings attention to both continuities and distinctions between policing and other domains. Chapter 2 turns to the foundational principle guiding this study, prioritizing the protection of life. Despite broad support for this principle, its meaning in practice remains unclear. Three puzzles emerge when trying to apply it: (1) justifying deadly force against grave but nonlethal threats, (2) balancing the right to life with other fundamental rights, and (3) weighing different lives under uncertainty. The ethics of policing sometimes overlooks these puzzles or offers inadequate explanations in response to them. I develop an understanding of prioritizing the protection of life to make sense of all three puzzles. Chapter 3 looks more closely at distributive justice's relevance to police deadly force. Though police killings disproportionately harm already vulnerable groups, perpetuating injustice in society, there is little agreement on how such concerns should inform the ethics of defensive force and policing. To tackle this question, I distinguish between distributive justice at the micro-level (individual encounters) and macro-level (society broadly). Depending on the level of analysis, different moral considerations have greater weight for evaluating deadly force. That distinction helps clarify the obligations of individual officers, police institutions, and other state institutions.

In Part II, each chapter takes up a specific problem that confronts policing today. Its opening two chapters—Chapter 4 and Chapter 5—illustrate more concretely the distributive justice framework outlined in Chapter 3. Chapter 4 explores the obligations that police have to aggressors with mental illness. Greater investments in mental health services have the potential to reduce police encounters with vulnerable populations but are unlikely to eliminate them, particularly in cases where individuals with mental illness have a weapon or are otherwise dangerous. I argue that such aggressors enjoy extra protections from deadly force due to their vulnerability and diminished culpability. Their vulnerability triggers *institutional* obligations to make those protections a reality, while their diminished culpability triggers *individual* obligations to do the same. Chapter 5 turns to the problem of racial disparities in police deadly force. This problem likely requires policy interventions that target the social determinants of violence, which highlights obligations for institutions beyond just the police. When systemic injustice contributes to police violence, interventions confined to policing have a role to play but by themselves are inadequate. Chapter 6 examines some of the most controversial incidents involving police—what I call *police-generated killings*. In these cases, bad police tactics create a situation where deadly force becomes necessary, becomes perceived as necessary, or occurs unintentionally. Such tactics betray a failure to prioritize the protection of life. To better uphold this principle, law and policy need to catch up by banning bad tactics. Chapter 7 considers how police should respond to fleeing suspects perceived as dangerous, even if they pose no imminent threat. Police often have more expansive permissions to use deadly force against these suspects because of their exemption from the imminence requirement, which restricts deadly force to imminent threats of grave harm. I explain what makes this exemption for police morally dubious.

The book closes by emphasizing that we should not see efforts to reduce police killings as a zero-sum game where officers necessarily lose. The police *already* lose under the status quo. Avoidable killings erode public trust while undermining the police's ability to work effectively and collaboratively with communities. It is in the police's interest to support policy changes that promote prioritizing the protection of life, especially of the vulnerable. For police administrators and policymakers ready to take up that task, the Appendix provides a model deadly force policy, which serves as a concise guide to the recommendations outlined in the preceding chapters.

PART I

ETHICAL FRAMEWORK
FOR DEADLY FORCE

1

Self-Defense, Policing, and War

In November 2002, a drone operated by the US Central Intelligence Agency (CIA) fired a missile at a car traveling through the desert of Yemen. The strike killed its intended target, Ali Qaed Senyan al-Harthi, a suspected terrorist whom the CIA believed had been involved in the bombing of the USS Cole in 2000. The strike also killed the five other occupants in the car. Though the US had used a drone once before to carry out a lethal strike in Afghanistan (Woods 2015), the 2002 strike in Yemen was the first time the US used the technology to kill a suspected terrorist outside a conflict zone (BBC 2002). It marked the start of the US's controversial program of targeted killings, which continues to this day.

A persistent dispute has been the relevant moral and legal framework for evaluating targeted killings. Should we understand them as policing or war (Downes 2004; Ratner 2007; Melzer 2008; Jones and Parrish 2016; Miller 2016, 237–70)? Much rides on that question due to the different rules governing force in the two contexts. The US government has taken the view that it is engaged in a global war against terrorist groups like al-Qaeda, so the rules of war should apply to operations targeting members of terrorist groups (Obama 2016). The rules of war are less restrictive than the rules for policing, especially against targets that pose no present danger. If we adopt the lens of war and treat suspected terrorists as enemy combatants, they enjoy fewer protections against deadly force than do criminal suspects. Since it is easier to justify targeted killings under the rules of war, it comes as little surprise that the US government opts for that framework when defending its program of targeted killings. But critics believe that the US has made a category mistake: applying the rules of war to a context where they don't belong. The result, in their view, is in an overly lax approach to using deadly force in anti-terrorism efforts.

The debate over targeted killings reveals that our judgments about the use of deadly force depend on which framework we use to evaluate it. We find deadly defensive force used in three principal domains: war, policing, and self-defense (for this discussion, self-defense includes force by civilians in defense of others). Each domain features its own moral and legal framework to evaluate force. The framework found in policing shares elements with the frameworks for self-defense and war but remains distinct from both.

Protecting Life. Ben Jones, Oxford University Press. © Ben Jones 2026.
DOI: 10.1093/9780197823316.003.0003

That point is evident from the core criteria for evaluating defensive force. In self-defense, policing, and war, three basic criteria—just aim, proportionality, and necessity—must be met to justify force. These criteria rightly set a high bar for using force. Because force is inherently harmful, there should be meaningful restrictions on its use. Someone shouldn't resort to force that lacks a just aim, is disproportionate, or is unnecessary. But though the same core criteria apply to force in self-defense, policing, and war, the details for the criteria can look different depending on the domain, changing their implications. What justifies deadly force in war may not justify it in policing, as the debate over targeted killings shows.

This chapter offers an overview of the moral landscape for defensive force. Individual self-defense represents the most fundamental level. The justifications for deadly force that apply to individual self-defense hold across all three contexts. Like civilians, police officers and soldiers can be justified in using deadly force to protect themselves or others from grave harm. But the reverse is not true. Soldiers have a justification for deadly force, gaining a military advantage in war, that civilians lack. So where does policing stand? Should police use deadly force only under the circumstances justifying its use in individual self-defense—protecting one's or another's right not to suffer grave interpersonal harm? Or is policing more like war in having an additional just aim? The idea that there is another justification for deadly force in policing—specifically, enforcing the law—has a long history going back to the common law. But current law has shifted at least partially away from this approach. As a result, there is now little consensus on which aims justify police deadly force. This chapter examines the reasons for the ambiguity. In doing so, we set the stage for returning to the subject in Chapter 2, which argues for a more restrictive view of the just aims for using deadly force in policing.

The sections below also explore the two other core criteria to justify force—proportionality and necessity—across the three domains. These constraints on force show up in both moral and legal thought. Our main focus is on the morality of deadly force. But we also consider the law when it illustrates core ethical criteria governing defensive force. By examining these criteria's similarities and differences across domains, we gain insight into them and their specific guidance for police.

The analysis shows that, in policing, proportionality and necessity more closely resemble the more restrictive form they take in self-defense than the form they take in war. There is, however, one important area of overlap between policing and war: their institutional natures. For most civilians, defensive force is a rare and peripheral concern. But police officers and soldiers belong to institutions with special authorization to use force in carrying out their objectives. This feature of the police and military comes with greater ethical responsibilities than civilians have. In particular, I suggest, the police and military have an *institutional obligation to raise the bar of necessity*. This obligation refers to the ethical requirement on police and military institutions to continually develop and improve defensive options available to officers and soldiers, better enabling them to minimize harm and protect life when taking defensive action.

Defensive Force

Defensive force represents one variety of force. What makes defensive force distinctive is its instrumental nature: its specific purpose is to prevent harm. Like all force, defensive force can and often does cause harm. But this effect should not be confused with its purpose. Harm from defensive force is never good in itself. For this reason, moral and legal frameworks for defensive force emphasize minimizing harm. Harm from defensive force is morally valuable only to the extent that it is needed to prevent other harm (McMahan 2009, 8).

Not all force is defensive. Take, for instance, lethal force used to execute a prisoner in punishment for a crime. In this case, lethal force's purpose is to inflict harm on the condemned. For proponents of retribution, the harm inflicted by the execution is intrinsically good because it ensures that the prisoner receives what they deserve.

But for defensive force, retribution should never be the motivation behind using it. If an aggressor is trying to kill you and you can prevent their deadly threat by tackling them, there is no justification for instead choosing a defensive option that would inflict greater harm, like shooting them. That is true even if the aggressor is fully culpable, motivated by cruelty, and guilty of horrific crimes. Regardless of what the aggressor deserves, defensive force's purpose remains the same: avert unjust threats through the least harmful means possible.

Keep that point in mind when thinking about defensive force by police. The police are one component of the criminal justice system, which has a range of goals that in many cases include retribution. If we believe that the state should punish certain criminals, the first step in delivering legal punishment is for police to investigate and arrest them. By contributing to this process, police advance the goal of retribution (at least in criminal justice systems with that goal). But police do not decide whether retribution is warranted. That decision comes *after* police arrest a suspect. Judges and juries ultimately decide legal punishment, not police. In some cases, a court concludes that someone arrested by police is not guilty of the charges. Police must recognize that their role in the criminal justice system is not to exact punishment, even when using force. And so in keeping with the rationale for defensive force, police should strive to minimize harm while carrying out their objectives like upholding individual rights and enforcing the law.

If police can arrest a suspect without causing physical harm to them or others, that approach is preferable to roughing someone up. So even when police are working within a system of criminal justice that embraces retribution, defensive force remains an apt lens for evaluating police force.

Some overlook or reject that the purpose of police force is distinct from retribution. We see this attitude in politicians who, trying to burnish their tough-on-crime image, encourage police to slam suspects' heads against cars and shoot shoplifters (Berman 2017; Haberman, Nehamas, and McFadden 2023). The better angels of our nature condemn such brutality, and for good reason. When police forcibly punish suspects, they invert the criminal justice process, punishing before the legal system has deliberated and determined guilt. What's more, punitive force is at odds with the prohibition on corporal punishment throughout much of the world today. The defensive force framework acts as a guardrail against police uses of force that corrupt and distort their role.

Similar guardrails are needed in self-defense and war. In these contexts, individuals confront grave threats and profound loss. Under such circumstances, there is the temptation to use force as punishment and vengeance. But as in policing, punishment must wait. Punishment is not the job of the soldier on the battlefield or the individual engaged in self-defense. Both are permitted to use force to fend off threats and, in the case of soldiers, to advance military objectives, but only under constraints prohibiting excessive and gratuitous force. Whether aggressors or enemy combatants merit punishment is a question handled by systems of justice and decided outside the heat of the moment, well after their threat has passed.

Core Justificatory Criteria: Just Aim, Proportionality, and Necessity

Even though the defining purpose of defensive force is the prevention of harm, not all defensive force is automatically justified from a moral perspective. Far from it. There is no shortage of moral pitfalls that someone using defensive force can fall victim to, which would render the force unjustified. To avoid those pitfalls, ethical thought has developed guardrails to constrain the use of defensive force. Specifically, there are three generally recognized criteria—just aim, proportionality, and necessity—that defensive force must satisfy to be justified. These criteria provide guidance to anyone considering defensive force, placing limits on its use and the harm associated with it.

First, does the force considered have a just aim? Satisfying that condition means only using defensive force to attain some moral good. The rationale behind this condition starts with the inherently harmful nature of force, a moral consideration that counts against its use. For the use of force to have a chance of being justified, it must have a positive moral reason in its favor. When force lacks a just aim, it risks harming others without any redeeming reason.

The area of just war theory known as *jus in bello*, which is concerned with the just use of force in war, includes a thin conception of just aim. Its principle of discrimination or distinction (terms used interchangeably) requires combatants to distinguish between civilians and military targets, only permitting combatants to direct force against the latter (Lazar 2017, 45). Force that kills civilians as an unintended side effect can be justified in war under limited circumstances where the force satisfies the other two criteria of proportionality and necessity. But discrimination categorically rules out force that intentionally targets civilians. Simply put, targeting civilians is an unjust aim (for an exception to that view, see Frowe 2014; for a rebuttal, see Lazar 2015).

Though the principle of discrimination *prohibits* an unjust aim, it falls short of *specifying* a just aim. Imagine a Nazi soldier during the Second World War who scrupulously followed the principle of discrimination, only firing at military objectives and never targeting civilians. Still, it would be a mistake to say that this soldier's use of force had a just aim. After all, his force contributed to a war of conquest and genocide. Since discrimination fails to guarantee a just aim, ethicists increasingly take the view that a soldier cannot fulfill their ethical obligations when it comes to using force simply by satisfying discrimination and the two complementary principles of proportionality and necessity (see Rodin 2002; McMahan 2009; Fabre 2012; Frowe 2014). To be morally justified, force in war must satisfy a richer conception of just aim, such as advancing a war that seeks to protect individuals' moral rights from being violated. For instance, Ukrainian soldiers have a just aim in fighting to fend off unjust aggression and protect their fellow citizens' rights. That is not so for Russian soldiers unjustly invading Ukraine.

For a collective endeavor like war, sometimes multiple motivations drive it. In such cases, we should focus on the primary reason for going to war when determining if its aim is just. In cases where that is unclear and we find a mix of aims, some of which are just, it may make the most sense not to let our justificatory analysis hinge on such ambiguous evidence. The analysis can turn to the criteria of proportionality and necessity to determine whether the war is justified.

In individual self-defense and policing, the just aim requirement shows up in the caveat that force's purpose should be to stop an *unjust* threat of harm. Without such a just aim, force lacks justification even if it is the only way to stop a threat. Imagine the following.

Two threats: An officer confronts a suspect with a kidnapped child and pulls out a gun to shoot the suspect because it is the only way to stop them from killing the child. The suspect's partner in crime also pulls out a gun to shoot the officer because it is the only way to stop the officer from killing the suspect.

For both the officer and the suspect's partner in crime, deadly force is required to prevent the threatened harm they confront. But there is an important moral difference between them. Only the officer has a just aim—preventing an innocent child from being killed—while the partner in crime unjustly aims to protect an aggressor who will go on to kill the child.

The second condition, proportionality, requires that force avoid inflicting harm that is notably greater than the harm it seeks to avert. Force can have a just aim yet lack justification because it would be a disproportionate response to a threat. This basic idea resonates with our intuitions. If someone attempts to slap you—an indignity, to be sure, but far from grave harm—responding with gunfire would be unjustified. It doesn't matter if deadly force is the only way to stop the slap. The disproportionate nature of the response morally rules it out.

Proportionality analysis involves comparing the harm expected from a defensive option against the harm expected from the non-defensive option—that is, doing nothing to avert a threat (McMahan 2014, 3; Quong 2023, 223; Clark 2023, 488). Now how we understand harm has a significant impact on proportionality analysis. One obvious way to assess harm is from a consequentialist perspective, which is concerned with assessing the magnitude of the negative effects from a harmful action. This perspective evaluates harm in metrics like total lives lost, number and severity of injuries suffered, physical and psychological pain experienced, and economic loss. All those factors matter from a moral perspective. But the consequentialist perspective leaves out other moral considerations. In evaluating harm, we care about deontological considerations, which refer to factors independent of a harm's magnitude that also impact our moral evaluation of it. Those factors include whether the harm falls on an innocent or culpable person, whether the harm is caused or merely allowed, or whether the harm is a means to averting a threat or a side effect of doing so. In each comparison, the second option is morally preferable. To illustrate, if one force option would kill a culpable aggressor and the other would kill an innocent bystander, it would be a mistake to treat the harms associated with these options as morally equivalent just because they each involve the loss of one life. The death of an innocent person is worse, all else equal, suggesting that we should understand the option associated with that outcome as causing greater harm.

The concept of "morally weighted harm" (Lazar 2012, 5–14)—which we will return to in Chapters 2 and 4—captures how both deontological and consequentialist considerations matter when comparing harms. This holistic concept accounts for a harm's sheer magnitude and further adjusts how it weighs a harm based on deontological considerations. If a deontological consideration counts against harm—say, it falls on an innocent person—that translates into greater morally weighted harm, and the reverse is true for a deontological consideration counting in its favor. The concept of morally weighted harm encompasses the range of concerns that are relevant when evaluating harm, making it well suited for proportionality analysis.

The third condition to justify defensive force is necessity. This condition prohibits force that causes harm beyond what is required to attain a just aim. Analyzing necessity involves asking: is there an alternative defensive option that would avert the threat while causing less harm? If so, we should choose it over more harmful options. The principle of necessity captures the widespread intuition that we should avoid inflicting more harm than is required to stop a threat. If someone attacks you with a bat—potentially a deadly weapon—and you can prevent them from harming you either by shooting them dead or tripping them, it is better to trip them. The latter protects you from injury while avoiding grave harm to the attacker, which cannot be said of the deadly force option.

This example highlights that satisfying proportionality does not guarantee satisfying necessity. Since the attacker with a bat wields a deadly weapon, shooting the attacker qualifies as a proportionate response. But despite being proportionate, deadly force in this example is not necessary. Conversely, force that satisfies necessity is not always proportionate. To return to our earlier example of someone trying to slap you, let's say that the only way to prevent the slap is to shoot the slapper. Deadly force qualifies as necessary to stop the slap since it is the only, and therefore least harmful, option for achieving that aim. Yet deadly force is clearly disproportionate in this instance. To be morally justified, defensive force must satisfy not merely proportionality or necessity. It must satisfy both.

Asking whether force is proportionate involves a different comparison than when asking whether it is necessary. Disproportionate force causes notably greater harm than it seeks to prevent. So what proportionality analysis compares is the harm from a defensive option against the harm that would result from the non-defensive option, doing nothing to avert a threat. In contrast, when analyzing necessity, we compare a defensive option's harm against the harm of other available options likely to avert a threat (McMahan 2014, 3; Clark 2023, 488). If there are several defensive options that would avert a threat, the principle of necessity recommends using the one likely to cause the least amount of harm. In sum, this constraint prohibits a defensive option when there is a less harmful alternative available for averting a threat.

Whether a defensive option is necessary depends on our underlying conception of harm. As with proportionality, both consequentialist and deontological considerations matter in the analysis. When comparing defensive options and their respective harms, it makes sense to adopt a concept like morally weighted harm, which considers both a harm's sheer magnitude and deontological concerns like who bears the harm. Under this approach, necessity can be understood as ruling out defensive options that, compared with an available alternative, fail to minimize morally weighted harm (Lazar 2012; McMahan 2016).

Which Aims Justify Police Deadly Force?

Though ethicists disagree about the just aims or purposes of policing, they continually return to certain leading proposals:

- *Protect individual moral rights enshrined in law* (Miller and Blackler 2005, 5–30; Miller 2016, 92–99)
- *Enforce the law* (Walzer 2021, 98)
- *Respond to and assist in emergencies* (Cohen 1985, 37–39; Kleinig 1996, 25–26)
- *Protect and rescue individuals threatened by violence* (del Pozo 2023, 26–46)
- *Maintain order* (del Pozo 2023, 61–88; Monaghan 2023, 126–49; Heath 2024, 36–41)
- *Promote public safety or peace* (Kleinig 1996, 27–29; Hunt 2021, 25–26)

Many of these aims overlap. When police help maintain order by resolving disputes over the use of public space, their action also can promote public safety, especially when there is the risk of unresolved disputes turning violent. The law guarantees many moral rights—like rights to life, freedom of expression, and basic human necessities provided through public goods—so protecting those rights can share the aim of enforcing the law. Much of the debate hinges on which aim is most fundamental. It could turn out that no proposal encompasses all the responsibilities properly within policing's scope, suggesting that policing has a variety of aims that cannot be reduced to a single overarching one.

We can draw insights from the debate over policing's aims without needing to fully resolve it when examining the ethics of police deadly force. Even if policing has various just aims, the aims that justify police deadly force likely constitute a shorter list. Because deadly force poses such significant harm, it faces a higher justificatory bar, which limits its justification to a narrower set of circumstances than most other police action. Given its narrower scope, an account of the ethics of police deadly force does not need to take a position on what the aims for all other police activity should be. In fact, remaining agonistic on some of these questions avoids assumptions that could unnecessarily limit the appeal of our account.

A good place to start in investigating which aims justify police deadly force is individual self-defense. Of the three defensive force domains, individual self-defense represents the most fundamental. The justifications for using force, including deadly force, in self-defense also apply to policing and war. Though the state has responsibilities to protect its inhabitants from violence, individuals retain rights to defend themselves and others threatened by unjust harm. Sometimes threats emerge where there is not enough time for the state to intervene and protect those threatened. In such cases, civilians have rights to use defensive force to protect themselves and others facing an unjust threat. A police officer and a soldier have these same rights. A civilian on the sidewalk, an officer walking a beat, and a soldier on patrol all have rights to use defensive force to fend off unjust attacks.

Only a few aims justify deadly force in self-defense. Using deadly force in self-defense can be justified when protecting someone's right to life and, more broadly, right not to suffer grave interpersonal harm—a slightly broader category that includes harms like rape and serious bodily injury along with death (see Chapter 2). That's it. Protecting other rights, such as property rights or rights against suffering minor injuries, are generally seen as insufficient reasons to justify deadly force in self-defense.

Few object to police having the same justification to use deadly force—defending against unjust threats of grave harm—as do civilians. It would be odd to say that every person's fundamental right to self-defense goes away for police officers. Indeed, taking away that right would impose an unreasonable burden on officers, as it would deprive them of moral grounds to defend themselves against unjust and deadly attacks.

Are there additional just aims for deadly force that apply to police but not civilians? Here the answer is less clear. Some of the just aims commonly associated with policing, like promoting public safety and enforcing the law, certainly overlap with the aim of protecting fundamental rights, like the right to life. The key question is whether any of these other aims justify deadly force in circumstances distinct from those where defense of life already provides a justification.

By contrast, in war, it is widely accepted that there is an additional just aim for deadly force not found in individual self-defense: military advantage. Both just war theory and international humanitarian law, which specifies the legal constraints on force in war, recognize military advantage as a just aim of deadly force by soldiers (Lazar 2017, 45). Some military targets, like enemy soldiers firing upon one's unit, pose a present threat of grave harm. Against such a target, deadly force by just combatants has an aim that also justifies force in policing and self-defense—protecting oneself and others from grave harm. But soldiers have justification to fire on military targets even if they pose no present threat. In such circumstances, force still can achieve a military advantage in the overall war effort. For instance, enemy fighter jets with their pilots nearby remain legitimate military targets even if the aircraft are parked on the runway posing no present threat. Just combatants have moral justification to strike these targets without having to wait for the pilots to take off and become active threats, since doing so achieves an important military advantage that advances the overall war effort.

Obviously, police cannot justify the use of deadly force by arguing that it would give them a military advantage. Police are not engaged in war, so striking targets to gain a military advantage makes little sense in this context. But perhaps policing is analogous to war in the following sense: it has a just aim for deadly force not found in individual self-defense. Most who take this position point to enforcing the law as the additional just aim of police deadly force (Miller 2016, 122–36; Leider 2018).

The idea that enforcing the law is a just aim of police deadly force has a long history stretching back to the common law. Under the common law, law enforcement had two recognized aims for using deadly force: (1) defense of life against threats of grave harm and (2) effecting the arrest of fleeing felony suspects (Kleinig 1996, 111). By allowing deadly force against any felony suspect where necessary to stop their escape, regardless of whether they posed a danger to others, the common law embraced enforcing the law as a distinct aim of police deadly force. That aim offers a rationale for deadly force against fleeing felons who pose no grave threat to others. In such cases, the goal of deadly force is to effect an arrest and enforce the law rather than protect others from grave harm.

Though the common law recognized enforcing the law as a just aim of police deadly force, it stopped short of taking that view for the enforcement of *any* law. Only laws whose violation constituted a felony could be enforced by deadly force. Even with that caveat, many came to doubt the common law's approach because it allowed police to shoot suspects like fleeing burglars and shoplifters where deadly force appeared disproportionate to the underlying offense.

The alternative justification that emerged further restricted the types of lawbreaking that justify police deadly force. The US Supreme Court ruling in *Tennessee v. Garner* (1985), whose approach is reflected in many state statutes, does not allow police deadly force whenever it is required to effect an arrest. Rather, such force is justified only when it is required to arrest those suspected of crimes "involving the infliction or threatened infliction of serious physical harm" (*Tennessee v. Garner* 1985, 11). By limiting police deadly force as a response to violent offenses, *Garner* looks to avoid allowing police deadly force in circumstances where it seems disproportionate.

As unease with the common law's approach led to a narrowing of the offenses that justify police deadly force, ambiguity came with it. The holding in *Garner* does not enumerate specific crimes that justify the use of deadly force when necessary to stop a suspect's escape. Rather, it limits deadly force to stopping the escape of dangerous suspects who pose "a significant threat of death or serious physical injury to the officer or others" (*Tennessee v. Garner* 1985, 1). Later in the text, the ruling explains that an officer has good reason to view a suspect as dangerous if there is probable cause that they committed a serious violent crime (*Tennessee v. Garner* 1985, 11). One might interpret this approach as endorsing enforcement of the law as a just aim of police deadly force for certain serious crimes. Yet according to *Garner*, these crimes justify police deadly force because they indicate a suspect's grave danger to others, implying that protecting individuals' rights to avoid grave harm remains the aim of police deadly force in such cases.

While the common law previously had two distinct aims for police deadly force—defense of life and arresting felony suspects to enforce the law—*Garner* mixed these aims together. Police are still justified in using deadly force to effect the arrest of certain suspects, but only those whose offense suggests that they are a grave danger to others. Is enforcing the law still a distinct aim of police deadly force—and should it be?

That question requires unpacking, and we will have to wait until Chapter 2 to take it up. The point to stress here is that there is no consensus view to report. Some see self-defense as the relevant analogy for the proper aims of police deadly force (Sherman 1980, 98; Reiman 1985, 242–46). Others see the police as having institutional responsibilities that, like the military, come with additional just aims for using deadly force (Miller 2016, 122–36). Neither view necessarily implies that the rules governing police deadly force can be wholly reduced to those governing either self-defense or war. After all, just aim is only one of three core ethical criteria for evaluating defensive force, supplemented by further rules depending on the context (e.g., the imminence requirement we will discuss in Chapter 7). Still, whatever conception of just aim we land upon significantly shapes our understanding of the proper scope of police deadly force. Fundamental disagreements about what constitutes a just aim lead to markedly different views about which circumstances justify police deadly force.

What Policing Shares with Self-Defense

When we turn to the other two core criteria for assessing when defensive force is justified, proportionality and necessity, there is greater consensus that policing should more closely follow the criteria for individual self-defense than for war. In war, the criteria are less restrictive and would have implications out of place for policing.

Let's begin with proportionality. The philosopher Jeff McMahan (2009, 20–21) makes a distinction between *narrow* and *wide proportionality*, which proves relevant when thinking about the proportionality constraint across different domains of defensive force. McMahan's distinction hinges on the concept of liability. If someone is liable, it means that through their action they have forfeited some rights people normally possess against being harmed—think an aggressor or combatant in war. When analyzing proportionality, we can ask if the harm from force would be disproportionate to those potentially *liable* to defensive harm. Alternatively, we can ask if it would be disproportionate to innocent parties *not liable* to defensive harm, like a bystander or civilian in war. Narrow and wide proportionality capture these two perspectives.

Narrow proportionality: concerns whether force would inflict disproportionate harm on aggressors or combatants (specifically, those potentially liable to defensive harm)

Wide proportionality: concerns whether force would inflict disproportionate harm on bystanders or civilians (specifically, those not liable to defensive harm)

Together, narrow and wide proportionality make up the proportionality constraint. If force is disproportionate, it inflicts excessive harm on those potentially liable to defensive harm (narrow proportionality considerations), on those not liable (wide proportionality considerations), or both. The distinction between narrow and wide proportionality helps ensure that harm to aggressors and bystanders both figure into proportionality analysis.

Analysis of wide proportionality receives greater emphasis in war than policing or self-defense. In war, the arms often employed—like missiles and bombs—pose significant risks to bystanders. Even if a soldier only intends to damage an enemy military base, the base's proximity to civilians can make it impossible to destroy the target without inflicting civilian casualties. Given those risks, the laws of war focus on avoiding *disproportionate* harm to civilians. The Geneva Conventions require that combatants consider force's potential harm to civilians and refrain from using force whose harm to civilians "would be excessive in relation to the concrete and direct military advantage anticipated" (Lazar 2017, 45). This instruction specifically focuses on wide proportionality considerations.

In contrast, just war theory and international humanitarian law pay minimal attention to narrow proportionality (McMahan 2014, 6; McMahan 2021, 17). This lack of attention is not because the concept of narrow proportionality proves incoherent in war. It is possible to imagine military force that is disproportionate in the narrow sense. If a military bombs and kills thousands of enemy combatants on a remote base, far from the primary theater of the war and contributing little to the war effort, such force appears disproportionate. The bombing kills many without gaining much military advantage to show for it. In actual wars, though, considerations of narrow proportionality receive short shrift because military assets doing little now to advance a war effort often have the potential to be deployed later in combat. The dominant view is that military targets are fair game: the military advantage gained from striking them almost always outweighs narrow proportionality concerns. Even just war theorists hoping to place meaningful constraints on military force largely concede this point. They focus instead on limiting harm to civilians by translating the principle of wide proportionality into constraints on military force.

We find a different emphasis in policing and self-defense. In these contexts, wide proportionality remains on the margins of moral analysis (McMahan 2014, 6; 2021, 17). Use of defensive force in policing and self-defense typically involves hand-to-hand combat and weapons like Tasers, knives, and guns, which pose lower risks to bystanders than missiles, bombs, and many of the destructive arms used by militaries. Compared with war, wide proportionality considerations arise less frequently in policing and self-defense.

And yet there are times when the use of force in policing and self-defense can raise wide proportionality concerns, as when gunfire directed at an attacker hits a bystander. In 2021, police responded to calls of a man threatening customers at a California department store during the winter holidays. After arriving, police saw the suspect viciously beat a woman with a bike lock, prompting an officer to fire and kill the suspect. One of his bullets struck and killed a 14-year-old girl, Valentina Orellana-Peralta, hiding in a nearby dressing room (Gorman and O'Brien 2021).

Given the risk of such outcomes, police use-of-force policies do sometimes address collateral harm to bystanders. They often are reluctant, though, to encourage wide proportionality analysis. That approach differs from the laws of war, which expect soldiers to engage in such analysis when considering force that could harm civilians. It is far less common for police policies to outline the relevant factors for determining whether force expected to harm bystanders would satisfy proportionality. Instead, policies tend to caution against using force that poses substantial risks to bystanders. The Metropolitan Police Department in Washington, DC, has in place a deadly force policy reflecting this approach: "To the greatest extent possible, members shall ensure that the use of deadly force presents no substantial risk of injury to innocent persons." The policy goes on to prohibit officers from firing their weapons into a crowd (Metropolitan Police Department of the District of Columbia 2024, 6).

Could police gunfire into a crowd ever be widely proportionate? We can imagine a thought experiment satisfying those criteria

> *Shooting into a crowd*: A suspect in a crowd is about to detonate a bomb that
> will kill 30 innocent people. The only way for police to prevent the bombing is
> to shoot in the vicinity of the suspect, which will kill the suspect and three in-
> nocent bystanders.

Despite the loss of innocent life that would result, police deadly force against
the suspect would be widely proportionate in this case. Shooting into the crowd
leads to significantly less harm than if the police held their fire—in fact, ten times
fewer innocent deaths.

Given such hypotheticals, one could conclude that Washington, DC's, policy
guidance is wrong in telling police to avoid deadly force that endangers innocent
life, like shooting into a crowd. Perhaps officers should engage in wide proportionality analysis just as soldiers do.

But the guidance in Washington, DC, is more defensible when we consider
the uncertainty that characterizes most threats police face. In contrast to *shooting
into a crowd*, police often lack full information about the severity, likelihood, and
imminence of an attacker's threat. Nor do they know for certain whether their use
of deadly force will avert the threat. Simply put, killing bystanders is a steep cost
to accept when defensive force offers only uncertain benefits. That uncertainty,
along with the fact that causing harm is worse than allowing it (as we discuss
in Chapter 7), creates a strong presumption in policing as well as self-defense
against using deadly force likely to cause grave harm to bystanders. A clear imminent threat to many lives—say, an active shooter—may in some cases override
the presumption against using deadly force that endangers bystanders. But outside such exceptions, there is understandable discomfort with making wide proportionality analysis a routine part of policing and self-defense. If force would
put innocent bystanders in harm's way, generally officers and self-defenders
should avoid it.

It is worth noting that one can appeal to similar reasoning to argue for a
stronger presumption in war against using force likely to cause civilian casualties
(McMahan 2021, 30–37). That view may be correct. Still, certain features of
war—like greater opportunities to gather intelligence and deliberate before carrying out strikes, as well as the high moral stakes of at least some conflicts where
defeat could lead to mass atrocities—distinguish it from the other two domains
of defensive force. Even if the presumption against causing civilian casualties in
war should be stronger than the standard view today, we should expect it to be
comparatively weaker than the presumption against such casualties in policing
and self-defense.

Since wide proportionality analysis tends to be discouraged in policing and
self-defense, these domains focus instead on narrow proportionality: whether

defensive force would inflict disproportionate harm on an attacker. The prevailing view treats deadly force as a proportionate response for only a small number of threats. The influential Model Penal Code recognizes four threats that justify deadly force in self-defense: death, serious bodily injury, kidnapping, and rape (Dubber 2015, 164). As discussed already, the US Supreme Court decision *Tennessee v. Garner* (1985, 1) takes a similar approach to police deadly force, only permitting it against suspects who pose "a significant threat of death or serious physical injury." War lacks the same stringent rule since the military advantage gained from deadly force can make it proportionate, even if it is not in direct response to a grave threat.

There are further parallels between policing and self-defense when we turn to the necessity constraint. As with proportionality, the necessity constraint can be broken down into narrow and wide components (Jones forthcoming).

Narrow necessity: concerns whether force would inflict unnecessary harm on aggressors or combatants (specifically, those potentially liable to defensive harm)

Wide necessity: concerns whether force would inflict unnecessary harm on bystanders or civilians (specifically, those not liable to defensive harm)

Among defensive options likely to avert a threat, narrow necessity identifies the option that would minimize harm to those who have made themselves potentially liable to defensive harm due to their unjust threats, such as aggressors. In contrast, wide necessity identifies which option would minimize harm to those who have done nothing to make themselves liable, such as bystanders.

The distinction between narrow and wide necessity proves helpful in highlighting the different ways that the constraint is applied in war, on the one hand, and self-defense and policing, on the other. Once again, wide necessity receives greater emphasis in war due to the risks military force often poses to civilians. The Geneva Conventions require combatants to "take all feasible precautions" to minimize civilian casualties when deciding on what weapons to use and how to carry out attacks. If there are several ways to achieve a similar military advantage, the principle of necessity calls for the option likely to inflict the least harm on civilians—ideally, an option that avoids all harm to civilians (Lazar 2017, 45).

The perspective of narrow necessity occasionally shows up in the ethics and laws of war. There are various prohibitions, for instance, on using weaponry that would cause unnecessary harm to enemy soldiers (McMahan 2021, 5). Narrow necessity plays a more prominent role, however, in policing and self-defense.

Within these domains, force tends to pose less serious risks to bystanders than in war, so the primary purpose of the necessity constraint is to avoid excessive harm against aggressors. The necessity constraint prohibits deadly force whenever it is not required to stop an aggressor's threat due to the availability of a less harmful option for achieving the same end. When there is a less harmful alternative, resorting to deadly force inflicts unnecessary harm.

Despite the shared emphasis on narrow necessity in policing and self-defense, the principle can have different implications for these two domains. Many ethicists and legal scholars recognize that self-defenders have a duty to retreat. If a self-defender can safely avoid an aggressor's threat by retreating, this duty prohibits using force and instead counsels getting away from the aggressor (Leverick 2006, 69–85). In effect, it requires self-defenders to include retreat among the options they consider when analyzing necessity. Defensive force lacks justification if someone instead could protect themself from harm by retreating. Under those circumstances, the option to retreat better satisfies necessity because it averts a threat without causing harm.

The duty to retreat remains limited, though, to self-defense. It generally does not apply to police, given their responsibilities. The public calls on police to intervene and confront threats, not run away from them. The duty on civilians to retreat makes sense, in part, because there are government services responsible for confronting and ensuring that threats do not persist. A civilian who retreats from an active threat should contact police, who can investigate, pursue, and take a threatening suspect into custody. Police carry out critical responsibilities related to addressing threats, allowing for the duty to retreat to apply to the rest of society (del Pozo 2023, 39–43). If police had a duty to retreat from threats, they would be unable to carry out a core aspect of their job.

Now it is important distinguish the duty to retreat from de-escalation tactics in policing, which include tactical repositioning to create distance between oneself and a suspect (del Pozo 2023, 39). Though police lack a duty to retreat, that does not mean they should rush to confront every threatening suspect. Sometimes the best way to bring a suspect into custody, consistent with the duty to avoid unnecessary harm, is to slow things down, create distance through repositioning, verbally de-escalate the situation, and wait for further back up (see Chapter 6). Such tactics do not involve retreating from a threat. Rather, they address a threat with the aim to end it while using patience to their advantage in minimizing harm.

Let's sum up, then. There is understandable reluctance in self-defense and policing to encourage analysis of wide proportionality and wide necessity. If defensive force poses substantial risks to innocent bystanders in these domains, the general rule is simply to avoid such force. In certain rare exceptions, police and civilians are justified in using force that harms bystanders—but only when it averts an especially grave and clear threat. In these two domains, analysis of wide proportionality and wide necessity lacks the established place it occupies in ethical thinking about war. Given the collateral risks that military force frequently poses, analysis of wide proportionality and wide necessity is indispensable for just war theory. Such analysis is less critical for policing and self-defense, where force typically carries a less substantial risk of physical harm to bystanders.

What Policing Shares with War

Though self-defense rather than war is generally the right analogy when considering how the principles of proportionality and necessity should constrain police use of deadly force, policing does share certain features with war. Notably, the institutional nature of both the police and the military has important implications for necessity. Unlike civilians engaged in self-defense, police and militaries have what I call an *institutional obligation to raise the bar of necessity*. This obligation captures the idea that institutions reliant on force should constantly be taking steps to minimize their need to use it.

> *Institutional obligation to raise the bar of necessity*: requirement on institutions authorized to use force, like the police and military, to provide their personnel with resources—training, equipment, weapons, and tactics—that minimize harm by narrowing the circumstances where force, especially deadly force, is necessary to achieve just aims.

To explain this obligation, it helps to look again at what necessity demands. The necessity constraint calls on those considering defensive force to compare its expected harm with the expected harm of other available options likely to avert a threat and to select the option that minimizes harm. The qualification to focus on *available* defensive options makes the analysis more manageable. We do not have to consider all hypothetical options, many of which have little practical relevance because it would be impossible for a defender to use them. But though at the moment of an attack there often is little that one can do to change the defensive options available, over a broader timeframe they can change. Preparation prior to an attack can impact the defensive options available when facing a threat. The level of force necessary to avert a threat depends, for instance, on what weapons and protective equipment the defender has on hand, as well as what defensive tactics they learned previously. Well before a threat ever arises, one can take steps to expand the defensive options available for future encounters. It is especially valuable, from a moral perspective, to add to one's repertoire defensive options that allow one to avert a threat while inflicting less harm. Having such options, compared with the counterfactual where they are unavailable, means that less harm is necessary to avert a threat.

It is doubtful that there is an obligation on civilians to expand their defensive options against potential future threats. We typically don't fault civilians who never train in defensive tactics or acquire protective equipment and weapons. And that makes sense. At least in relatively peaceful societies, civilians rarely end up facing grave threats of force. The necessity constraint still of course applies to civilians. But there is no moral expectation that they extensively prepare for such attacks and have a wide array of defensive options on hand.

There is that moral expectation for police officers and soldiers, however. Since using force is a core function of their jobs, it is standard for officers and soldiers to receive training in use of force and defensive tactics. Police and military institutions are responsible for this training, as well as for equipping officers and soldiers with tools to assist in encounters with suspects and enemy combatants. In the preparation they provide, the police and military have an obligation to implement training, equipment, weapons, and tactics that put officers and soldiers in the best position to minimize harm while pursuing their objectives. In other words, the police and military have an institutional obligation to take steps that raise the bar for when force—especially its most harmful varieties—is necessary.

This obligation aligns with common intuitions about policing and war. If a military has a weapon that is generally effective at destroying enemy targets but is so imprecise that its use frequently causes significant civilian casualties, then the military is expected to develop or acquire alternatives that better protect civilian life. Similarly, if officers use deadly force in circumstances where nonlethal tactics could have preserved human life, the public often demands the adoption of de-escalation training and tactics. Such demands go beyond just wanting officers and soldiers to exercise greater restraint. They communicate that institutions responsible for training and equipping officers and soldiers must do more to support their personnel in upholding the moral goal of minimizing harm.

So the institutional nature of policing and war impacts necessity's demands in both domains. Like individual self-defenders, police officers and soldiers have obligations to satisfy necessity and related constraints on defensive force. But unlike civilians acting in self-defense, officers and soldiers make decisions about force as part of larger institutions that have obligations to minimize force's harm. Police and military institutions continually prepare their personnel for force encounters. As a result, they are in a unique position to affect the calculations of necessity that their personnel will face. Through training, equipment, weapons, and tactics, these institutions can provide officers and soldiers with resources to minimize harm without compromising their ability to avert threats and achieve their aims. The institutional obligation to raise the bar of necessity demands those resources in both the military and policing contexts.

Policing as Its Own Domain of Defensive Force

Scholars on the ethics of defensive force haven't exactly ignored policing. But they have paid less attention to it than to individual self-defense or war. Titles like *War and Self-Defense* (Rodin 2002) and *Defensive Killing* (Frowe 2014), which examine self-defense and war but not policing, reflect where the bulk of the focus lies in the field (for a notable exception, see Miller 2016). In particular, the extensive literature on just war theory dwarfs the ethical literature on police force. Given the moral horrors of war, it is understandable why ethicists dedicate so much attention to the subject. But the comparable lack of attention on policing is somewhat puzzling. War should be, and for many countries is, an exceptional occurrence. In periods of peace, soldiers drill and train without ever going to battle. By contrast, policing is part of government's core functions. It is not uncommon for people to encounter police in their lives. Unethical use of force by police represents a persistent danger to a state's legitimacy and its people. We have good reason to remain vigilant about that danger by developing moral frameworks to minimize it.

As this chapter hopefully makes clear, policing constitutes a distinct domain of defensive force that deserves dedicated study. To be sure, the lines between domains sometimes get blurred, like with the practice of targeted killings discussed at the chapter's opening or when governments mobilize their militaries for domestic law enforcement (see González 2021; Flores-Macías and Zarkin 2021). The controversies surrounding such edge cases highlight the ethical intuitions we have about the boundaries between the domains and when force is justified in each. Cases that clash with those intuitions spark debate, as we struggle with which domain to categorize them into and which rules to apply.

Edge cases at the boundaries between the different domains represent a rich area of study but are not the focus here. This book focuses instead on deadly force by sworn officers whom we readily recognize as police due to their authorization from the state to use force in carrying out their responsibilities to enforce the law and promote public safety within a domestic context. As we delve into the topic, we generally remain well within the domain of the policing, not at its edges, which is left to others to investigate.

Now as we have seen, the ethical issues that arise with deadly force in policing overlap with many concerns we encounter when considering self-defense and war. Where there is overlap, we can draw insights from these other domains to apply to policing. Importantly, though, policing presents its own unique constellation of moral considerations. It would be a mistake to try to wholly map the ethics of police defensive force from our expectations for the other domains. But by comparing and contrasting policing with self-defense and war, we give ourselves a foundation for evaluating police deadly force to build on over the coming chapters.

2

The Priority of Protecting Life

In her memoir on becoming a reserve officer with the Metropolitan Police Department in Washington, DC, law professor Rosa Brooks details an encounter she had while looking into a potential burglary. An apartment alarm had gone off while the tenant was away, so police checked to see if anything was wrong. Brooks and her partner found the apartment door cracked open, suggesting that perhaps there was a burglar. They unholstered their guns and kept them at their sides when entering. As the two officers slowly moved through the mostly dark apartment, a figure abruptly appeared down an illuminated hallway, let out a yelp, and disappeared. It is just these circumstances—a sudden movement when officers already are primed to suspect foul play—that can lead to a burst of gunfire and someone dead. In this case, Brooks and her partner held their fire and tried calmly talking with the person in the apartment. A wet teenager soon emerged from the bathroom. It turned out that the tenant's son had come over to take a shower and do laundry but had forgotten the alarm code. There was no burglary to report. And even more importantly, everyone left the encounter alive and unharmed (Brooks 2021, 313–15).

If we take an objective perspective, knowing all the facts of the incident, the actions of Brooks and her partner were consistent with prioritizing the protection of life. The teenager in the apartment posed no danger to anyone. He was just taking a shower and doing laundry in his dad's apartment, hardly actions that make someone liable to deadly force. In light of that information, there was no moral reason for deadly force. Police should have held their fire, as Brooks and her partner did. Their restraint preserved everyone's life and avoided unnecessary grave harm. With the benefit of hindsight, this is an easy case.

Calling this an easy case, though, doesn't do justice to the officers' experience in the moment. When responding to the figure who suddenly appeared, they were operating with imperfect information. For all they knew, the person in the hallway could have been a burglar or, worse, a violent offender about to do them harm. Brooks acknowledges that she and her partner may have taken on additional risk by keeping their weapons at their side rather than pointed ahead. That decision reduced the risk of killing someone who was innocent and not a threat, which turned out to be the case. But if circumstances were different and the person in the hallway had fired at them, their decision to keep their firearms

Protecting Life. Ben Jones, Oxford University Press. © Ben Jones 2026.
DOI: 10.1093/9780197823316.003.0004

at their sides could have delayed their responses and increased their risk of being killed. In that alternative set of circumstances, their tactics look more questionable. One challenge for police is that, in many cases, they must decide whether to fire before all the facts are known.

This example illustrates some of the complications of trying to prioritize the protection of life amid the uncertainties of real life. The principle itself is popular, enjoying broad support inside and outside of policing. But just endorsing the principle does not get us very far. What is important is upholding it in practice. That is easier said than done, for the principle's implications are less clear when conditions are uncertain, when saving one life conflicts with others' rights, or when there is a serious but nonlethal threat. Despite the consensus about prioritizing the protection of life, we run into a host of questions once we try to implement it.

We need to figure out the implications of prioritizing the protection of life for messy scenarios like the one Brooks and her partner found themselves in so that officers have actionable guidance for such moments. This chapter tackles that task, with the goal of developing a fuller account of what it means to prioritize the protection of life in policing. It starts by considering the moral rationale behind the principle. The idea of prioritizing the protection of life is closely linked to the right to life. Indeed, the most straightforward justification for deadly force comes when such force is needed to prevent someone from being killed and having their right to life violated. But outside those paradigm cases, puzzles arise on whether the use of deadly force would prioritize the protection of life.

In the sections below, we consider three puzzles.

Puzzle 1: How do we reconcile justifications for deadly force against nonlethal threats with prioritizing the protection of life?

Puzzle 2: How do we balance protecting the right to life with other fundamental rights? Can the latter ever justify taking a life?

Puzzle 3: How do we prioritize the protection of life under uncertainty where a defensive option reduces the risk of harm to one life while increasing it for another?

Working through these puzzles yields a more nuanced account of prioritizing the protection of life, capable of offering concrete guidance to police.

A Principle with Broad Support

In their jobs, police have an ethical obligation to prioritize the protection of life. As the political theorist Michael Walzer (2021, 102) puts it, "the first responsibility of the police is the protection of life." This idea enjoys broad acceptance, including in law enforcement, which is evident from use-of-force policies. The National Consensus Policy on Use of Force developed by nearly a dozen law enforcement organizations, including the International Association of Chiefs of Police and Fraternal Order of Police, opens with a commitment to "value and preserve human life" (Association of State Criminal Investigative Agencies et al. 2020, 2). The US Department of Justice (2022) adopts the same language in its policy on use of force. In an executive order, President Joe Biden (2022) ordered federal law enforcement agencies to develop use-of-force policies that "reflect principles of valuing and preserving human life." When outlining its principles on use of force, the Police Executive Research Forum (2016, 34) states: "The *sanctity of human life* should be at the heart of everything an agency does." Likewise, the United Nations' (1990) principles on police force call on officers to "respect and preserve human life."

The idea that officers have an ethical obligation, tied to their professional role, to prioritize the protection of life aligns with common intuitions about police work. When an elusive suspect flees but poses no threat to life, it is wrong for police to use deadly force to stop them. Such force is a disproportionate response since preserving the suspect's life trumps the government's interest in catching them. Similarly, if police must choose between catching a thief escaping with stolen goods or saving a bystander from a potentially deadly trap left by the thief, they should save the bystander. Though police have a responsibility to enforce laws against theft, the value of life exceeds any piece of property, and thus protecting life takes priority.

Several complementary reasons explain why protecting life has such importance. Loss of life involves considerable and irrevocable harm. It robs someone of all future opportunities to participate in the joys and pleasures of this world. The harm extends to friends and family who miss out on goods from the relationship with their loved one. Understandably, we judge loss of life—especially when sudden and unexpected—as one of greatest harms a person can suffer. It is a harm that cannot be undone. If someone's car is stolen, there is a straightforward way to make them whole: replace their car. It is impossible, though, to restore a life lost. When a family receives monetary compensation after a loved one's wrongful death, the harmed parties are by no means made whole. Certain tragedies preclude that possibility.

It is true that other losses have an irreparable quality. Perhaps some property, like rare art, can never be replaced. Still, most without hesitation favor saving a human life over rare art because of the former's incomparable value (Rodin 2002, 43–48). Human beings have incommensurable value or dignity, to use the language of Immanuel Kant (1996, AK 4:434). Despite disagreement over the source of human dignity—suggestions range from our rationality and autonomy to being made in God's image (Kleinig 1991)—there is broad consensus that human life possesses that feature and demands respect. This core value informs normative expectations for a wide range of human activity. Police work is no exception.

The Right to Life

The respect we hold for human life shows up most directly, both in law and morality, in the right to life. Foundational documents, like the Universal Declaration of Human Rights and US Declaration of Independence, often begin with the right to life when enumerating core rights that must be protected. The right to life has the distinction of being the most fundamental right for obvious reason: without life, the exercise of all other rights becomes moot (Jones 2023b, 79).

Rights come with corresponding duties. In the case of the right to life, these duties are far from settled, especially duties to provide life-saving aid. What sacrifices does the right to life demand from those in a position to save a life under threat? It seems clear that positive duties exist, but the extent of these duties is less clear (Bedau 1968; Singer 1972). There is greater agreement that, at a bare minimum, the right to life imposes on us obligations not to interfere with the exercise of this right by others. In the vast majority of interpersonal interactions, respecting the right to life means that we should not take another's life.

Because of life's value and the respect that it demands, one might be tempted to endorse a categorical prohibition on taking human life: do not kill, no exceptions. Notably, pacifists take that view. There is reason, though, to question the pacifist position. Though individuals have the right to life, the sad reality is that not everyone respects that right. When rights are under attack, those targeted (as well as third parties) have moral and legal justification to defend them. Otherwise, rights would prove impotent in the face of those who seek to violate them.

In certain cases, deadly force represents the only option that can prevent an unjust aggressor from violating another's right to life. Consider a hostage taker about to kill a hostage, where the only way to prevent the hostage from being killed is for a police sniper to shoot the hostage taker. These circumstances offer the paradigmatic justification for deadly defensive force. The three conditions to justify such force discussed in Chapter 1—just aim, proportionality, and necessity—are all met. Deadly force is a proportionate response to the hostage taker's deadly threat. Such force is also necessary because no less harmful means can stop the threat. And deadly force has a just aim: protecting the hostage's right to life.

Deadly force comes with the substantial risk, of course, of taking a life. Ideally, action to protect life would avoid taking life. That outcome is most consistent with prioritizing the protection of life. But in some zero-sum scenarios, an unjust threat pits one life against another, precluding the possibility of saving every life. For such dilemmas, most share the intuition that the innocent life under attack takes priority over the unjust aggressor's life. By not respecting the right to life and putting another's life in jeopardy, the aggressor makes themself liable to deadly force. Such force against the aggressor inflicts considerable harm but is morally and legally justified. The moral good achieved—protecting the right to life against an unjust threat—outweighs the harm of taking the life of an aggressor attempting to violate that right.

When the right to life is at stake, we have the most straightforward justification for deadly force. Though taking any life inflicts substantial harm, which seems in tension with prioritizing the protection of life, such action makes moral sense when necessary to defend life from unjust attack. In those circumstances, deadly force is consistent with upholding the right to life.

Puzzle 1: Nonlethal Threats that Justify Deadly Force

The National Consensus Policy on Use of Force developed by various law enforcement organizations contains an explicit commitment to protecting human life. Shortly after stating that commitment, it includes the threat of serious bodily injury as one of the justifications for using deadly force (Association of State Criminal Investigative Agencies et al. 2020, 2–3). This provision is commonplace in laws and policies on deadly force, for both police and civilians. Yet on its face, recognizing a nonlethal threat as justification for deadly force seems at odds with prioritizing the protection of life. If protecting life should be our priority, why would preventing any harm less than death justify deadly force? Does the Consensus Policy contradict itself in embracing the protection of life as a priority while recognizing a nonlethal threat as a justification for deadly force?

To handle this puzzle, we could say that deadly force lacks justification against nonlethal threats. But that position proves unpalatable. It goes against deeply held intuitions about the amount of force permitted to fend off certain serious threats. Consider the following.

Serious bodily injury: An aggressor will paralyze an innocent person if their unjust attack is allowed to proceed. The only way to avert the attack and avoid permanent paralysis is for the person under attack to use deadly force against the aggressor.

Current criminal law takes the view that an innocent party in such circumstances is justified in using deadly force to protect themselves, even though the harm threatened against them falls short of death. Few of us, I suspect, would be comfortable denying someone the right to defend themself with deadly force against such a serious and unjust threat.

"Morally weighted harm," a concept we encountered in Chapter 1, helps explain why deadly force is justified in cases like *serious bodily injury* (Lazar 2012, 5–14). This concept captures the mix of consequentialist and deontological factors that matter in moral evaluations of harm. We care about the sheer magnitude of a harm's consequences but also deontological considerations like whether the harm falls on an innocent or culpable party. Examining situations through the lens of morally weighted harm has implications for cases in which individuals face similar potential harms, but their culpability differs. If a culpable aggressor will kill an innocent victim unless the victim kills the aggressor first, it is morally preferable for the victim to kill the aggressor. Both outcomes come with significant harm—loss of human life—but there is less morally weighted harm when the culpable party bears this harm.

We also can use morally weighted harm to evaluate defensive force in cases like *serious bodily injury*, where the potential harms facing the culpable and innocent differ. Though we generally treat death as a worse harm than serious bodily injury, both are significant. In terms of magnitude, the harm of serious bodily injury (like permanent paralysis) is significant enough that, when we factor in who bears it, serious bodily injury of an innocent victim ends up entailing greater morally weighted harm than a culpable aggressor's death.

There are limitations on the extent to which considerations like culpability and innocence affect the moral analysis. For instance, it is wrong to say that it is better to kill a culpable aggressor than allow the aggressor to slap an innocent victim. Being killed just about always entails greater morally weighted harm than being slapped. The disparity in magnitude between these harms overwhelms other factors like culpability. The concept of morally weighted harm adds nuance to the analysis without justifying deadly force against any threat, no matter how small.

This conclusion fits with the principle of proportionality. The proportionality constraint prohibits force in which the harm would far exceed the harm that it aims to prevent. The rule does not categorically bar force whose harm, in terms of its magnitude, is greater than the harm it seeks to prevent. Those trying to avert an unjust threat have some leeway to employ force greater than what they face. In *serious bodily harm*, deadly force against the aggressor to avert the threat of permanent paralysis proves consistent with the principle of proportionality.

The deadly force scenarios throughout this book often focus on cases involving a threat of *grave harm*. I use this term with a precise meaning in mind.

Grave harm: a harm significant enough that deadly force represents a proportionate response to avert it

The most obvious grave harm is death. If one faces the threat of death from an unjust aggressor, deadly force represents a proportionate response that carries the potential of inflicting the same harm threatened by the aggressor. Death, though, does not exhaust the category of grave harm. As *serious bodily harm* illustrates, there are other harms that, if they fall on the innocent, entail greater morally weighted harm than killing the party culpable for the threat. Since deadly force is a proportionate response to preventing such harms from falling on the innocent, they qualify as grave harms as defined here.

What specific harms beyond death fall in the category of grave harm, whose threat could justify deadly force as a response? This should be a short list. Taking human life in a defensive force encounter, even of a culpable aggressor, entails a significant moral loss. We should not run this risk to prevent merely minor harms like a bloody nose or the sting from a slap to the face. The moral stakes must be higher. The Model Penal Code offers a proposal consistent with this idea. It suggests a concise list of threatened harms—death, serious bodily injury, being raped, and being kidnapped—that justify deadly force as a proportionate response (Dubber 2015, 164).

This list matches common-sense intuitions about the sort of threats for which deadly force would be a proportionate response. All the threats listed in the Model Penal Code as justifications for deadly force come with the risk of acute pain and suffering during the attack, as well as adverse long-term consequences, both physically and psychologically. Serious bodily injury, being kidnapped, and being raped are grave harms that, even if not as bad as death, are considerable.

Inevitably, there will be tough cases. For instance, what specific injuries fall within the category of serious bodily injury? Though it is difficult to offer an exhaustive list free from objections—we should expect some ambiguity at the borders of this category—there is general agreement about which injuries qualify as serious. We treat injuries that permanently and significantly alter one's body and capacities, like losing a limb, organ, or sight, as serious. In contrast, injuries that will heal without long-term effects to one's capacities, like cuts and bruises, fail to qualify as serious (Rodin 2002, 43–44). Because of their more profound and lasting impacts, harms in the former list carry greater moral significance. It follows that an innocent defender is justified in using greater force to prevent such harms.

Drawing on the Model Penal Code's list of harms that justify deadly force, we can update our definition of grave harm.

> *Grave harm*: a harm significant enough that deadly force represents a proportionate response to avert it; specifically—death, serious bodily injury, being raped, or being kidnapped

As a result, use-of-force policies like the Consensus Policy are correct to include threats of grave harm short of death as justifications for deadly force. The concept of morally weighted harm explains why deadly force is justified against certain nonlethal threats. For a finite list of grave yet nonlethal harms, if they fall on an innocent party, they are morally worse than killing the culpable party who poses the nonlethal threat.

Now if certain nonlethal threats are among the justifications for deadly force, is that fact at odds with prioritizing the protection of life? I don't think we need to abandon the principle of prioritizing the protection of life. The principle rightly communicates that police work should reflect a commitment to valuing and protecting life. We just need to approach the principle with nuance. Rarely does any moral goal have absolute priority. We can recognize the protection of life as a top priority while drawing on the concept of morally weighted harm for more detailed guidance on how to weigh it against other priorities. Understood through this lens, protecting life is one component of a broader commitment to protecting individuals from grave interpersonal harm—a category that encompasses death as well as serious bodily injury, being raped, and being kidnapped. If protecting one individual from grave harm comes into conflict with protecting another from grave harm, the concept of morally weighted harm calls for giving priority to the innocent. These considerations should be at the forefront of decisions about defensive action.

Puzzle 2: Balancing the Right to Life with Other Rights

The lesson from Puzzle 1 is that the justifications for deadly force should extend beyond just the threat of death and include other threats of grave harm. Perhaps these additional justifications for deadly force do not go far enough. Individuals possess a panoply of rights in addition to the right to life, which often are enshrined in law. Though the extent of our fundamental rights is contested, most recognize a range of social, political, cultural, and economic protections that people should enjoy, from freedom of expression to rights to access basic public goods like education. In some cases, deadly force is the only way to prevent the violation of such rights and enforce laws protecting them. As mentioned in Chapter 1, this fact leads some to conclude that enforcing the law represents a just aim for deadly force distinct from defending oneself or others from grave harm (e.g., Miller 2016; Leider 2018). If that claim is right, those responsible for enforcing the law, like the police, have a justification for deadly force that civilians lack.

This proposal represents one approach to solving the puzzle taken up here. The right to life is widely recognized as the most fundamental right. As such, it should receive some priority over protecting other rights. At the same time, life would be impoverished if we *only* had the right to life with no guarantee of exercising many other rights we value. How should police balance protecting the right to life with protecting other rights guaranteed by law when making decisions about deadly force?

Seumas Miller offers perhaps the most compelling defense for treating enforcing the law as a distinct justification for police deadly force. In staking out that position, he avoids the implausible claim that police are justified in using deadly force whenever necessary to uphold the law. Some offenses like shoplifting are too minor to justify deadly force as a response, even if that is the only way to stop the suspect from escaping with stolen goods (Miller 2016, 122–23).

But other violations of the law are weightier and can justify police deadly force, in Miller's view. He illustrates that point with an example that we'll call *bank robbery*.

> *Bank robbery*: Someone robs a bank, taking millions of dollars of people's savings. Police track down the robber who will shoot officers if they try to arrest him but will not shoot anyone if left alone to enjoy his money. Officers understand the conditional nature of the threat: the risk of grave harm only arises if they try to make an arrest. (Miller 2016, 123)

Miller rejects that deadly force should be the first option police choose in response to such resistance. Initially, police should try nonlethal tactics, like containment and negotiation, in their efforts to carry out the arrest and resolve the standoff without grave harm (Miller 2016, 123–24). But Miller (2016, 126) emphasizes, "police officers need to retain as a last resort the use of lethal force to enforce the law." If containment and negotiation fail, police are morally justified in taking additional steps to make the arrest. That point holds even if attempting the arrest will prompt lethal resistance by the suspect and the need for deadly force in response.

For Miller, reasons of self-defense fail to justify deadly force in such circumstances. If the overriding goal of the officers were to protect themselves from grave harm, their option would have been "to get back into their patrol cars and return to the police station" (Miller 2016, 126). When officers instead go toward danger, try to make an arrest, and use deadly force, they aim for a different objective: enforcing the law.

I agree with Miller that the officers in *bank robbery* are justified in using deadly force as a last resort in their efforts to make an arrest. The suspect in this example differs from a merely elusive suspect who poses no grave threat to police or others but will get away, absent deadly force to stop him. Even if the elusive suspect gets away, police can continue their work, tracking and pursuing the suspect with the aim of bringing him into custody. In contrast, the suspect in *bank robbery* challenges the police's right to enforce the law at all. His deadly threat against officers seeks to preclude all enforcement efforts. If police had to give up pursuit anytime a suspect threatened lethal harm, those willing to make such threats would effectively become empowered to break the law and violate rights with impunity—an unpalatable outcome, to say the least.

Though I largely agree with Miller's substantive conclusions about how officers should handle a scenario like *bank robbery*, I am less confident that the example shows that enforcing the law offers a distinct justification for police deadly force. To see why, it's helpful to clarify what "justification" typically refers to in the context of defensive force.

If an action is justified, there is positive moral reason for it. As something that is good to do, justified action differs from merely permissible action, which is neither good nor bad from a moral perspective. It is worth noting that having *a* moral reason for action is not always sufficient for justification. After all, competing moral considerations can outweigh a reason for action so that it is no longer justified (McMahan 2009, 43). For instance, if I promised to meet a friend for lunch today, I have a moral reason to show up at the restaurant on time. But if just before our lunch meeting my spouse has a heart attack and needs me to rush her to the hospital to save her life, going to the lunch as planned no longer has moral justification. Now I still have a moral reason (keeping my promise) to meet my friend for lunch. It's just that a more compelling moral consideration (saving my wife's life) has entered the picture and changed the analysis of which action has justification.

In the context of defensive force, the potential moral reasons for using deadly force are virtually endless. Someone facing an unjust and life-threatening attack may use deadly force to avoid a painful death, to be able to provide for children and elderly parents, and to continue cultivating valued friendships. These are all moral motivations. Another person unjustly attacked may share some of these motivations while having others for using deadly force.

When we outline justifications for deadly force that could translate to law and policy, the goal isn't to list every potential moral reason for deadly force. The resulting list would be unwieldy and not a particularly helpful guide for when deadly force is justified. Some moral reasons for deadly force are not sufficient or necessary to justify such force. Whether they are present in an encounter has little bearing on questions of justification. For instance, the desire to continue caring for one's children is morally admirable, yet whether a defender has that motivation rarely is decisive for justifying deadly force. In determining whether deadly force is justified, we care about factors like the gravity of the threat and availability of nonlethal options to fend it off, not whether the defender is a parent or childless.

What we look for in justifications for deadly force are necessary and sufficient conditions that, if satisfied, puts a defender on strong moral footing for using such force. Though enforcing the law can offer a moral reason for deadly force, on closer inspection it falls short of being a necessary or sufficient condition for justifying deadly force.

Let's return to *bank robbery*, the hypothetical raised by Miller. In this scenario, whether the crime of robbery occurred ultimately has little impact on the justificatory analysis for police deadly force, at least from a moral perspective. Consider an altered version of *bank robbery*.

Bank robbery with no threat: Someone robs a bank, taking millions of dollars of people's savings. While pursued, the robber makes no threats against police. In fact, police know with certainty that the robber poses no present or future threat of grave harm to officers or others. Police also know that only deadly force will prevent the robber from escaping.

Here deadly force is necessary to enforce the law and prevent the robber's escape. Yet most would be troubled if police shot someone just to retrieve stolen property. The value of life rules out deadly force in such circumstances. Absent a threat of grave harm, police lack compelling grounds to justify deadly force, even though such force is needed to enforce the law.

The same appears true for other rights violations not involving grave harm, as defined here. People steal, embezzle, commit fraud, discriminate, pollute, and disenfranchise others. Such actions can involve egregious violations of people's rights and the law, demanding responses from government to stop them. Still, no matter how awful a rights violation is, it is difficult to justify police deadly force when no threat of grave interpersonal harm is present.

Consider the following scenario with higher stakes than *bank robbery*.

White-collar crime: Someone embezzles hundreds of millions of dollars from a retirement program before it collapses, resulting in thousands of workers losing their retirement savings. The white-collar criminal flees by piloting their plane solo to a country where they would avoid extradition. The criminal will get away unless police use deadly force to shoot down the plane.

The crime described in this case causes enormous harm—greater than the harm from the loss of property in *bank robbery*. So there is an even stronger interest in enforcing the law in *white-collar crime*. Moreover, deadly force is necessary, a last resort, to prevent the guilty party from completing their crime and getting away with hundreds of millions of dollars. If enforcing the law represents an independent justification for police deadly force, *white-collar crime* appears to satisfy the conditions to justify deadly force on those grounds. But despite part of us perhaps wanting the white-collar criminal to meet their demise, it would be morally alarming for police to shoot down the plane. When the prevention of grave harm is not at stake, enforcing the law fails to offer sufficient grounds to justify deadly force.

Cases with a threat of grave harm but no preceding crime show that enforcing the law fails to represent a necessary condition to justify deadly force. Consider this twist on *bank robbery*.

> *Grave threat from bank robbery observer*: A pedestrian who saw the bank robbery and had been following the law abruptly pulls a gun at close range as police try to ask about what they saw. Only deadly force can prevent the grave harm threatened against police.

These conditions—an unjust threat of grave harm that requires deadly force to prevent it—justify deadly force by police. Whether the person who pulls the gun on police participated in the bank robbery is irrelevant to the moral analysis. Of course, pulling a gun on police would violate the law in just about every legal system, but that legal violation does not appear to be doing the work in justifying deadly force in this scenario. Even if we imagined some Bizarro World where the law failed to prohibit the pedestrian's actions, the police still would have moral justification to use deadly force since it was necessary to protect them against an unjust threat of grave harm.

The above examples cast doubt that enforcing the law constitutes either a necessary or sufficient condition to justify police deadly force, suggesting it should not be included in formulations of the moral factors justifying such force. Notably, though, criminal law does often list violent offenses among the justifications for police deadly force. Pennsylvania's statute—which resembles the law in many other states (Stoughton, Noble, and Alpert 2020, 82–84)—states that police are justified in using deadly force if they reasonably believe such force is necessary to stop the escape of a suspect who "committed or attempted a forcible felony" (Pennsylvania General Assembly 2025, 18 Pa. Code §508). This statute provides *legal* justification for deadly force in cases where I argue that it lacks *moral* justification. Take *bank robbery with no threat*. In this case, the suspect poses no threat of grave harm. But since the suspect committed a forcible felony (robbery) and deadly force is necessary to stop their escape, the legal conditions are met to justify deadly force against them. Some may point to the inconsistency between the law and my account of the moral justification for police deadly force as reason to reject the latter.

One way to deal with this objection is to point out that moral justification is distinct from legal justification. Sometimes there is a gap between ethics and law. That is certainly true, and Chapter 7 raises specific moral concerns with the Pennsylvania statute in question (and similar ones). But there is another reason why we can reject this objection. Laws like the one in Pennsylvania do not fundamentally challenge my claim that enforcing the law fails to provide a distinct justification for police deadly force.

To see why, let's return to *bank robbery with no threat*. In this example, police know with certainty that the suspect poses no present or future threat of grave harm. Of course, in the real world, police often lack certainty about who poses such threats. The law handles this challenge by treating an attempted or completed violent offense by a suspect as an indicator that they pose a threat of grave harm. The justification for deadly force against suspects who engaged in violence and could escape is not so much about enforcing the law but about preventing them from committing future grave harm. We can question whether past violence is in fact a reliable indicator of future grave harm, which we do in Chapter 7. But the overall goal of the laws in question appears in line with the approach adopted by the US Supreme Court in *Tennessee v. Garner* (1985, 1), which only allows police deadly force against dangerous suspects who pose "a significant threat of death or serious physical injury." *Garner's* proposal resembles my own in this sense: it restricts justifications for police deadly force to threats of grave harm. In this legal framework, violent offenses indicate a threat of grave harm, which is what justifies police deadly force. So it turns out that most law in the US is consistent with my proposal that only unjust threats of grave harm justify police deadly force.

An important concern raised by Miller in *bank robbery* still needs to be addressed in working through Puzzle 2. His example highlights a troubling dynamic: the robber exploits for his own gain the value that others have for human life. Officers have a right to enforce the law. But by threatening them with death if they try to enforce the law, the robber seeks to preclude them from exercising this right. Other scenarios share this dynamic. During Reconstruction and Jim Crow, groups like the Ku Klux Klan threatened to kill Black Americans who ventured to the polls to vote. Today, protests sometimes face bomb threats to prevent the political expression planned. The rationale for making such threats is that those targeted may stop exercising guaranteed rights because they ultimately value human life more. In effect, the value we hold for human life becomes a cudgel to prevent the exercise of other rights, which utterly distorts this value. The right to life is fundamental precisely because it allows for the exercise of other rights.

For this reason, in cases like *bank robbery*, a grave threat should not be allowed to stand and interfere with people's rights. When rights protected by law are in jeopardy, police have a responsibility—tied to their professional role in upholding the law and people's rights—to ensure that rights can be freely exercised. If deadly force is necessary to remove a grave threat frustrating the exercise of basic rights, police can be justified in using it.

In Miller's view, the only way to reach that conclusion is to treat enforcing the law as a distinct justification for deadly force. But as *white-collar crime* illustrates, that approach opens the door to morally dubious uses of force. I think it's possible to restrict the justification for police deadly force to threats of grave harm, which avoids the troubling implications in cases like *white-collar crime*, without empowering those who make unjust threats from thwarting others from exercising their rights. Rather than understand enforcing the law as an independent justification for police deadly force, we should treat it as a constraint when analyzing if such force is necessary. Specifically, a defensive option entailing the permanent or indefinite loss of a fundamental right is not one officers must consider when determining which option satisfies necessity. Since enforcing the law counts as a fundamental right of police, a defensive option that completely blocks officers from enforcing the law falls outside those that merit consideration in the analysis of necessity.

This approach rules out deadly force in cases like *white-collar crime* where such force would not prevent grave harm and instead has an aim—enforcing the law—that fails to justify deadly force. At the same time, it provides justification for deadly force in *bank robbery*. In that case, preventing grave harm remains police's goal when using deadly force to confront a lethal threat while exercising their right to enforce the law.

The idea that officers and others should be free to exercise their rights without having to abandon them under threat of force has intuitive appeal. This principle comes in tension, though, with another bedrock principle from the ethics of defensive force. Notably, the duty to retreat requires abandoning a location that one has a right to occupy, if one has an opportunity to get out of a threat's way while avoiding the need for defensive force (Leverick 2006, 69–85). Despite some stand-your-ground laws that have done away with a legal duty to retreat, there remains a strong moral basis for it. Retreating from a location may be an inconvenience. Still, that inconvenience morally pales in comparison with the alternative: potentially taking a life. Though the duty to retreat is typically understood as only applying to civilians—someone who retreats from a threat should call police to handle it—we can imagine scenarios in which police have an analogous duty to de-escalate to avoid the loss of life. When police engage in forms of de-escalation like tactical repositioning, they hold off on immediately making an arrest and exercising their right to enforce the law.

How do we make sense of these competing intuitions: individuals should be free to exercise their rights, yet in certain instances they should delay doing so because it would endanger life? The answer, I believe, lies in distinguishing between temporary and indefinite obstructions of fundamental rights.

Because human life has such value, merely *temporary* delays in exercising a right can prove insufficient to justify deadly force. A civilian who is attacked in public and then retreats loses their ability to enjoy a particular space for only a short period. They can return once the threat passes. This modest burden is worth it when what is at stake is avoiding the loss of life. Likewise, if negotiation and containment delay police in enforcing the law but still result in an arrest several hours later, police have good reason to accept the delay. A life ends up being saved as a result, while police eventually succeed in enforcing the law. Similarly, when there is a grave threat against a political protest, police sometimes are justified in temporarily delaying or moving the gathering if such steps help ensure everyone's safety and avoid grave harm.

It is more difficult to accept *indefinite* obstructions of rights stemming from grave threats. In these cases, a few people hijack the value that others place in human life to undermine basic rights. If the threat is allowed to stand, the exercise of certain rights becomes precarious and perhaps even impossible. When grave threats prevent individuals from exercising legally guaranteed rights—like voting, protesting, assembling, and worshipping—the responsibility primarily falls to police to remove such obstructions. Their right to enforce the law empowers police to confront and stop threats to fundamental rights from continuing indefinitely. When those trying to block the rights of others respond to police intervention by threatening grave harm, police are justified in using deadly force, if it is necessary to prevent such harm.

So if someone poses an imminent threat to your life to stop you from expressing protected speech and you have an opportunity to escape with your life by retreating, it makes moral sense to take that option rather than responding with deadly force. In a society where police are living up to their ethical role and responsibilities, you also should call the police. They can intervene to ensure that the threat does not persist. If the person jeopardizing others' rights looks to stop free expression at all costs by threatening police who intervene, we want police committed to protecting fundamental rights and prepared to confront the threat. This is the moral rationale for sending federal troops to the US South during Reconstruction. They operated as a "standing Federal police," in the words of W. E. B. Du Bois (2007, 518), to ensure that Black Americans could exercise fundamental rights, which White supremacist groups were trying to prevent. Police in such circumstances have a right to enforce the law. Doing so in the face of a grave threat sometimes requires police to use deadly force, as a last resort to stop the threat.

To sum up, resolving Puzzle 2 does not require expanding the justifications for police deadly force beyond threats of grave harm—death, serious bodily injury, being raped, and being kidnapped. Those criteria erect a high bar and notably exclude enforcing the law as an independent justification for police deadly force. Importantly, though, police officers' right to enforce the law empowers them to confront grave threats that seek to block the exercise of fundamental rights. As part of their ethical responsibilities, police should function as a bulwark that protects fundamental rights and ensures that threats to their free exercise do not stand.

Puzzle 3: Weighing Lives Under Uncertainty

What it means to prioritize the protection of life proves especially challenging in cases where a threat pits the preservation of one life against the preservation of another. As discussed earlier, the concept of morally weighted harm helps navigate this challenge. It treats the loss of innocent life as morally worse than the loss of a culpable aggressor's life. In police training, officers commonly receive the instruction to prioritize life in the following order: (1) innocent civilians, (2) police officers, and (3) suspects (Klinger 2021, 131; del Pozo 2023, 45). If we operate under the assumption that most suspects are culpable, this rule on its face bears some resemblance to the moral principle that innocent life should receive priority over culpable life. Uncertainty, though, profoundly complicates the task of weighing lives—so much so that it can render the guidance that many officers receive unhelpful or even counterproductive.

There are two types of uncertainty worth highlighting: (1) uncertainty about the level of force needed to stop a threat and (2) uncertainty about a suspect's culpability. Many thought experiments leave out these types of uncertainty to allow for a cleaner analysis. In real life, however, it is much tougher to avoid such uncertainty in use-of-force decisions.

The first type of uncertainty often arises when confronting a threat. Officers have imperfect information on which tactics would stop a threat and the level of harm each would cause. Even in similar circumstances, the same tactic can have dramatically different consequences. Depending on where bullets land, gunfire can kill, seriously injure, cause only minor injuries, or leave others completely unscathed. It is helpful, then, to think of tactics in terms of probabilities. In an encounter, a tactic has a certain probability of stopping the threat at hand—as well as a certain probability of causing a specific level of harm. When choosing between tactics, few officers have exact probabilities in mind. But they often have a sense that one tactic gives them a better chance than another in achieving an objective like stopping a suspect's threat.

Lethal tactics can reduce the risk of grave harm for one party while increasing it for another. Such tradeoffs raise thorny questions. It counts in a tactic's favor if, compared with the alternatives, it reduces the overall risk that anyone will suffer grave harm. But what if the same tactic that reduces the overall risk of anyone suffering grave harm in an encounter nonetheless increases the risk of such harm for a particular individual in the encounter? Nonlethal defensive tactics may have this quality in some circumstances. Such tactics can lower the risk of either the aggressor or defender suffering grave harm, but when you consider the defender in isolation, they can take on some additional risk when opting for a nonlethal over a lethal tactic.

Though it is common for officers to receive instruction on prioritizing certain lives, with innocent civilians receiving the highest priority, there is less detailed guidance on how to handle tradeoffs in risks between lives. One strategy is lexical ordering. This concept, which gained prominence in philosophy through the work of John Rawls (1999, 214), takes its name from how we order words alphabetically. A word's first letter determines where it goes in an alphabetical list, unless it shares the same first letter with another word, in which case you move to each word's second letter to see which one comes first in the alphabet. If the words have the same first two letters, you go to the third letter of each word to determine their ordering, and so on. As a strategy for evaluating between options, lexical ordering specifies that any difference on the first evaluative criterion outweighs differences on all subsequent criteria (Barry 1973, 275).

Say we judge racecars on three criteria, with top-end speed being the most important criterion, acceleration rate the second most important, and gas mileage the third most important. If the Chevy has a slightly higher top-end speed than the Ford, it doesn't matter for ranking the options that the Ford beats out the Chevy on acceleration and gas mileage. The Chevy still is the better racecar under lexical ordering.

We could interpret the rule common in policing for prioritizing among lives—first innocent civilians, then police officers, and finally suspects—as lexical ordering. According to this interpretation, a tactic that slightly reduces the risk to innocent civilians should be favored even if it significantly raises the risk for police officers or suspects.

It quickly becomes evident that this interpretation runs into problems. First off, it imposes excessive burdens on police. Certainly, as part of their professional roles, police have a responsibility to protect civilian lives, which requires taking certain risks. There is disagreement on whether police should value the lives of innocent civilians more than or equally with their own (Gardner 2013; Page 2023). But even if police should give some priority to innocent civilians, treating civilians' lives as having absolute priority—as lexical ordering suggests—makes unreasonable demands on police. In some cases, it would require officers to adopt tactics that put themselves at enormous risk for only slight gains in the likelihood of saving civilians.

The police response to the September 11th attacks illustrates that there are limits on the risks we expect officers to take. After terrorists crashed two planes into the twin towers in lower Manhattan, officers from the New York City Police Department (NYPD) and other emergency responders rushed to evacuate the buildings. Many officers put their lives at risk, and some died as they tried to save those in the towers. But after the south tower fell, the NYPD ordered its officers to leave the north tower, which then collapsed 21 minutes after the order. Because of the directive to leave immediately, most officers in the north tower escaped (Dwyer and Flynn 2002). It is difficult to fault the NYPD for ordering its officers out of the north tower, given the imminent danger they were in. That point remains true even if police staying in the north tower would have marginally increased the chances of survival for civilians there. No one knew exactly when the north tower would fall. It is conceivable that continuing the evacuation efforts in the north tower could have given some civilians there a slightly better shot of escaping. Under those assumptions, the NYPD's order for its officers to leave the north tower would have been at odds with giving *absolute* priority to the lives of innocent civilians. A strict commitment to lexical ordering would require officers to accept immense risks to their lives for any increase—no matter how small—in the likelihood of saving innocent civilians.

That demand goes beyond our moral expectations for police. Officers should take on risks to save civilian lives. Yet at some point, the risks become too great and prospects for success too low for police to have an obligation to put their lives in peril. Officers' lives also matter morally—a consideration that sometimes outweighs the goal of saving civilian lives. Lexical ordering that gives absolute priority to civilian lives precludes that possibility, which casts doubt on it as a guide for policing.

Given its implausible implications, the lexical approach may appear unworthy of much attention. But it merits discussion because of its links to so-called warrior policing. Influential in the US, this approach to police training seeks to instill in officers that they are warriors in a dangerous world charged with protecting law-abiding citizens from bad guys. Warriors need to always be on the lookout for threats, suspicious of those they encounter, and unafraid to use violence for the noble end of keeping society safe from its enemies (see Sierra-Arévalo 2024). In a popular metaphor, police are sheepdogs guarding the sheep from wolves on the prowl (Stoughton 2015, 2016; Hunt 2021). If the lines between good guys and bad guys are as sharp as the warrior mindset implies, protecting the latter pales in comparison with protecting the former. The warrior mindset pushes police to take risks to protect good guys (innocent civilians and officers), not bad guys (criminal suspects). In this way, the mindset resembles a lexical approach to prioritizing life, especially when it comes to how much weight to give suspects' lives.

Here the second type of uncertainty, regarding a suspect's culpability, raises problems for the warrior mindset. The assumption that suspects are "bad guys"—or perhaps more precisely, aggressors culpable of threatening others' rights—can prove mistaken. Some suspects have done nothing wrong and are wholly innocent. Others have committed a crime but one less serious than what police suspect them of. The most rigorous studies suggest a wrongful conviction rate of between 3 and 6 percent for those in the US convicted of serious violent crimes, like rape and murder (Zalman and Norris 2021, 652). These mistakes occur *after* deliberation and reviewing the evidence. Police do not always have that luxury. So it is plausible that police judgments of culpability have a higher error rate, especially when officers are trying to determine under duress whether someone is responsible for a grave threat.

When this uncertainty mixes with the warrior mindset and a lexical approach to ordering life, the results can be morally disastrous. Recall the chapter's opening example. Brooks and her partner entered an apartment that, based on what they saw, may have been burglarized and confronted a potential suspect in the hallway. We gain a better sense of the lexical approach's shortcomings by examining what it would recommend in versions of this case where the suspect could have been a burglar. We will examine the case in two steps: initially with just the first type of uncertainty (concerning the level of force needed to stop a threat) and then also with the second type of uncertainty (concerning the suspect's culpability). The scenarios admittedly are simplified in that they assign precise probabilities to each type of uncertainty, which police rarely have. In addition, we limit the possible outcomes for each party to two: living or dying. The simplifications are primarily for the sake of illustration. They show more clearly the implications of the lexical approach under plausible risks for the officers and suspect.

In our initial analysis, there is certainty about the suspect's culpability. Say in this version of the case, officers know for certain that the suspect in the hallway committed burglary. They lack certainty, however, about the level of force needed to stop any threat the suspect may pose. Burglary is a nonviolent offense, so it is reasonable to assume that most burglars will not pose a grave threat to police. Still, the risk of grave harm to officers is not zero. Facing such uncertainty, officers can opt first for a nonlethal tactic like verbal de-escalation, as Brooks and her partner did. Or they can use deadly force in response to any sudden movement, with the goal of precluding the suspect from having a chance to cause them grave harm.

Each option comes with distinct risks. If the officers initially choose a nonlethal tactic, the suspect's risk of dying is low but not zero (e.g., the suspect could precipitate a struggle where he ultimately dies). Immediate deadly force by the officers obviously increases the suspect's risk of dying. Though police deadly force does not always reduce the risk to officers since it can prompt a lethal response, let's assume in this hypothetical that such force lowers officers' risk of death. Specifically, compared with the nonlethal tactic, police deadly force increases the suspect's chance of dying from 2 to 40 percent, while it decreases the risk of one officer dying from 2 to 1 percent and the risk of two officers dying from 1 to 0.5 percent.

Given the risks associated with each tactic, if the scenario played out a hundred times, we would expect the following difference in lives lost between the lethal and nonlethal tactic.

Lethal tactic: 2 innocent officer deaths, 40 culpable suspect deaths (42 total deaths)

Nonlethal tactic: 4 innocent officer deaths, 2 culpable suspect deaths (6 total deaths)

Lexical ordering, which the warrior mindset seems to favor, recommends police deadly force as the better of the two options because it saves more innocent lives, regardless of the dramatic disparity in overall lives lost.

For many, that implication is reason enough to reject lexical ordering as a guide to police deadly force. The problem with lexical ordering is not that it gives priority to innocent life. That principle is fundamental to the ethics of defensive force. The problem instead with lexical ordering is the extent to which it discounts the lives of those culpable for some wrong. It is willing to put their lives at dramatically greater risk for only slight improvements in protecting innocent life.

Lexical ordering, in which suspects' lives receive the lowest priority, proves even less appealing when we introduce the second type of uncertainty. Brooks and her partner did not know if the person they saw in the hallway was a burglar. Say that a potential suspect in such circumstances is innocent 20 percent of the time. That wrinkle has a morally meaningful impact on the expected outcomes for the two tactics over a hundred iterations of our hypothetical.

Lethal tactic: 2 innocent officer deaths, 8 innocent suspect deaths, 32 culpable suspect deaths (42 total deaths)

Nonlethal tactic: 4 innocent officer deaths, 0.4 innocent suspect deaths, 1.6 culpable suspect deaths (6 total deaths)

The lethal tactic still saves more officer lives than the nonlethal tactic. As in the initial version of this example, a rule that gives lexical priority to officers over suspects favors police deadly force. But now the rule no longer saves the most innocent lives. In fact, it recommends action that takes more culpable *and* innocent lives.

Since the category of suspect is only a proxy for who is culpable and is regularly mistaken, innocent people get swept into it. Deeply discounting suspects' lives in decisions regarding deadly force, as the warrior mindset does, leaves innocent people at significant risk. Despite priding itself on protecting the "good guys," the warrior mindset too often undermines the protection of innocent life. The encounter recounted by Brooks is a case in point. If she and her partner had entered the apartment with the warrior mindset, an innocent teenager may well have died.

A rigid ordering of life, where some lives receive absolute priority over others, proves morally untenable in a world full of uncertainty. The warrior mindset stands as a barrier to appreciating that uncertainty. If police are going to prioritize the protection of life in any sort of defensible way, they must reject the warrior mindset.

So far, the recommendations of this section have been wholly negative. The focus has been on how *not* to solve Puzzle 3. In rejecting lexical ordering as a rule for prioritizing among lives, we advance our ethical knowledge in a practical and valuable way, given the rule's influence on policing via the warrior mindset. Still, it is natural to ask: what should police do instead?

The thorny nature of Puzzle 3 may not lend itself to precise solutions. Part of the appeal of lexical ordering is that, in uncertain circumstances, it offers a clear rule for officers to follow. The rule's implausible and alarming conclusions ultimately doom it. Yet rejecting it comes at a cost: officers face Puzzle 3 without a clear rule to guide them.

We could try to develop a formula consisting of variables for the types of uncertainty discussed here. We might plug in probabilities for these variables, and the formula would recommend a defensive option for police. It is hard to see this approach succeeding given our imprecise intuitions over how much weight to give different lives when prioritizing among them. A formula relying on exact weights would cover over rather than reflect that uncertainty. What's more, officers rarely have exact probabilities for a suspect's culpability or a tactic's effectiveness. A formula demanding values we do not know would be little help in practice.

Our best hope for offering police guidance to Puzzle 3 lies instead, I suggest, in a more piecemeal approach. We can identify scenarios involving uncertain threats that police regularly confront. Close analysis of such cases brings to the fore our moral intuitions about how best to prioritize among lives in the context of characteristic threats that arise in policing. For instance, whether a suspect has a knife or gun affects the risks to officers and others, with implications for what police response strikes the best balance in protecting the different lives at stake. Much of Part II engages in exactly this sort of analysis.

A More Nuanced Account of Prioritizing the Protection of Life

The three puzzles discussed in this chapter complicate the question of how to prioritize the protection of life. That is why these puzzles are valuable. They reveal nuances that, if ignored, would leave police on shaky moral ground when making decisions about using deadly force. Without these nuances, the principle of prioritizing the protection of life risks being little more than empty rhetoric. But with these nuances, the principle takes shape in a way that can offer more concrete guidance to officers in navigating challenges in their jobs.

What emerges is a conception of prioritizing the protection of life that places stringent constraints on deadly force. Only the threat of grave harm can justify such force by police. Contrary to what some suggest, enforcing the law fails to offer its own distinct justification for police to use deadly force. At the same time, a commitment to protecting life does not require police to retreat from grave threats that block the exercise of fundamental rights. Uncertainty over suspects' culpability and tactics' effectiveness makes it difficult to decide how best to prioritize various lives at stake. While there are no easy answers, we can clearly reject one approach: the warrior mindset and its suggestion that officers should deeply discount the value of suspects' lives. In its stark vision of good against evil, the warrior mindset offers a vision of the world that leaves little room for uncertainty and moral ambiguity. Instead of dismissing those inextricable features of police work, officers need to learn to live with them. Nowhere is that truer than when considering the weightiest decision they can face—whether to use deadly force.

3

Distributive Justice and Deadly Force

By his early thirties, Philando Castile had been pulled over around fifty times, mostly for minor infractions. Just trying to get to work, pick up food, and run errands, Castile's life kept getting interrupted by police. Still, he didn't show any frustration in July 2016 when he was pulled over yet again in a suburb of Saint Paul, Minnesota. The reason given for the stop was a broken taillight—an infraction police typically ignore. Video of the stop shows Castile complying with the officer, politely answering his questions, and calmly letting the officer know that he had a gun and license to carry it. While Castile reached for his identification—something drivers across the country do every day during traffic stops—Officer Jeronimo Yanez shot him multiple times as Castile's horrified girlfriend looked on from the passenger seat (LaFraniere and Smith 2016). Throughout the encounter, Castile never did anything threatening. He was enmeshed, though, in a world that perceived him as a threat. It ultimately took his life.

Several factors put Castile at greater risk. He needed to drive to get to work. But challenges for low-income drivers—like no insurance and operating older vehicles with broken taillights and other defects—kept resulting in traffic stops, compounding the fines that he owed (LaFraniere and Smith 2016). Castile's race also made him a target. Data from across the US show that police stop and search Black drivers at significantly higher rates than White drivers. Notably, searches of Black drivers are less likely to turn up contraband, implying a lower bar for searching them, and disparities in traffic stops are less pronounced at night when it is harder to discern a driver's race (Pierson et al. 2020, 738–39; see also Epp, Maynard-Moody, and Haider-Markel 2014; Baumgartner, Epp, and Shoub 2018). These findings strongly suggest that Black drivers face pervasive racial bias from police in traffic enforcement.

Despite the obstacles stacked against him, Castile tried his best to overcome them. He worked in a school cafeteria, where "Mr. Phil" was beloved by the students, and saved up enough money to pay off many of his fines and buy auto insurance (LaFraniere and Smith 2016; Smith 2016). But these efforts weren't enough. From the start, the officers who pulled Castile over that final time treated him as a threat. They mistakenly believed he matched the description of a robbery suspect due to, in their words, his "wide-set nose" (Peralta and Corley

Protecting Life. Ben Jones, Oxford University Press. © Ben Jones 2026.
DOI: 10.1093/9780197823316.003.0005

2016). How officers perceived Castile throughout his life increased his vulnerability to police violence.

As illustrated by this incident, police killings hit marginalized groups the hardest. Such patterns of police violence exacerbate entrenched disadvantages for certain groups, which make them especially troubling. Deadly force incidents like the one that killed Castile are moral failures: they needlessly take human life. We would have strong reason to prevent them even if everyone had roughly the same chance of suffering such violence. But in reality, police killings are not evenly distributed throughout the population. They especially harm already vulnerable groups. That aspect of policing raises worries related to distributive justice, which concerns how to fairly allocate benefits and burdens in society. Police practices prove at odds with a widely recognized principle of distributive justice: giving some priority to the vulnerable and marginalized when allocating benefits. The state has obligations to advance distributive justice, and as an institution of the state, the police should be a partner in, rather than barrier to, that work.

Existing scholarship on the ethics of defensive force has trouble making sense of the distributive justice concerns raised by police killings. First off, there is disagreement on whether distributive justice is relevant to the ethics of defensive force. Even among those who claim it is, there is a tendency to evaluate force encounters in isolation, disconnected from background conditions of injustice. That approach leaves little room for considering the moral implications of how patterns of deadly force interact with broader injustices in society.

This chapter looks to clarify distributive justice's relevance for the ethics of defensive force, especially police deadly force. I distinguish between two levels of distributive justice: the micro-level (individual interactions) and the macro-level (society broadly). This distinction highlights the different moral considerations that matter depending on our level of analysis. At the micro-level, individuals' culpability especially impacts how we understand justice. It seems unfair for someone who has done nothing or little wrong to suffer grave harm from deadly force. The rules guiding individual use of deadly force should provide extra protection to those with diminished culpability. At the macro-level, the consideration of vulnerability takes on a more salient role in prescribing action. It is unfair that members of certain groups, due to factors beyond their control, are more vulnerable than others to experiencing force and its harms. State institutions, including the police, have obligations to reduce the risk facing the vulnerable. Together, micro- and macro-level principles ultimately complement each other. They advance societal justice without abandoning basic notions of justice in interpersonal interactions.

Distributive Justice

Distributive justice captures the idea that there are just and fair ways—as well as unjust and unfair ways—to allocate benefits and harms among individuals. Exploring what distributive justice demands involves stepping back from how goods and resources in society are currently distributed and asking instead how they should be distributed. Commonly proposed principles for distributing resources include equality, desert, and need (Michelbach et al. 2003, 524–25; Schmidtz 2006, 13–16; Vallentyne 2007, 554–55). Even among principles widely recognized as relevant, there are disagreements over what weight to give each principle, which to prioritize, and in which contexts.

The exact borders of distributive justice and what it encompasses are also contested. John Rawls's (1999) influential text *A Theory of Justice*, first published in 1971, spurred interest and debate over distributive justice, yielding competing theories and perspectives (Van Shoelandt and Gaus 2018). This literature often focuses on economic goods, like income and wealth, and what form the state should take to ensure their just distribution. But despite being the dominant approach, a focus on economic goods always has had its critics (Olsaretti 2018).

Few question the importance of goods like income and wealth for individuals' welfare, but a conception of distributive justice limited to these goods strikes many as inadequate. For instance, the same economic resources could affect people's lives differently, depending on their circumstances. At a particular level of wealth and income, one person may have everything they need to strive, while someone with a disability who has the same wealth and income faces greater societal barriers and needs additional resources to overcome them. This point suggests that, when considering distributive justice, we cannot just look at economic metrics. We also must consider how they interact with people's capabilities to pursue their goals (Robeyns 2005). In addition, various factors beyond an individual's bundle of economic resources contribute to their welfare and ability to flourish. Without public goods like clean air, drinkable water, and a safe environment, people's health and well-being suffer, sometimes in irreparable ways. Even if there is compensation to those harmed from lack of access to public goods, more money often fails to make them whole given the nature of these harms.

A second line of critique questions the narrow focus on state institutions as the site of distributive justice. Obviously, the law and state institutions have a major impact on the distribution of benefits and harms in society. Yet structures and practices outside the state's formal institutions also have an impact. Individual decisions, habits, norms, and cultural practices all play a role in distributing goods in society, from honor to wealth (Walzer 1983; Cohen 1997). If the study of distributive justice limits itself to the state, we risk an incomplete picture of the complex processes that influence how the goods people care about are distributed.

Debates over distributive justice spill into the ethics of defensive force. When individuals are justified in, permitted to, or prohibited from using force may seem tangential to the issue at the heart of many debates over distributive justice—how to allocate economic resources within society. Nonetheless, rules on defensive force affect the distribution of considerable benefits and harms, up to and including life and death. From this perspective, distributive justice is an apt subject for the ethics of defensive force to take up. We turn next to how the ethics of defensive force literature has grappled with its relationship to distributive justice.

A Muddled Debate: Distributive Justice and Defensive Force

According to one conception of justice, the same principle (or set of principles) holds across all contexts. Perhaps the just thing to do in every context is to maximize overall utility. Though some hold this view, inevitably situations arise where a proposed principle seems out of place and leads to implausible conclusions. Should a doctor still maximize overall utility when it means having to cut open a healthy patient and distribute their organs to five other patients who will die without an organ transfer? Rather than trying to fit principles into contexts where they appear out of place, some find it more plausible that there are spheres of justice, each with its own and sometimes distinct principles for guiding action (Walzer 1983; Jacobs 2020). But even in this picture, the borders between spheres of justice are not always sharp. Matters of distributive justice, for instance, overlap with criminal justice since the distribution of resources in society has effects on crime. The lines between distributive justice and the ethics of defensive force can similarly become blurred, as when disadvantaged groups in society are disproportionately the targets of police deadly force. A natural question follows: to what extent, if at all, are distributive justice principles relevant for guiding and evaluating defensive force?

According to some, distributive justice should directly inform the ethics of defensive force. Let's call this view the *distributive justice lens* for evaluating defensive force. Most trace this position back to a 1981 article by Phillip Montague, "Self-Defense and Choosing Between Lives" (Kaufman 2008, 95; Burri 2022, 544). There he considers cases of self-defense where harm is unavoidable: either an innocent person under attack will be killed or, if they defend themself with necessary and proportionate force, the unjust aggressor will be killed. In such cases, he argues, it is *"a matter of basic justice"* that harm should fall on the person at fault for creating circumstances where grave harm is unavoidable (Montague 1981, 215). Montague (2010, 86) reiterates this position in a later article, where he endorses more explicitly the idea that "distributive justice" best explains the permission to kill "culpable attackers in self-defense." In his view, there are just and unjust ways to distribute unavoidable harm in cases of self-defense. Specifically, the culpable should bear such harm.

Others have followed Montague in adopting the distributive justice lens (e.g., Draper 1993). Its embrace by Jeff McMahan—the most influential just war theorist of the 21st century—elevated distributive justice's prominence in debates over the ethics of defensive force. McMahan develops a theory of who is liable to defensive force—that is, who loses the rights they normally possess against being attacked and harmed. In his view, the best explanation of who is liable draws on the idea that self-defense is "a matter of justice in the distribution of harm" (McMahan 2005b, 772; see also McMahan 2005a, 395; 2011, 552).

McMahan departs from Montague in identifying moral responsibility for unavoidable harm (rather than culpability) as the factor that makes someone liable to defensive force. This move expands who is liable to defensive force since moral responsibility is a broader category than culpability. When someone acts with agency and has control over their actions, we typically understand them as being morally responsible for those actions and their foreseeable consequences. One can be morally responsible for praiseworthy or blameworthy actions. Culpability is a subset of moral responsibility—to be culpable for an action means that one is also morally responsible for it—but only applies in cases of blameworthy action (Lazar 2009, 701). Despite endorsing a different basis for liability, McMahan (2002, 403, fn. 124) acknowledges his debt to Montague in making sense of self-defense in scenarios involving a forced choice where harm must fall on one party or the other.

The different conclusions reached by Montague and McMahan highlight how appealing to one theory of distributive justice over another can alter the analysis. When McMahan and others (e.g., Otsuka 2016) point to moral responsibility as the basis for liability to defensive force, they appeal to principles associated with luck egalitarianism (Gordon-Solmon 2018). This theory of distributive justice says that everyone should have equal opportunities to succeed, which it takes to mean that justice requires remedies for misfortunes beyond someone's control but not misfortunes from voluntary risks that turn out badly. In the context of self-defense, luck egalitarian principles suggest that someone who engages in morally permissible action involving foreseeable risk can be liable to defensive force when that risk transpires.

Consider the thought experiment most often cited to illustrate this idea.

Conscientious driver: Due to a freak accident, a conscientious driver loses control of their car and will kill a pedestrian unless the pedestrian blows up the car with a grenade.

The driver does nothing wrong—conscientious driving is, after all, a permissible activity—but they are morally responsible for their decision to drive and thereby impose risks on others.

According to McMahan's luck-egalitarian approach, since the conscientious driver is morally responsible for a grave threat, they are liable to deadly force (McMahan 2005a, 393–94; 2009, 165–66). In contrast, a theory of distributive justice grounded in notions of desert suggests that the driver is not liable to deadly force because they did nothing wrong.

Not all who study the ethics of defensive force welcome the distributive justice lens. Some reasons for skepticism are easy to address. Take the claim that distributive justice concerns only benefits—wealth, healthcare, property, and the like—so the concept is ill-suited for determining who should bear harms in encounters involving force (Kaufman 2008, 106). This objection overlooks an obvious point: the benefits considered in theories of distributive justice also entail certain burdens, like taxes and constraints on liberty to preserve public goods. Distributive justice is as much about how to distribute those burdens as it is about how to distribute the benefits resulting from them (Montague 2010, 90). Yes, the ethics of defensive force deals with the distribution of harms and burdens, but so does distributive justice. That is hardly a reason to see distributive justice as irrelevant to the ethics of defensive force.

There remains the broader worry that analyzing the ethics of defensive force through the lens of distributive justice brings normative principles to a sphere where they do not belong. Susanne Burri (2022, 540) expresses this concern: "liability to defensive harm is a distinctly localised affair, whereas determinations of distributive justice are sensitive to wider societal considerations." In her view, distributive justice specifies the allocation of benefits and harms for the whole of society and is not meant to guide interpersonal interactions on who can harm whom. Jonathan Quong takes a similar position. Distributive justice has priority, he claims, in the sense that we first must figure out what rightfully belongs to everyone in society. Only after we settle those distributive justice questions can we turn to the ethics of defensive force, which offers distinct principles on when individuals are permitted to use force to protect against threats to their possessions, including life and limb. This view outlined by Quong offers an alternative to the distributive justice lens. It treats "the morality of defensive force" as "downstream from questions of social or distributive justice" (Quong 2020, 7).

Those embracing this view draw sharp distinctions between their position and the distributive lens, but the distinctions turn out to be blurrier than suggested. After criticizing the distributive justice lens, Burri (2022, 550–52) concludes that culpability (or something close to it) is likely the most compelling ground for determining who is liable to defensive harm. Montague, who champions and first introduced the distributive justice lens into the ethics of defensive force, also believes culpability is the relevant criterion to determine which party should bear unavoidable harm. The person to blame for such harm should be the one who suffers it, in his view. Given their similar conclusions, much of the dispute between Burri and Montague comes down to differences in terminology rather than differences in substantive recommendations. In encounters involving unavoidable harm, both Burri and Montague believe that there is justification for defensive force that shifts harm to the culpable party (assuming that the force is proportionate and necessary). Their disagreement comes down to whether to use the term "distributive justice" to describe that approach. Burri chooses to reserve that term for normative principles guiding the distribution of benefits and harms at the societal rather than individual level.

In Quong's argument, his method obscures distributive justice's relevance for defensive force. As he admits, his account of the ethics of defensive force engages in "a fair bit of idealization" (Quong 2020, 13). He assumes a society characterized by the just allocation of rights and property. Under those conditions, he considers individuals' permissions to use force to defend what rightfully belongs to them from threats. "The real world looks nothing like this," Quong (2020, 13) notes. What results is an odd form of idealization: a society that perfectly embodies distributive justice yet remains plagued by violence, judging from Quong's thought experiments, in which Victim repeatedly faces down mortal threats. Even if we accept Quong's claim that the distributive justice lens is ill-suited for this context, it is less clear that this lens is inappropriate for the real world, which *is* characterized by background conditions of injustice.

When persistent injustice distorts the distribution of certain benefits and harms, which appears true in the case of police deadly force, it is important to be sensitive to how this reality affects individual obligations. Combating unjust forms of disadvantage often requires a broad range of actions by grassroots movements, policymakers, and everyday people changing their behavior. In short, advancing justice is a shared project that individuals have an obligation to contribute to. Our thinking about ethics should reflect that point.

The flaw with Quong's approach is that it leaves little room, in the context of the ethics of defensive force, to consider how an unjust world may alter the obligations of individuals and institutions. If, when formulating principles for the ethics of defensive force, we operate under the assumption that rights and resources are fairly distributed in society, our principles may prove limited in messy social conditions marked by injustice. In particular, they are apt to miss how obligations to advance justice interact with the ethics of defensive force. This is a point we return to later in the chapter and illustrate more concretely in Chapters 4 and 5 when considering police deadly force against two marginalized groups, persons with mental illness and Black Americans.

Unfortunately, theorists who endorse applying a distributive justice lens to the ethics of defensive force do not fare much better in accounting for how unjust conditions in society may affect their theory. They often apply distributive justice principles to thought experiments detached from the rest of the world, with little attention to background social conditions and whether they reflect distributive justice. What results, as critics point out (Burri 2020a), is selective and questionable reliance on distributive justice principles. Take, for instance, theorists who appeal to luck egalitarianism to argue that someone who takes a voluntary risk should be liable to harm if their action ends up endangering others. Notably, that argument almost always occurs in contexts where one of luck egalitarianism's core principles—equality of opportunity—is *not* met. It is far less clear that people should bear the burdens of voluntary risks that turn out badly if being unjustly disadvantaged pushed them to take such risks to survive. Those championing the distributive justice lens have staked out a position with a major limitation: it grounds the ethics of defensive force in principles of distributive justice while ignoring systemic injustice in society.

So despite all the talk about distributive justice in recent years, scholarship on the ethics of defensive force has failed to grapple with how systemic injustice interacts with our moral obligations regarding force. At best, one finds an acknowledgment that this "often . . . ignored" and "very difficult" question deserves "much more attention," followed by dozens of thought experiments that put it off further (Quong 2020, 13). Questions of distributive justice prove especially pressing for policing, given the link between groups disproportionately harmed by police deadly force and those unjustly disadvantaged. The remainder of the chapter turns to developing an account of how distributive justice should inform the ethics of defensive force.

Micro- and Macro-Level Justice

As we have seen, distributive justice can mean different things in debates over the ethics of defensive force. Some understand the concept as only referring to the just distribution of benefits and harms at the societal level. Others believe that it also applies to individual interactions. The first step in clarifying its relationship to the ethics of defensive force is to offer a more precise account of distributive justice.

The framework proposed here distinguishes between two levels of distributive justice:

Micro-level justice: just or fair distribution of benefits and harms among individuals in their interpersonal interactions

Macro-level justice: just or fair distribution of benefits and harms among groups that make up society

This distinction captures different but related notions of justice (for a similar distinction, see Daly 2025, 713). At the micro-level, there are just and unjust ways to treat individuals in encounters with them. If a teacher steals a bike from her student because it is her son's favorite model and the store no longer has it, most observers agree that the teacher wrongs the student. Likewise, at the macro-level, there are just and unjust ways of distributing benefits and harms to groups in society through policies, institutions, and societal practices. If a state imposes higher taxes on the poor to subsidize luxury housing for the wealthy, that policy strikes most as unfair. Whether an action is just or unjust will not always be as clear-cut as in these cases. But our reactions to these cases illustrate that few of us entirely reject notions of justice and fairness, either at the interpersonal or societal level. They are a deep-rooted part of how we experience and describe the moral world.

There is value in distinguishing between micro- and macro-level justice because different considerations have greater normative force depending on the level. To be sure, many moral considerations matter at both levels. The principle of equality is relevant for a host of questions, from how to distribute cake among kids at a birthday party to how to distribute voting rights among a population. Still, some considerations have greater influence at one level than the other. Culpability is a notable example. When someone engages in culpable action that makes harm unavoidable, it appears more just that they bear this harm rather than shifting the harm to an innocent party. At the macro-level, though, it is harder to ascribe culpability to demographic groups. There is almost always variation within a group. Plus, rarely do all its members act in coordination with each other, so it makes little sense to say that the group exercises collective control over its actions. Large and diffuse groups lack agency—typically a requirement for culpability—which explains why this consideration proves less apt at the macro-level.

We can distinguish between micro- and macro-level justice without severing all links between them. Indeed, macro-level goals have a role in informing conceptions of justice and individual obligations at the micro-level.

This point is not always obvious since principles endorsed at the macro-level often seem ill-suited for decision-making at the micro-level. When cautioning against relying, in interpersonal contexts, on principles meant to guide the distribution of benefits and harms in society, Quong (2020, 7–8) offers a hiring decision as a counterexample. Even if we suppose that improving the welfare of the least advantaged is the correct distributive justice principle for the macro-level, it does not follow that an employer should hire the least advantaged applicant. It would be absurd to expect a clinic to hire an applicant with no medical training as a physician simply because that applicant was the least advantaged candidate.

We can concede that key considerations at the macro-level often have less weight at the micro-level without concluding that such considerations are irrelevant at the micro-level. Moving toward a more just society requires action by both institutions and individuals. Individuals are not morally off the hook when it comes to combating injustice in society. They have obligations to do their part in working toward a more just society. The exact nature of these obligations depends on what roles people occupy, which offer different opportunities to alter unjust structures and practices (Zheng 2018; Young 2011).

That insight applies to the hiring example. The employer's obligations to contribute to a more just society may mean making extra efforts to recruit candidates from disadvantaged groups and considering the hardships they face when evaluating candidates. This approach is informed by macro-level principles but does not guarantee that the least advantaged candidate will be hired. We can incorporate such principles from the macro-level and still arrive at plausible conclusions about individuals' ethical obligations. And if we fail to consider macro-level justice, we are stuck with an impoverished view of our ethical obligations—one disconnected from broader injustices in society.

In this framework, micro-level justice is a variety of distributive justice. The term distributive justice remains apt since questions of how to distribute benefits and harms come up in interactions between individuals. The notion of a just distribution of goods at the individual level also has a long pedigree, going back to Aristotle (2000, V.3). Still, some may object to the terminology used here, preferring to reserve the term distributive justice for the macro-level. Not much hangs on that dispute. It ultimately comes down to preferences in terminology. One could use another term for distributive justice at the micro-level—say, interpersonal morality—without anything substantively changing about the framework outlined here.

The distinction between micro- and macro-level justice holds across a range of contexts. Take education. Here macro-level justice refers to the just distribution of education resources across society. This lens of analysis is apt for evaluating policy and institutional design. Micro-level justice, on the other hand, focuses on interactions between individuals in the education system, like how to assign grades to students in a class or which applicant should receive a scholarship. We similarly could apply these two levels of analysis to other parts of society, from healthcare to wealth distribution to criminal justice.

It is beyond this study's scope to offer a comprehensive account of micro- and macro-level justice across every context. More narrowly, the goal is to clarify the relationship between distributive justice and deadly force. The framework of micro- and macro-level justice distinguishes two separate (but linked) levels of analysis for the ethics of defensive force, bringing attention to different moral considerations for each level. The next two sections identify key considerations, one at the micro-level and one at the macro-level, for determining the fair distribution of benefits and harms related to force.

Culpability's Importance for Micro-Level Justice

Ethicists and legal scholars have long debated when defensive force is justified. One can come away from those debates with the impression that there is little agreement on the subject. But if we step back from the fine points of disagreement and take a broader view, there is significant consensus in certain areas. Take the following case.

> *Wrongful violence*: Someone without any features that would diminish control over their actions—like youth, mental illness, or intellectual disability—attacks and threatens grave harm against an innocent person who is doing nothing to endanger the rights of others. The attack does not prevent some greater harm. In fact, the aggressor lacks any justification or excuse for their violence.

In cases of wrongful violence, most without hesitation prioritize protecting the innocent victim over the culpable aggressor. Ideally, the threat could be averted without any harm at all. But if harm proves unavoidable, it is more just for the harm to fall on the aggressor than the person attacked. To achieve that outcome, the person attacked is morally justified in using necessary and proportionate force against the aggressor. There are competing explanations for this conclusion but, aside from pacifists, little debate over the conclusion itself.

The overlapping consensus in favor of protecting the innocent over the culpable reflects basic notions of fairness at the micro-level. All individuals enjoy rights against being harmed. I have an obligation to respect your rights, and there is the expectation that you will respect my rights, too. When an aggressor fails to respect another's rights and only force can stop their unjust threat, the aggressor is at fault for introducing unavoidable harm into the encounter. It would be unfair for the person who has done nothing wrong to bear this harm.

The fairer outcome, it seems, is for the harm to fall on the person culpable for creating circumstances—which could have been avoided—where someone must suffer harm.

Culpability corresponds with blameworthy action that violates or attempts to violate another's rights. This consideration especially influences our ethical thinking at the micro-level. When determining the just distribution of harm in individual encounters, we pay special attention to who is culpable, more so than other considerations like who is more disadvantaged. Which groups face societal structures that unfairly disadvantage them matters for distributive justice. As we will see, those unfair disadvantages matter for our normative judgments at the macro-level. But who has moral justification to use force in an individual encounter cannot be reduced to which party is more disadvantaged.

Consider violence during the Rwandan genocide. The history of colonialism in Rwanda led to divisions between the two largest ethnic groups in the country, with the Hutu occupying a more disadvantaged position than the Tutsi. Studies of the genocide find that wealthier Tutsi (and Hutu) were more likely to be killed, and that those who did the killing tended to be poorer (Friedman 2016). Occupying a disadvantaged position, however, fails to justify acts of genocide. It would be abhorrent to look at the murder of a defenseless Tutsi during the genocide and conclude that it was morally preferable for the aggressor to survive due to their disadvantaged position. If such an attack created unavoidable lethal harm, it would have been better to shift the harm onto the aggressor through self-defense or defensive force by a third party. Why? Because at the micro-level, culpability for wrongful harm matters more than relative disadvantage. Our intuitions in such cases, where disadvantage and culpability are coupled together, highlight the greater weight we give culpability when thinking about justice at the micro-level.

A point by Tommie Shelby further helps explain our reactions to such cases. In his book *Dark Ghettos*, Shelby explores how conditions of persistent injustice alter the moral landscape for residents of poor Black communities who are unfairly disadvantaged. Still, he notes, certain natural "duties are not suspended or void because one is oppressed" (Shelby 2016, 219). Natural duties apply to all, the advantaged and disadvantaged alike, and include refraining from violence that would violate others' rights over their life and body. So, despite being disadvantaged, the Hutu still had duties to the Tutsi. Those who participated in genocide acted culpably because they unfairly exempted themselves from duties that apply to all.

The claim that certain duties apply to everyone can coexist with the idea that persistent injustice weakens other duties. An influential view in political philosophy is that the state has its strongest claim to political authority—the moral right to rule and corresponding duty on its inhabitants to obey its laws—when its institutions foster a mutually beneficial system of cooperation (Rawls 1999, 301–8). If a state unfairly excludes some from this cooperative scheme, it fails to meet a key condition for political authority. Shelby (2016) and others (e.g., Hendrix 2019) argue that, in such cases, the unjustly disadvantaged have weaker obligations to obey the state. For instance, those unfairly trapped in poverty may have permission to break some property laws entrenching injustice and engage, say, in minor theft (Shelby 2016, 220). We do not need to take a position on that question. The important point is that, even if the poor have such permissions, certain acts like rape and murder remain wrong. As moral agents, we have duties to our fellow human beings to avoid unjust aggression against them. To suggest that the disadvantaged lack these duties carries the troubling suggestion that they are less than full moral agents (Tadros 2009, 392).

The conception of micro-level justice outlined here, which treats the culpable as more liable to defensive force, does not imply a blanket justification for using force against the culpable. Liability is limited to those culpable for a *current* threat, not those culpable for a past threat but who no longer pose one (Frowe 2014, 30, fn. 16). Relatedly, defensive force is bound by necessity, as we discussed in Chapter 1. This principle reflects the idea that harm from defensive force is never good in itself but only as a means to avoid another harm. Necessity prohibits force beyond what is required to achieve a just aim. In sum, we can understand the culpable as more liable to defensive force while still recognizing constraints on using force against them.

This section has focused on culpability's importance at the micro-level even in the face of countervailing considerations that matter at the macro-level. So is there any room for macro-level considerations at the micro-level? I suggest that there is—specifically, in informing the relationship between liability and culpability.

Culpability exists on a spectrum, in which individuals can be more or less culpable depending on whether factors mitigate blame like youth, mental illness, or intellectual disability. If a child threatens another's rights, we understand them as less culpable than an adult aggressor who, in full control of their actions, poses the same threat, absent any mitigating excuses. For a particularly young aggressor, youth can diminish their culpability to such an extent that they bear no culpability for their unjust threat. But in other cases, a factor like youth diminishes culpability without eliminating it entirely. An open question is whether the variable nature of culpability should impact notions of justice at the micro-level.

One option is to treat culpability as a threshold: anyone slightly culpable for an unjust threat is as liable to defensive force as the fully culpable (Ferzan 2005,

2012; Alexander 2013). The problem with the threshold approach is that it has dubious implications for vulnerable groups. For members of vulnerable groups who are more susceptible to police violence due to factors beyond their control, low levels of culpability put them at greater risk of harm than others who are equally culpable. They live under heightened vulnerability, where small missteps can lead to outsized harms. We see a similar dynamic in drug enforcement. Though both White and Black Americans use drugs at roughly the same rates, Black Americans are arrested for minor drug offenses at significantly higher rates (Mitchell and Caudy 2015, 303).

Policy responses to uneven drug enforcement offer insight into how an alternative to the threshold approach would enhance protections for the vulnerable. Reduced penalties for drugs apply to all, but this change disproportionately benefits Black Americans, who are most vulnerable to drug enforcement. Similarly, treating those with diminished culpability as less liable to defensive harm—either as liable to a smaller amount of harm or as liable to harm in a narrower range of circumstances—implies greater restraint in using force against them. Such restraint disproportionately benefits groups that are most vulnerable to suffering force and its harms. In this alternative approach, where liability varies with culpability, vulnerable groups end up with greater protections from defensive harm than they enjoy under the threshold approach and the legal status quo. On its face, treating liability as varying directly with culpability is not a rule that specifically benefits the vulnerable, yet it has that effect.

This feature counts in the rule's favor. It offers a coherent account of how micro- and macro-level justice fit together in the context of defensive force. Macro-level considerations inform the interpretation of culpability at the micro-level without supplanting this key consideration. As we will see in Chapter 4, the idea that liability varies with culpability aligns with many people's intuitions in cases involving an aggressor with diminished culpability, like a child or person with mental illness. A common reaction is that police and others should exercise greater restraint in using force against child aggressors and aggressors with mental illness, which is exactly what the approach to culpability defended here suggests.

My account of culpability's relationship to liability has parallels to the moral responsibility account, which we discussed earlier in the section on the debate over distributive justice's relationship to the ethics of defensive force. In my account, liability varies with culpability. In the other account, liability varies with moral responsibility. Moral responsibility is a broader concept that encompasses culpability. Being culpable means that one is morally responsible. The converse is not always true, as one can be morally responsible without being culpable. The partial overlap between the concepts means that the moral responsibility account and my account yield similar conclusions for aggressors with diminished culpability—and by implication, diminished moral responsibility—like child aggressors and aggressors with mental illness. Both accounts understand such aggressors as less liable to defensive force and call for greater restraint in encounters with them.

Despite the similarities, some prefer the moral responsibility account. In their view, it better explains liability in cases where moral responsibility and culpability come apart. This account treats those morally responsible but not culpable for a threat—like the conscientious driver who loses control of their car in a freak accident and threatens a pedestrian—as liable to harm from defensive force. According to the moral responsibility account, the responsible driver knowingly took a risk by driving their car. If that risk eventuates by putting a pedestrian in harm's way, the pedestrian or a third party is justified in using defensive force against the driver to stop their threat.

It is questionable, though, whether the moral responsibility account's implications in such cases count in its favor. In the case of a culpable aggressor, their greater liability to defensive force appears fair: it allows for shifting unavoidable harm onto the party who introduced such harm by disregarding duties that apply to everyone. The fair distribution of harm is less clear in cases where someone is morally responsible but not culpable for a threat. They have fulfilled their duties. To become liable to defensive force without doing anything wrong seems potentially unfair. In cases of bad luck, like the responsible driver who loses control of their car, there may be no fair way to distribute harm, suggesting that neither party in the interaction loses their rights against being harmed. A further reason to treat neither party as liable is that *both* introduce foreseeable risk into the encounter. After all, the responsible driver is not the only one who engages in risky action. So does the pedestrian who carries around a grenade ready to blow up out-of-control cars. As Seth Lazar (2009, 719) notes, the pedestrian's decision that day to stroll beside the road with a deadly weapon is a necessary component for the zero-sum encounter that occurs. Since we all engage in risk-imposing activity, this criterion at the heart of the moral responsibility account proves to be a shaky basis for distinguishing who is liable to harm.

So I stick with culpability as the basis for determining liability to defensive harm and the just distribution of harm at the micro-level. It is worth noting that opting for this approach rather than the moral responsibility account has little impact on much of the analysis that follows. Moral responsibility and culpability generally do not come apart in the cases examined, which represent persistent challenges in policing. In other words, starting from the moral responsibility account leads to similar conclusions about the ethics of police deadly force, at least for the specific challenges covered in Part II.

Vulnerability's Importance for Macro-Level Justice

At the micro-level, considerations of unfair disadvantage have limited influence on the evaluation of defensive force. Culpability typically outweighs those considerations for this level of moral analysis. If we restrict our attention to micro-level justice, it is easy to come away with the impression that issues central to debates over distributive justice, like who is unfairly disadvantaged, play only a minor role in the ethics of defensive force. The philosophical literature on defensive force often contributes to this impression by focusing on individual encounters, detached from background social conditions. But this approach, by itself, leaves us with an incomplete picture. Law, policy, and societal structures all shape how individuals use force, and therefore shape larger patterns of violence. Such factors stack the deck against certain groups, increasing their vulnerability to force and grave harm. Rather than ignore these realities, the ethics of defensive force needs to make room to consider macro-level justice.

A previous example illustrates this point. If cars keep hitting pedestrians with such regularity that more people begin carrying around grenade launchers to protect themselves, debates at the micro-level only will get us so far. There is a place for examining who is justified or permitted to use force in these encounters. But we also need to look at structural factors—like the design of cities, placement of roadways, and investment in public transportation—that contribute to the risks that pedestrians face from cars. If we spent all our time at the micro-level, scrutinizing myriad variations of out-of-control cars threatening pedestrians and ignoring those structural factors, our analysis would be morally impoverished. We can avoid that pitfall by considering force incidents from the perspective of macro-level justice.

When we turn our attention to the macro-level, the consideration of vulnerability stands out, just as culpability does at the micro-level. As understood here, vulnerability means susceptibility to harm due to factors outside one's control. We are all vulnerable to a certain extent. That is an inescapable part of the human condition. But some individuals and groups face a greater risk of suffering certain harms (see Goodin 1985; Mackenzie, Rogers, and Dodds 2013). In the context of macro-level justice, the concept of vulnerability captures who lives under a heightened risk of suffering force and its harms due to structural factors in society. This heightened risk of harm unfairly disadvantages vulnerable groups.

How police in the US use force causes some of this vulnerability from a macro-level perspective. Patterns of police violence are not evenly distributed across society but instead fall disproportionately on certain groups, such as Black Americans and persons with serious mental illness (Saleh et al. 2018; Edwards, Lee, and Esposito 2019).

The chapter's opening example illustrates conditions of heightened vulnerability. Everyday activities like driving around town carried greater risks for Philando Castile due to pervasive perceptions that young Black men represent a threat. As Bryan Stevenson (2017, 4) notes, "People of color in the United States, particularly young black men, are burdened with a presumption of guilt and dangerousness." This reality negatively impacts Black Americans across the criminal justice system, from decisions on bail (Arnold, Dobbie, and Yang 2018) to capital sentencing (Eberhardt et al. 2006). The same appears true for policing. Black men in the US face a risk of being killed by police during their lifetime that is more than double what White men face (Edwards, Lee, and Esposito 2019). Notably, police are significantly more likely to kill unarmed individuals who are Black—a finding that cannot be explained by whether the person killed was attacking police or others (Nix et al. 2017, 324–26). Such disparities are consistent with officers seeing Black men as more dangerous and being more likely to resort to deadly force against them. For Black Americans, being perceived as dangerous comes with real harms.

Castile never had a choice whether to live under a heightened risk of police violence. Factors outside his control forced it upon him. As a Black American, he was born into conditions of greater vulnerability. Members of less vulnerable groups experience the world differently. They go about their lives without the same level of lethal risk hanging over them.

The vulnerability of certain groups to force reveals unfairness at the macro-level. Their increased vulnerability puts them at a disadvantage. Members of vulnerable groups face tougher odds of succeeding in their pursuits due to the greater risk of their lives being cut short. Their vulnerability robs them of a fair chance at life. This concern represents an area of overlapping consensus in ongoing debates over distributive justice. Surveys and experiments reveal consistent support for the idea that individuals should at least have an equal chance to succeed (Marshall et al. 1999, 358–59; Bruner 2018; Burri, Lup, and Pepper 2021, 23–25). Heightened risk of suffering lethal violence closes off equal opportunity for vulnerable groups.

In short, vulnerable groups suffer injustice when societal structures beyond their control produce patterns of force and harm that put them at a serious disadvantage. Macro-level justice calls for addressing such unfair distribution of harm. This point has implications for how we think about distributive justice at the macro-level. Most recognize the state's responsibilities to advance distributive justice in areas like healthcare, education, and wealth allocation. Given the considerable harm that patterns of violence inflict on certain groups, the state also has responsibilities to advance distributive justice in this area. State institutions must identify which groups in society are most vulnerable to violence and develop strategies to reduce the risks they face. Importantly, when we consider the macro-level perspective, the ethics of defensive force ceases to be just about individuals. It also has implications for the state, whose laws and institutions shape patterns of force and harm in society.

The factors that contribute to patterns of violence are wide-ranging and complex. Some relate directly to the use of force, like laws on gun ownership and what justifies police use of deadly force (see Kivisto, Ray, and Phalen 2017; Rogna and Nguyen 2022; Tennenbaum 1994). Given their impact on patterns of violence, such factors belong among those that the state should consider in efforts to advance distributive justice for vulnerable groups. But the work of advancing justice at the macro-level does not end there. Other factors like poverty, homelessness, lack of mental health services, and racial bias also impact groups' vulnerability to violence. These challenges should figure into the state's overall strategy to lower the risks faced by vulnerable groups.

If changes in the distribution of resources and protections from force would reduce the risk of violence, it makes moral sense to distribute these benefits in ways that give priority to the vulnerable. That principle advances justice by improving conditions for vulnerable and unfairly disadvantaged groups. One question that comes up in debates over distributive justice is whether to give priority to those absolutely worse off or to those comparatively worse off. Prioritarians endorse the former view, while egalitarians endorse the latter (Parfit 2002). Since groups in society at the greatest risk of suffering violence tend to be the same whether their vulnerability is measured in absolute or comparative terms, it is not critical to take a position on that debate here.

It is worth noting that the principle to prioritize the protection of life (discussed in Chapter 2) places constraints on how to achieve a fairer distribution of risk. A policy that raises the lethal risks for the group in society least vulnerable to force while leaving unchanged the risk for the most vulnerable group would be a step toward equalizing the risks between the two groups. But it would put more lives at risk overall and therefore would not be worth pursuing. After all, the reason why macro-level justice focuses on the vulnerable is to highlight their unfair disadvantage and prompt action to *improve their lives*. Prioritizing the protection of life rules out implausible forms of egalitarianism that address disparities in vulnerability by "leveling down" and increasing lethal risks for others without improving conditions for the vulnerable.

Police's Role in Advancing Distributive Justice

Police deadly force proves so controversial, in part, because it exacerbates injustice in society. The chapter's central point is that distributive justice has a critical role in informing the ethics of defensive force. That point proves especially true for policing.

Police have a different relationship to force than civilians do. Officers occupy a role that comes with higher expectations to use force in ways consistent with distributive justice. Many civilians go their entire lives without ever facing a threat from an aggressor and the decision whether to respond with defensive force. Since the use of force usually plays a marginal or nonexistent role in civilians' lives, there are lower expectations on what civilians should know about when force is justified. They of course need to know the basics—for instance, that it is wrong to go around attacking innocent and defenseless people. Most civilians have this basic knowledge without needing extensive study of the ethics of defensive force. But on more nuanced points, like how to advance macro-level justice in individual encounters, it is plausible that the moral obligations on civilians are less stringent than those on police. In contrast, police agencies have obligations to put their officers through more extensive use-of-force training given its centrality to their jobs. Police administrators have obligations to implement training and policies consistent with promoting distributive justice at both the micro- and macro-levels. Well-designed training and policies, grounded in ethics, help officers better understand how the use of force interacts with their obligations to advance distributive justice. In short, because of their professional roles, police have less of an excuse for being ignorant of these obligations.

Some might push back, saying that it is unreasonable to expect police administrators and officers to be versed in the finer points of distributive justice on top of all their other responsibilities. Though reasonable on its face, this objection overlooks the ethical challenges inherent in policing. Questions of distributive justice regularly confront police in their interactions with disadvantaged and vulnerable groups (del Pozo 2023, 213–15). How police understand their obligations to these groups is informed by underlying views about distributive justice. They ultimately cannot avoid questions of distributive justice in their work.

Now not every police professional needs to be an expert on the scholarship on distributive justice. But police should consult ethicists—as professionals in fields like medicine often do (Monaghan 2021b)—to better understand their obligations to disadvantaged and vulnerable groups, especially in scenarios that regularly arise in policing. When police put off that task, they act negligently. Negligence is not a legitimate reason to shirk their obligations to vulnerable and disadvantaged people in the communities they serve.

Moreover, the nature of policing makes it even less plausible that the police lack obligations to advance distributive justice. As we have seen, some philosophers are skeptical that individuals have obligations to advance distributive justice. This chapter pushes back on that skepticism. But even if the skeptics are right, it does not follow that the police lack obligations to advance distributive justice. The police are an institution of the state—the entity for which there is the most consensus that it has responsibilities to advance distributive justice (see Monaghan 2022). As part of the state, the police have responsibilities to promote rather than hinder its distributive justice goals.

A more complete picture of the ethics of police deadly force comes into view once we recognize those responsibilities. To analyze police deadly force in a vacuum, ignoring persistent injustice in society, precludes us from developing an account that speaks to the real-life challenges facing police, policymakers, and communities. The framework outlined here offers guidance for those challenges by breaking down what justice demands at the micro- and macro-level. In short, when making micro-level decisions related to using deadly force, officers need to pay special attention to individuals' culpability, and at the macro-level, police and other state institutions need to pay special attention to groups' vulnerability. This framework provides a foundation for clarifying the moral expectations that police officers and institutions must fulfill to be partners in the project of advancing distributive justice. In Chapters 4 and 5, which open Part II, we explore those expectations in more concrete detail.

PART II
CONTEMPORARY CHALLENGES

4

Aggressors with Mental Illness

In October 2020, protests broke out in Philadelphia, Pennsylvania, after police shot and killed Walter Wallace Jr. His family had called 911 for help because he was experiencing a mental health crisis and acting violently. Video captured Wallace in the street pointing a knife at officers, who shot him after he failed to drop it (Dale 2020).

Such killings by police are all too common. Each year, police in the US fatally shoot around one thousand people. One out of every five killed was experiencing a mental health crisis (*Washington Post* 2024). The ethics of defensive force scholarship offers little direct discussion of police obligations in these cases. Scholars do examine the question of killing innocent aggressors—those who intentionally pose an unjust threat but lack moral responsibility and culpability for their threat (Otsuka 1994, 74; Quong 2009, 507). Thought experiments illustrating these encounters often have an artificial quality, like someone developing the intent to kill after being drugged against their will (Thomson 1991, 284). Though not impossible, such incidents are incredibly rare. Focusing on them can distract from more likely scenarios involving aggressors who, even if not fully innocent, have severely diminished culpability due to factors like mental illness. Since police regularly encounter these vulnerable populations, determining when deadly force is justified in such cases is a pressing moral and policy question.

As can be seen from the mass protests in Philadelphia and elsewhere, police killing vulnerable individuals strikes many as a moral failure, regardless of whether deadly force is justified under current law. This chapter examines that intuition, with a focus on aggressors with mental illness who pose an intentional threat of grave harm, like death or serious bodily injury. Drawing on the ethics of defensive force literature, it considers five ways to understand police obligations to these and other *vulnerable aggressors with diminished culpability* (VADCs).

(1) *Diminished protections account*: VADCs enjoy fewer protections from deadly force.

(2) *Traditional account*: VADCs do not enjoy extra protections from deadly force.

(3) *Culpability account*: Innocent VADCs are not liable to deadly force.

> (4) *Vulnerability account*: VADCs' vulnerability renders them less liable to deadly force.
> (5) *Fusion account*: VADCs enjoy extra protections from deadly force due to their vulnerability and diminished culpability.

I reject the diminished protections and traditional accounts because they go against basic notions of distributive justice discussed in Chapter 3. VADCs' vulnerable status leaves them worse off—they are at greater risk of being harmed—which suggests that they should receive some priority in the distribution of benefits and protections. Both the diminished protections and traditional accounts fail in this regard. The culpability and vulnerability accounts offer potential solutions, but their approaches to liability run into problems. As an alternative, I develop the fusion account, which pulls from the culpability and vulnerability accounts to explain why VADCs should enjoy extra protections from deadly force.

Before we jump into these competing accounts, let's first situate my argument within current debates over policing. In 2020, protests in response to high-profile killings by police led to calls to reimagine public safety and limit police interactions, especially with vulnerable populations (Jones and Mendieta 2021, 2; Jones and Lim forthcoming). Proposals included more robust social services and teams of mental health professionals that could respond to individuals in crisis, rather than leaving this responsibility to police. Behind these proposals lies the idea that avoidable violence stems from both overreliance on the police and societal failures to address the needs of vulnerable populations. Indeed, in the US and elsewhere, policing often proves challenging because it occurs against a backdrop of inadequate funding and services for vulnerable populations (Morabito 2014; Wood, Watson, and Barber 2021).

Though actors besides the police have obligations to vulnerable populations, it remains important to understand police obligations to these groups. Even if more robust social services were to reduce the need for police interactions with vulnerable populations, occasions will arise (albeit less frequently) where a vulnerable individual has a weapon or is otherwise dangerous and police must respond. For instance, civilian crisis response teams—often championed as an alternative to the police (McLeod 2019, 1630)—have had promising results in assisting individuals in crisis while decreasing their contact with police and the criminal justice system (Dee and Pyne 2022). Still, such services rely on police as the primary responders for those in crisis who are violent or have a weapon (Midgette and Reuter 2024, 784–85). Unfortunately, perfect compliance and the elimination of violence exist only in theory, not in any actual society—not even those most proactive in addressing the root causes of violence. So even under the most favorable conditions, police must be prepared to respond to VADCs.

Of course, conditions often are far from favorable. Despite growing calls to address the needs of vulnerable populations, those needs remain unmet in many places. Officers today face the challenge of responding to VADCs in difficult circumstances, where gaps in social services make such encounters more likely. In those cases, police continue to have obligations to VADCs, as this chapter explores.

Culpability, Vulnerability, and Mental Illness

Aggressors with mental illness have two salient features that matter from a moral point of view: diminished culpability and heightened vulnerability. Culpability refers to the extent that someone is morally blameworthy for unjust or wrongful action, meaning that it violates or attempts to violate others' rights. There are different degrees of culpability. Fully culpable aggressors lack moral justification, permission, or excuse for the intentional harm they threaten or inflict on others (McMahan 2009, 159). For other aggressors, features like youth, mental illness, or intellectual disability diminish their culpability by limiting their deliberative agency and control over their actions (Rodin 2011, 83). Some exculpatory factors like serious mental illness can diminish an aggressor's agency to such an extent that they lack any culpability for their threat. That limit case is an innocent aggressor.

As understood here, vulnerability refers to susceptibility to harm due to factors outside one's control. All humans are vulnerable—to disease, injury, aging, and other factors (Fineman 2008). But some are more vulnerable than others (see Goodin 1985; Mackenzie, Rogers, and Dodds 2013). Though certain physical and psychiatric disabilities come with inherent vulnerabilities, social conditions remain a significant source of vulnerability (Scully 2013, 207–9). Societal structures often create and exacerbate the vulnerabilities of marginalized groups by failing to respond to their needs.

A feature can impact vulnerability but not culpability, and vice versa. For instance, being Black in America where systemic racism persists comes with greater vulnerability to various harms, including police violence (see Chapter 5). But someone is not more or less culpable because of their race (though it can impact *perceptions* of culpability when bias is present).

Mental illness can impact both culpability and vulnerability. This impact is often most evident for serious or severe mental illness, such as schizophrenia, bipolar disorder, major depression, and other psychotic disorders (Latalova, Kamaradova, and Prasko 2014, 1926). If someone in a mental health crisis is undergoing delusions or hallucinations, we understand these conditions as impairing their judgment and control over their actions, thus diminishing their culpability. Less severe forms of mental illness also can diminish culpability by affecting judgment and agency but to a lesser extent. How mental illness interacts with background social conditions has implications for vulnerability. Many aspects of society prove inhospitable to individuals with disability, including psychiatric disability or mental illness, which leaves them more susceptible to suffering harm.

Robust evidence across the world reveals that persons with mental illness are more vulnerable to being victimized by violence. Several reviews and meta-studies all reach this conclusion (Choe, Teplin, and Abram 2008; Maniglio 2009; Hughes et al. 2012; Latalova, Kamaradova, and Prasko 2014; de Vries et al. 2019). Some of the largest studies investigating the link between mental illness and violent victimization come from northern Europe, where data collection practices allow for comparing outcomes between those with and without mental illness across a national cohort. These studies find that persons with mental illness face a significantly higher risk of violent victimization compared with the rest of the population (Dean et al. 2018; Sariaslan et al. 2020).

Similar disparities characterize the criminal justice system. In the US and around the world, persons with serious mental illness make up a disproportionate share of the prison population (Fazel and Seewald 2012; Maruschak, Bronson, and Alper 2021). That finding also holds when we look at the harshest forms of incarceration. In US prisons, persons with serious mental illness end up in solitary confinement at higher rates and stay there longer than do prisoners without such a diagnosis (Simes, Western, and Lee 2022, 553–56). Persons with serious mental illness also are more likely to be killed by police—seven times more likely, according to US data from 2015 (Saleh et al. 2018, 114).

A common conclusion about the disparate harms experienced by persons with mental illness is that they can be attributed to dangers posed by this population. In recent decades, especially with growing concerns over mass shootings, much of the narrative around mental illness has focused on its role in perpetrating violence (Metzl and MacLeish 2015; Swanson and Rosenberg 2023). If persons with mental illnesses are more likely to engage in violence, crime, and other risky behaviors, it follows that they are more likely to end up in the criminal justice system, as victims of violence, and killed by police. In other words, their actions endangering others make them more susceptible to criminal penalties and violence. This perspective challenges the idea that we should understand persons with mental illness as a vulnerable group, whose heightened risk of suffering violence and other harm stems from societal factors beyond their control.

The problem with that perspective is that it oversimplifies the relationship between violence and mental illness. Many common types of mental illness have little or no association with perpetrating violence (Van Dorn, Volavka, and Johnson 2012, 490–97; Metzl and MacLeish 2015, 241). There is more evidence linking serious mental illness to violence, but even in this case, the evidence comes with important caveats. The conclusion that Richard Van Dorn, Jan Volavka, and Norman Johnson draw from US survey data sums up the consensus view to emerge in recent decades: "there is a modest, yet statistically significant relationship between severe mental illness (SMI) and violence." In addition to emphasizing the modest nature of the relationship, they point out that other factors like substance abuse contribute more strongly to the risk of perpetrating violence than does mental illness by itself (Van Dorn, Volavka, and Johnson 2012, 487; see also Fazel et al. 2009; Yukhnenko et al. 2023).

Importantly, the modest relationship between serious mental illness and committing violence appears unable to explain the greater risk of violent victimization faced by this population. A national cohort study from Denmark controlled for criminal offending among persons with mental illness, including serious mental illness, when examining their risk of violent victimization. Criminal offending explained some but hardly all this population's heightened risk of experiencing violence (Dean et al. 2018, 692–94). Research looking at police violence comes to similar conclusions. A survey study of residents in Baltimore, Maryland, and New York City found that persons with serious mental illness were significantly more likely to experience police violence, even after controlling for criminal offending (Jun et al. 2020, 33–85).

Investigations of US police departments and high-profile incidents of brutality have revealed practices in line with these empirical findings. One particularly egregious incident caught on video occurred in Fullerton, California, where police in 2011 killed Kelly Thomas, a homeless man with schizophrenia. Though Thomas was unarmed and posed little threat, six officers beat him continuously for close to ten minutes as he cried to his dad for help (Barber 2014; La Tour 2020). US Department of Justice (2012, 2014, 2016) investigations have found patterns of excessive force against persons with mental illness in numerous police departments, including in Portland, Oregon; Cleveland, Ohio; and Baltimore, Maryland. All this evidence strongly suggests that persons with mental illness are a vulnerable population at greater risk of suffering violence from police and others.

So when an aggressor has mental illness, they possess a feature that both increases their vulnerability and diminishes their culpability. I define this class of aggressors as follows.

Vulnerable aggressors with diminished culpability (VADCs): aggressors with a feature (or features) beyond their control—like youth, mental illness, or intellectual disability—that (1) significantly diminishes their culpability for their unjust threat and (2) significantly increases their vulnerability to violent harm, making them worse off.

There are a few points to note about this definition. First, it characterizes VADCs not as inherently worse off but as worse off in the social conditions in which they live—conditions marked by vulnerability. Second, due to factors beyond their control, VADCs live under prolonged vulnerability to violent harm. Wholly culpable aggressors may face a greater risk of violence when attacking others, but they bring this risk on themselves, so they do not qualify as vulnerable in the sense that VADCs are. Third, VADCs range from the partially culpable, who have some responsibility for their wrongful actions, to innocent aggressors, whose culpability is fully diminished. Fourth, VADCs have a condition that *significantly* impacts their culpability and vulnerability. Inevitably, there are marginal cases where it is debatable whether an aggressor's condition has a significant impact on culpability and vulnerability. We can lack clarity on how to handle marginal cases (e.g., mild mental illness), while still arriving at firmer conclusions for more clear-cut cases (e.g., serious mental illness). I take that approach here, with the goal of offering guidance for an important range of cases involving aggressors with mental illness, even if tough cases remain.

Proposal 1: Diminished Protections Account

How should police respond to VADCs? This section considers what I call the diminished protections account. As the name implies, it offers the fewest protections to VADCs of the accounts considered in this chapter. The diminished protections account takes the view that at least some VADCs have fewer protections against deadly force than aggressors typically enjoy. This idea comes up in response to a classic thought experiment.

> *Psychotic aggressor*: Someone who lacks culpability due to insanity attacks and threatens the life of another person while both are in an elevator. The only way to stop the aggressor's threat is to kill them. (see Fletcher 1973, 371)

Some legal theorists compare such aggressors to wild animals, suggesting that their lives have less value than other human lives at stake (Bouzat 1963, 272).

The wild animal analogy also shows up in philosophy. Michael Otsuka (1994) defends the diminished protections account for a subset of VADCs: innocent aggressors with severe permanent impairments. This claim comes up within a larger argument by Otsuka that innocent aggressors are *not* liable to defensive force—that is, they have not forfeited their moral right to be free from being attacked and harmed by others. But in his view, there is moral justification to kill innocent aggressors with severe permanent impairments when deadly force is necessary to prevent them from inflicting grave harm on others. These aggressors merit fewer protections than innocent aggressors with only temporary impairments, like hypnosis. Otsuka explains his reasoning:

> The simple explanation of why you may kill a lethal agent that happens to be a grizzly bear on the attack is that you are a human person, whereas it is merely a grizzly bear, and human persons are worth more than grizzly bears. I believe that the same can be said about a contest between a normal human person and certain types of psychotics. A normal human being is worth more than a human being whom mental illness has permanently rendered incapable of moral agency. . . . I do not believe that dangerous psychotics who have been permanently ravaged by certain types of mental illness are persons. (Otsuka 1994, 92–93)

So for Otsuka, if innocent aggressors have severe impairments that prevent moral agency from returning, their lives have less value and merit less moral weight in deadly force decisions.

The diminished protections account has several worrisome features. It dehumanizes individuals with severe permanent impairments and treats them as not persons, which is a prima facie reason to question it (Fletcher 1973, 374–75; Kaufman 2010, 87–88). There is a strong presumption against that view, given the long history of abhorrent treatment of marginalized groups deemed to have less value than "normal human beings" (Otsuka's term). Even if we entertained the diminished protections account in theory, it is important to recognize how easily it could be abused in practice. Those without mental illness can have difficulty understanding the experiences of those who live with it. That disconnect can lead to mistaken conclusions about people's welfare, intelligence, and agency (Carter 2023). The diminished protections account could encourage judgments that mistakenly dehumanize vulnerable populations and exacerbate violence against them.

This view has potentially troubling implications for policing, too. If the moral value of individuals with severe permanent impairments is similar to that of wild animals, one could reason that their lives should receive lower priority than even the lives of culpable aggressors with full agency. Such a principle implies that, in an encounter where an officer provokes violence and the need to use deadly force against someone with a severe permanent impairment, the life of the culpable officer should be prioritized. But that conclusion seems clearly wrong, which is further reason to reject the diminished protections account as a guide for policing.

Proposal 2: Traditional Account

As the prevailing approach in law, the traditional account has significant influence on the rules governing deadly force. This view rejects the idea that VADCs should receive extra protections from deadly force. Its position results from excluding culpability and vulnerability as relevant considerations for determining whether deadly force is justified. According to the traditional account, deadly force is justified if one reasonably believes that such force is necessary to stop an aggressor's unjust threat of grave harm. As long as those conditions are met, deadly force is justified regardless of whether the aggressor is innocent, culpable, or vulnerable. Conditions like insanity and mental illness ultimately do not influence an aggressor's liability to defensive force (Fletcher 1973; Thomson 1991). Like anyone else, VADCs who pose a grave threat put themselves at serious risk of being liable to deadly force. The Model Penal Code adopts this approach (Dubber 2015, 157), which shows up in criminal law and often provides legal justification for police killings of aggressors with mental illness.

On its face, the traditional account has certain advantages. Sometimes it is difficult to determine an aggressor's culpability and vulnerability, especially when police respond quickly to a threat. By treating aggressors the same regardless of their culpability or vulnerability, the traditional account avoids imposing on police and others unreasonable epistemic burdens (Klinger 2021, 125–26). Furthermore, though many recognize a role for culpability in determining an aggressor's punishment *after* an attack, it is more controversial to claim that an aggressor's culpability (or vulnerability) impacts their liability to defensive force to *prevent* an attack. An innocent aggressor still can violate others' rights against being harmed. The traditional account makes the plausible, though debated, claim that one is justified in using proportionate and necessary force to fend off an innocent aggressor's unjust attack.

Despite its apparent advantages, the traditional account has shortcomings. Notably, some of the worries motivating it are exaggerated. It would be unfair to expect police to respond differently to VADCs who, based on an officer's reasonable belief, do not appear vulnerable or to have diminished culpability. Yet in other cases—like when serving a mental health warrant or responding to a mental health crisis call—officers know an aggressor is likely a VADC. So the idea that police have special obligations to VADCs does not entail unrealistic demands. We can rely on a standard like reasonable belief to determine when those obligations most clearly apply.

The more fundamental problem with the traditional account is that its one-size-fits-all approach leaves little room for a broadly shared intuition: it is morally preferable, when distributing benefits, to give priority to those who are worse off (Parfit 2002). This principle from prioritarian and egalitarian thought proves most compelling when there is a close link between the disadvantage in question and the benefit being distributed. Not all disadvantages are morally relevant for distributing a benefit like protections from police violence. Greater vulnerability to, say, wildfires is not a compelling moral reason for extra protections from police violence. But police violence is a harm to which persons with mental illness are more vulnerable. Their vulnerability renders them worse off, suggesting that they should receive some priority in protection from police violence. That claim does not mean vulnerable lives *always* take precedence over others, since many factors matter when morally evaluating force. Rather, more modestly, vulnerable lives should be prioritized, all else being equal. The traditional account's failure to accommodate that intuition gives us reason to explore whether other accounts can.

Proposal 3: Culpability Account

The culpability account's approach to liability offers a potential remedy to the traditional account's shortcomings. Developed by Kimberly Kessler Ferzan (2005, 2012) and others (e.g., Alexander 1987), it treats culpability as a necessary condition for liability. The culpability account emphasizes that there should be a high bar for losing one's right against being harmed. And culpability—engaging in morally blameworthy action—is a higher bar than what the traditional account proposes. Aggressors who lack culpability and are innocent still can be liable to deadly force, according to the traditional account. In contrast, the culpability account understands innocent aggressors as not liable to deadly force, even if such force is necessary to prevent them from killing innocent victims.

Though the culpability account rejects the idea that innocent aggressors can be liable to deadly force, this position does not imply that deadly force may never be used against them. For instance, if deadly force is necessary to prevent an innocent aggressor from killing several innocent victims, there can be a lesser evil justification for killing the innocent aggressor. In other words, neither the innocent aggressor nor the innocent victims are liable to harm, but killing the innocent aggressor is justified because it prevents a greater harm—several innocent people being killed (Alexander 2005, 612).

Even with that caveat, the culpability account grants innocent aggressors greater moral protections than does the traditional account, which has implications for VADCs—specifically, those who are innocent aggressors. Treating innocent aggressors as not liable to deadly force gives priority to the lives of certain VADCs, who by definition are worse off. So compared with the traditional account, the culpability account better accommodates the intuition that those worse off should be prioritized in the distribution of benefits, like protections from deadly force.

On closer inspection, though, the culpability account makes only limited room for that intuition, which raises questions over whether it overcomes the traditional account's deficiencies. The culpability account's emphasis on innocence turns out to be a double-edged sword. It provides moral protections to the wholly innocent but fails to extend these protections to aggressors who fall anywhere below that bar, such as aggressors with diminished but partial culpability.

This point is evident in the claim by Larry Alexander (2013, 169), a defender of the culpability account, that liability to deadly force applies to "all culpable aggressors, no matter how low their level of culpability, if they threaten an act that *could* cause great harm." Relatedly, Ferzan (2005, 744–45) stresses that an aggressor's probability of killing someone can be quite low—yet they remain liable to deadly force if they are culpable of intending such harm. So if an aggressor is at all culpable for a threat posing any risk of grave harm, protections against deadly force no longer apply to the aggressor, according to proponents of the culpability account.

It is doubtful that most aggressors with mental illness qualify as innocent aggressors. Mental illness often diminishes VADCs' culpability without eliminating it (Pickard 2015). Such VADCs occupy a worse-off position in society without having the benefit of extra protections from deadly force, if we accept the culpability account. This view offers little to prioritize their lives.

Notably, some who defend moral protections for innocent aggressors are reluctant to extend those protections to individuals with mental illness. When arguing that innocent aggressors are not liable to deadly force, David Rodin carves out exceptions in cases of mental illness. In his view, only innocent aggressors whose mental "aberration . . . has its source entirely outside of the mental and psychological world of the subject"—like a blow to the head—are not liable to deadly force. But individuals whose aggression arises from factors internal to their psychology do not enjoy the same moral protections, according to Rodin (2002, 94–95). In some cases, mental illness emerges from internal factors beyond an individual's control and is so severe that it renders them not culpable for their aggression. These aggressors certainly appear innocent yet, for Rodin, exist outside the moral protections purportedly for innocent aggressors.

Even for innocent aggressors covered by moral protections in the culpability account, its implications for law and policy are somewhat limited. Most defenders of the culpability account treat deadly force against an innocent aggressor as excused if such force is necessary to stop their grave threat (Ferzan 2005, 748). An excuse suggests that the person who uses force should be exempt from blame and penalties. So though the culpability account sees innocent aggressors as not liable to deadly force, it is a mistake to conclude that this view implies penalties for officers who use deadly force against such aggressors when needed to stop their grave threat.

None of the points raised so far deny the culpability account's central claim that innocent aggressors are not liable to deadly force. How to respond to innocent aggressors threatening grave harm, where deadly force is necessary to stop their threat, is a thorny question that involves competing moral considerations. Since causing harm is seen as worse than allowing it, that consideration counts against using deadly force (McMahan 1994). At the same time, many believe that giving some preference to preserving one's own life is permitted or justified (Quong 2020, 58–96). Here I remain agnostic over whether someone who has only two options—kill or be killed by an innocent aggressor—is morally excused, permitted, or justified in using deadly force. What's important is that all three positions suggest that moral blame and legal penalties are inappropriate for someone who employs deadly force in this predicament.

Though the culpability account provides greater moral protections to VADCs than the traditional account, these protections prove limited and fail to cover most VADCs. As a result, it runs into similar problems as those facing the traditional account. The culpability account offers little to prioritize the lives of many VADCs who, it seems, should receive some priority due to their vulnerability and worse-off position in society.

Proposal 4: Vulnerability Account

The fourth proposal comes from Jeff McMahan. In the ethics of defensive force scholarship, McMahan (2005a, 2009) is best known for the moral responsibility account, which argues that someone's liability to defensive harm varies directly with their moral responsibility (see Chapter 3). He also suggests a complementary yet distinct idea regarding liability that has received less attention: aggressors' *vulnerability* renders them less liable to deadly force (McMahan 2009, 198–202; see also Fabre 2018). This section focuses on that proposal—what I call the vulnerability account—because of its implications for VADCs. The vulnerability account singles out greater susceptibility to harm as a reason to grant VADCs extra protections from deadly force.

This idea comes up in McMahan's discussion of how military forces should respond to child soldiers:

[W]hen just combatants could use lesser force against child soldiers without seriously compromising their ability to achieve their just aims, they may be morally required to fight with restraint, even at greater risk to themselves. . . .

> I suspect that any commander would earn the respect of his troops if he were
> to order them to take additional risks to try to drive back, incapacitate, subdue,
> or capture child soldiers, while sparing their lives. (McMahan 2009, 201–2; see
> also McMahan 2010)

For McMahan, just combatants have an obligation to make extra efforts to avoid
deadly force against child soldiers, even if doing so puts the combatants at greater
risk. This claim has intuitive appeal. Most of us would be troubled if combatants
treated child soldiers like any other adversary.

Child soldiers make moral demands on combatants that other aggressors
do not. In explaining why, McMahan notes that their diminished culpability
and responsibility count in favor of restraint. What he emphasizes, however,
is their vulnerability: "[T]hese soldiers are *children*—that is, individuals who
have hardly had a chance at life and have already been terribly victimized . . . .
[W]hen child soldiers are conspicuously young, there is moral reason to exercise
restraint simply because of their special vulnerability to exploitation and loss"
(McMahan 2009, 201–2). That description applies to children in war zones vulnerable to being coerced into military service and suffering violent harm. Given
their vulnerability, diminished culpability, and worse-off position due to societal
failures to protect them, child soldiers clearly are VADCs.

On its face, child soldiers represent a compelling case in support of the vulnerability account. This example, though, does not represent the cleanest test of
the vulnerability account. As VADCs, child soldiers are characterized by vulnerability *and* diminished culpability, which both could impact liability. It is important to disentangle the respective impact of these factors.

Cases of aggressors characterized by vulnerability or diminished culpability,
but not both, help with that task. Consider the following scenario.

> *Diminished culpability without vulnerability*: A society implements robust
> measures to protect children so that overall they are among those least vulner-
> able to violence. Such measures cannot eliminate all risks, however. A child
> within the society finds a deadly weapon and wields it in a way that threatens
> others. The child is not vulnerable like a VADC, yet their youth leaves them
> barely culpable.

The vulnerability account suggests that someone threatened in this case is justified in responding with less restraint than against a vulnerable child aggressor,
like a child soldier, all else being equal. But that claim seems wrong. The obligation to exercise restraint against the child aggressor strikes us, I suspect, as largely
similar in both cases. Whether the aggressor comes from vulnerable conditions
appears to have little impact on liability in these unfortunate circumstances. If

the aggressor is a 10-year-old, that fact alone is reason for restraint, regardless of the child's background. It is the aggressor's status as a child, with significantly diminished culpability, that demands others to exercise restraint in how they respond.

We also can imagine the converse—a fully culpable aggressor from a vulnerable group. As the experiences of child soldiers illustrate, conditions of vulnerability often go hand in hand with factors that diminish culpability, like abuse, trauma, and duress. But it is possible to be part of a group that overall is more susceptible to harm without personally experiencing factors that diminish culpability. Take the following scenario.

> *Vulnerability without diminished culpability*: In a society with high levels of inequality, the poor suffer systemic injustice, including a heightened risk of police violence. Like other groups, a small percentage of the poor engage in culpable acts of violence. One poor member of the society, who is an adult in complete control of their actions, tries to kill an innocent person without justification or excuse. Since they are fully culpable, this vulnerable aggressor is not a VADC.

The vulnerability account treats this culpable and vulnerable aggressor as less liable to deadly force than an equally culpable but not vulnerable aggressor. A potential victim, then, has an obligation to exercise greater restraint and accept greater risks against a culpable and vulnerable aggressor than against a merely culpable one. Yet that claim appears in tension with justice at the micro-level, which prioritizes protecting the innocent over the culpable in individual interactions.

To be sure, the micro-level perspective by itself is incomplete. It leaves out the context of the encounter: systemic injustice that makes certain groups more susceptible to harm and worse off. From a macro-level perspective focused on distributive justice broadly in society, vulnerable groups—like the one the poor aggressor is a part of—should on prioritarian and egalitarian grounds receive protections against the greater risks they face. But even given those macro-level considerations, the vulnerability account's prescriptions in this case remain questionable. Why should the burden of remedying systemic injustice fall so heavily on innocent persons threatened by vulnerable yet culpable aggressors? That responsibility does clearly lie with state institutions charged with advancing distributive justice, which should strive to fulfill their task in ways consistent with considerations of justice at the micro-level. The vulnerability account makes the controversial move of relying on macro-level considerations for a micro-level domain: liability and justice in individual encounters (see Burri 2022).

These two examples suggest gaps in the vulnerability account. In cases disentangling vulnerability and culpability, the vulnerability account has less intuitive appeal than it does for child soldiers and other VADCs. Given these limitations, the next section looks to identify a firmer moral basis for determining what extra protections from deadly force should apply to VADCs.

Proposal 5: Fusion Account

In Chapter 3, we saw how vulnerability and culpability both matter when thinking about the ethics of defensive force. Each represents a relevant moral consideration for determining individuals' protections from defensive force, with vulnerability receiving greater weight at the macro-level and culpability greater weight at the micro-level. Since VADCs are both vulnerable and culpable, ethical analysis needs to incorporate both considerations to gives us a full picture of what protections VADCs should enjoy. The fusion account does exactly that. It treats vulnerability and culpability as distinct and complementary grounds for enjoying extra protections from deadly force. As a result, this approach offers VADCs more robust protections from deadly force than either the culpability or the vulnerability account.

The fusion account encompasses micro- and macro-level perspectives on justice. This feature distinguishes it from much of the ethics of defensive force scholarship, which is characterized by a hyperfocus on micro-level justice and who is liable to harm in hypothetical scenarios, disconnected from any consideration of background social conditions and institutions. Protections from deadly force are not just found at the micro-level, however. The fusion account is sensitive to that point. It also emphasizes that, at the macro-level, institutions have responsibilities to protect vulnerable groups from deadly force.

In explaining the fusion account in more detail, let's begin at the micro-level with its approach to liability. Recall from the previous section the case of *diminished culpability without vulnerability*, which features a child aggressor. In this case, the aggressor's diminished culpability provides reason for restraint, regardless of their vulnerability. This example suggests that diminished culpability reduces liability to defensive force, which is how the fusion account understands the relationship between liability and culpability. This approach departs from the culpability account's threshold view that any level of culpability, no matter how diminished, makes someone just as liable to deadly force as a fully culpable aggressor. That view of liability excludes many VADCs from its moral protections. In cases of a child soldier or an aggressor with mental illness, additional restraint often seems appropriate, even if the aggressor bears some culpability. The fusion account has the advantage of matching that intuition. It understands these aggressors as less liable to deadly force due to their diminished culpability.

The fusion account's view of liability has the further advantage of advancing macro-level distributive justice goals without conflicting with notions of justice at the micro-level—the problem we noted with the vulnerability account. Because of society's gaps in support for vulnerable groups like those with mental illness, they are more likely to find themselves in violent situations that could have been avoided. VADCs face a greater risk of harm than others who are *equally culpable* yet do not live under the same conditions of vulnerability. For VADCs, even a low level of culpability carries a heightened risk of a deadly encounter. By providing greater protections to those with diminished culpability, the fusion account has the indirect effect of disproportionately benefiting vulnerable groups.

Some ethicists question whether distributive justice considerations are relevant when we consider liability and the ethics of defensive force generally (Quong 2020; Burri 2020a, 2022). The fusion account shows that it is possible to have an approach to liability that advances broader distributive justice goals while also focusing on a consideration, culpability, apt for evaluating justice at the micro-level. In sum, we need not take a radically novel approach to liability to establish broader protections for VADCs.

It is at the level of institutions that the distributive justice principle of prioritizing the vulnerable offers more direct guidance. In McMahan's discussion of child soldiers—the source of the vulnerability account—he emphasizes that combatants should take on extra risks to protect these children (McMahan 2009, 198–202). That point is correct but incomplete. Those who take on extra risks to protect VADCs act admirably, yet it would be morally preferable to have in place measures that lower the risks for all parties. On prioritarian and egalitarian grounds, the fusion account recognizes that institutions have obligations to take steps to reduce the risk of grave harm for vulnerable groups before encounters even occur.

The police are among the institutions with such obligations. Their activities have important consequences for the distribution of harms and benefits in society (see del Pozo 2023; Monaghan 2021a, 2023). One of the most widely recognized functions of the police is to promote peace or public safety (Kleinig 1996, 27–29; Hunt 2019, 24–26). Law, policy, and tactics influence how that public good is allocated. To ensure its fair distribution, principles of distributive justice need to inform policing.

Often various institutions bear responsibility for a group's vulnerability to harm, even in a discrete area like deadly force. Since many factors contribute to conditions of vulnerability, police agencies cannot remedy the problem by themselves. But they have a clear role to play in addressing it. The first step is ongoing study of how best to prioritize the vulnerable in policy and practice. Such study should inform the development of training and tools to help officers uphold that principle in the field. Proper training in use of force and de-escalation prepares officers for encounters with VADCs, while bringing with it higher expectations. Due to the institutional support and specialized training they receive, officers have more extensive and stringent obligations than do civilians to protect the lives of VADCs.

Addressing Objections to the Fusion Account

By treating liability as varying with culpability, the fusion account faces two related objections: its protections to VADCs are meaningless in practice or lead to implausible conclusions. An example illustrates these worries.

> *Certainty that deadly force is necessary*: A barely culpable VADC attacks an innocent victim, who will be killed for certain unless they kill the VADC.

In this case, it is impossible to divide harm between the victim and the aggressor. If the fusion account treats deadly force by the victim as justified on the ground that indivisible harm should fall on the more culpable party, the VADC does not appear any less liable than a fully culpable aggressor. Both are liable to deadly force (for an objection along these lines, see Quong 2020, 103–4). Conversely, if the fusion account avoids that conclusion by treating the VADC as liable to a lesser amount of defensive force—say, only force that would cause moderate injuries—the victim no longer is justified in using the deadly force needed to stop the threat. On that interpretation, the fusion account requires the victim to allow the unjust aggressor to kill them, which strikes many as an implausible conclusion (Quong 2012, 50–51).

Such a demand would be unreasonable, and it is a mistake to attribute that view to the fusion account. But the alternative interpretation—the VADC in the example is liable to deadly force—does not mean that their liability matches that of a fully culpable aggressor. That objection assumes that liability varies in only one sense: the magnitude of force that justifiably can be imposed on someone. But there is another sense of being more or less liable to defensive force: the range of circumstances in which one is liable to a particular level of force. In the above example, it is certain what will stop the aggressor's threat. That's hardly typical. For many and likely most cases of aggression, the person being attacked lacks the luxury of such certainty. Often there is ambiguity over the level of force needed to stop a threat. It is these cases, I argue, that VADCs' diminished culpability becomes most relevant in reducing their liability and the level of force justified against them. A revised view of necessity helps explain why and complements the fusion account's approach to liability.

As covered in Chapter 1, force must be both proportional and necessary to justify its use. Proportionality prohibits force whose harm greatly exceeds the unjust threat that it aims to prevent. Necessity prohibits force that, even if proportionate, causes more harm than required to stop the threat. When the amount of force needed is uncertain, the traditional view of necessity prohibits force that would cause more harm than other options with an equal or better chance of stopping a threat (McMahan 2016, 185). This rule permits questionable uses of force, however. A proportionate option with a better chance of stopping a threat than all the alternatives is justified even if another option with *nearly* the same chance of success would inflict much less harm. So, if deadly force has a 95 percent chance of stopping a VADC's grave threat and de-escalation tactics offer a 94 percent chance of success, police are justified in using deadly force according to the traditional view of necessity. Yet that seems wrong. Police should take on a small additional risk to avoid the grave harm that deadly force would inflict on the VADC (see Lazar 2012, 12; McMahan 2016, 187).

An alternative approach to necessity offers more plausible guidance in such cases. It draws on a concept we already encountered in Part I, "morally weighted harm." This view of harm accounts for the range of ethical considerations that matter for evaluating force. Features that count in a defensive option's favor from a moral perspective lower its morally weighted harm. The opposite is true for features that count against a defensive option from a moral perspective. For instance, a greater likelihood of averting an unjust threat would lower a defensive option's morally weighted harm. Causing grave harm to innocent bystanders would increase its morally weighted harm. Such considerations can pull in opposite directions. That point is important for VADCs since allowing them to carry out their unjust threats leads to obvious harm, yet their diminished culpability increases the morally weighted harm of using force against them. A conception of necessity grounded in morally weighted harm captures those tradeoffs. We specifically can understand necessity as specifying that force is justified only if, when compared with other available defensive options, it minimizes morally weighted harm (Lazar 2012, 5–14; see also Lazar 2018; McMahan 2016).

To illustrate this approach to necessity, let's consider two cases involving different risks of grave harm. The first comes from Baltimore. In July 2020, while experiencing a mental health crisis, Ricky Walker Jr. pulled a gun on nearby officers who responded with fire that proved nonfatal. The incident prompted calls by civil rights groups for increased funding of mental health services and police alternatives for those in crisis (NAACP Legal Defense Fund 2020). There is much to commend in those demands. In a well-funded and functioning mental health system, Walker may never have found himself in a situation requiring a police response. But given the nonideal conditions in which police had to operate, it is difficult to fault their response.

Walker's family called 911 because he was suffering from paranoid schizophrenia, refusing to take his medication, and acting strangely in the basement of their house. Both medics and police came to the house. Emergency responders on the scene decided that police should enter first since Walker's wife mentioned that he may have had a gun, which turned out to be true. Body camera footage shows officers spending over 10 minutes calmly talking with Walker amid a mental health crisis (Mosby 2020). Walker eventually pulled a gun out of his pocket and aimed it at an officer. At this point, officers fired at Walker, who was injured but survived (CBS News 2020). Since Walker threatened officers with a gun, nonlethal options—like trying to tackle him—had a low chance of succeeding and preventing the grave harm he posed. The significant gap between lethal and less lethal options in their expected effectiveness strengthens the moral case for deadly force. A decision by police to refrain from deadly force would have brought a high likelihood of grave harm to an innocent party (one of the officers), whereas using such force came with the high likelihood of grave harm to a VADC. Both harms are significant, but it is unlikely that the latter exceeds the former from the perspective of morally weighted harm. In this encounter, then, deadly force by the officers would qualify as necessary and justified.

Now consider the example that opened this chapter, the police killing of Walter Wallace Jr. in Philadelphia. Whereas Walker in Baltimore had a gun, Wallace had a knife. Despite qualifying as a deadly weapon, a knife is significantly less deadly than a firearm. In fact, for the last decade of available data (2014–2023), only three officers in the US have been killed in knife attacks, according to the Federal Bureau of Investigation (2024). That low number cannot be explained by US officers' being so quick to shoot aggressors with knives. Officers in the United Kingdom also rarely die in knife attacks, even though they are trained to respond without relying on a firearm (Zimring 2017, 100–2). Such data suggest that police resorted to deadly force against Wallace when less lethal tactics, while not guaranteed to succeed, had a real chance of success. That consideration and Wallace's diminished culpability increased the morally weighted harm of using deadly force so that it likely exceeded that of other options, suggesting that such force violated necessity.

The approach to necessity defended here, grounded in the concept of morally weighted harm, brings important nuance too often missing from evaluations of police deadly force. Notably, in the US, many police killings of VADCs with knives are treated as justified based on the law and departmental rules (e.g., Danahy 2019; *Venice Gondolier* 2020). That conclusion proves easier to reach under the traditional view of necessity, which continues to influence law and policy. Since a knife is a deadly weapon, deadly force is generally understood as a proportionate response to a knife attack. In addition to being proportionate, deadly force against an aggressor like Wallace would satisfy the traditional view of necessity—as long as officers reasonably believed that such force offered a slight advantage in the likelihood of stopping the threat over alternatives like de-escalation. That claim is not implausible, given deadly force's effectiveness at incapacitation.

The fusion account's view of necessity offers a rationale to exercise greater restraint. For aggressors generally, this view can require officers to pursue measures that involve taking on additional risk than that associated with deadly force, especially if the extra risk is small. A significantly greater chance of stopping the aggressor's threat *and* preserving their life morally outweighs a small additional risk to officers. Since killing VADCs involves greater morally weighted harm, police in encounters with them can be obligated to take on greater risks than what necessity would demand in encounters with fully culpable aggressors, all else being equal. Correspondingly, VADCs are liable to deadly force in a narrower range of circumstances than are fully culpable aggressors.

Whether there is an obligation to take on extra risk depends on the availability of options that would meaningfully divide risk between the defender and aggressor. In the encounter with Wallace, de-escalation tactics with the option of less lethal force would not have eliminated all risk to the officers and VADC. But these tactics would have distributed risk more justly than did the actual response. Other scenarios preclude the division of risk because the nature of the conflict nearly guarantees that either the defender or aggressor will be killed. In such a case, avoiding deadly force means the defender bears all risk of harm. The fusion account rejects blame or penalties for officers who use deadly force in such difficult circumstances. Its view of necessity sees aggressors' culpability as one, but not the only, factor to consider when comparing the morally weighted harm of potential responses. The likely effectiveness of available options also impacts whether deadly force is morally justified.

Implications for Police Administrators

In many places, police interactions with persons with mental illness would look much different if the fusion account guided them. A case illustrating the status quo drives home that point: the 2020 fatal police shooting of Adrean Stephenson in Sarasota, Florida. Stephenson was a frail 63-year-old woman who lived with chronic pain. She had a history of mental illness and was suicidally cutting herself with glass on the day that her family called police. Video of the incident shows two deputies in the street with their weapons aimed at Stephenson, who placed a fillet knife to her neck and then pointed it at police (see Figure 4.1). The deputies commanded her to drop the knife. One fired his Taser. When that failed, the other officer quickly resorted to shooting and killing Stephenson (Munoz 2020).

Figure 4.1 Police's encounter with Adrean Stephenson (republished with permission from the *Sarasota Herald-Tribune*)

Afterward, Sarasota County Sheriff Tom Knight called it a "tragic situation," bemoaning the lack of mental health services available to help. He emphasized that his deputies acted properly and only used deadly force after exhausting "all attempts at de-escalation" (*Venice Gondolier* 2020).

The Sheriff's response is not surprising. Criticizing the officers who killed Stephenson would have called into question the agency's policies and training. Even when police administrators require officers to receive training in verbal de-escalation for responding to a mental health crisis, such training often remains paired with a version of the 21-foot rule. That rule instructs officers to use deadly force against aggressors with a weapon less lethal than a firearm, like a knife or club, who get within twenty-one feet (Stoughton, Noble, and Alpert 2020, 168–71). When officers are taught the 21-foot rule or, more generally, to resort to deadly force if verbal de-escalation fails and an aggressor still approaches, attempts at de-escalation often do not last long (for further discussion of the 21-foot rule, see Chapter 6). So the deputies who killed Stephenson may have acted in accordance with their training and departmental policies. But the more important question is whether measures to ensure extra protections for the vulnerable were in place to begin with.

Police administrators can advance that goal by adopting policies, training, and equipment that raise the bar for when deadly force is necessary in encounters with VADCs. When police administrators take those steps, incidents like the one with Stephenson will likely end differently. Consider, for instance, how UK police responded in 2011 to a more dangerous aggressor with mental illness—a large man wielding a machete. Compared with most US officers, UK officers receive more robust training in de-escalation tactics aimed at resolving such incidents without deadly force. When UK officers responded to a person with mental illness wielding a machete, video shows their proactive efforts to maintain distance while keeping him surrounded until additional officers with shields arrived (CBC 2016). This equipment rendered deadly force unnecessary and allowed police to disarm the aggressor using other tactics. Wide-scale adoption of such tactics by US police would especially benefit those with mental illness, who are overrepresented among those armed with a knife when shot by police (Saleh et al. 2018, 114; Ward et al. forthcoming).

These reforms would save the lives of other aggressors carrying a weapon less lethal than a firearm. Indeed, extra efforts to protect VADCs can raise the bar for when deadly force is necessary in other contexts. That outcome mirrors how efforts to create a more accessible environment for those with disabilities have broader benefits. For example, curb cuts make it easier for those in wheelchairs to navigate on and off sidewalks, while also benefiting cyclists and parents with children in strollers.

Though the fusion account has policy implications whose benefits would extend beyond VADCs, it is a mistake to see it as indistinguishable from simply calling for greater restraint against all aggressors. Importantly, the fusion account emphasizes giving priority to VADCs when police administrators make decisions on how to deploy limited resources.

Another potential implication for policy illustrates that point. In addition to changes in training for officers generally, the fusion account may require police administrators to put in place teams designed to further reduce the need for deadly force against VADCs. Through intensive training, specialized teams would have expertise in de-escalation and corresponding equipment to help resolve crises without deadly force. These units likely would be a scarce resource that could not be deployed in response to every aggressor. Police administrators would have an obligation to prioritize protecting VADCs when deploying the resource.

Calling for such investments hardly seems unreasonable given current practices. Law enforcement in the US has made significant investments in training teams to conduct militarized drug raids (see Kraska 2007). In a world where police administrators engaged in proactive efforts to protect the most vulnerable, police units highly effective in resolving encounters with VADCs through nonlethal means would be the norm, rather than SWAT teams that often exacerbate the vulnerability of already vulnerable groups (see Mummolo 2018a).

Police administrators' efforts in the US to protect VADCs have been insufficient. The most common approach is Crisis Intervention Team (CIT) training, which a minority but growing number of agencies have adopted. CIT teaches officers about mental illness, de-escalation, and coordinating with mental health resources in their community (Rogers, McNiel, and Binder 2019). To be sure, increased interest in CIT is a welcome step. But it would be a mistake to see the program as a panacea for police violence against persons with mental illness. Investigations have revealed that some CIT training programs present incorrect and demeaning information about persons with mental illness. CIT training materials for the Minneapolis Police Department, for instance, included the claim that a child with autism "will power struggle with you to the death" (US Department of Justice 2023, 64). CIT's de-escalation training also has limited effectiveness when outdated tactics like the 21-foot rule remain in place.

Such limitations were evident in the police response to Stephenson. Two years before the incident, the Sarasota County Sheriff's Office (2018) boasted that all its "law enforcement members . . . are . . . trained in crisis intervention and de-escalation tactics." The deputies who encountered Stephenson had a combined 120 hours of CIT training, yet that failed to prevent them from killing a 63-year-old woman in a mental health crisis (Henning 2020).

Despite anecdotal reports by some departments that adopting CIT reduced police shootings of persons with mental illness (Miller and Hanson 2016, 77–94), empirical studies find little evidence that the training lowers the risk of injury or death for this population (Rogers, McNiel, and Binder 2019; Fagan and Campbell 2020, 998–99; Marcus and Stergiopoulos 2022). These findings suggest that police administrators have an obligation to pursue strategies beyond just CIT training to protect aggressors with mental illness (see Engel et al. 2022 discussed in the next section).

Implications for Officers

Because of failures by police administrators, some officers end up in situations where they lack the most effective training and tools available to protect the lives of aggressors with mental illness. But even under nonideal conditions, officers have special obligations to VADCs. Deficient policies, training, and equipment mitigate but do not eliminate blame for officers who fail to exercise greater restraint in encounters with VADCs. In the context of institutional failures, the fusion account still implies certain moral obligations on officers.

Those obligations include taking on extra risks to preserve the lives of VADCs. Consider the police encounter with the 63-year-old Stephenson. Though the two deputies lacked training and equipment that would have been helpful in avoiding deadly force, they could have done more to save Stephenson's life. They resorted to deadly force quickly, spending less than a minute on other tactics (Munoz 2020). Given that Stephenson posed no immediate threat to anyone besides the officers, they could have prolonged attempts at de-escalation by repositioning and maintaining distance from her and the knife. Even if those tactics imposed a small additional risk on the officers, there is the moral expectation that they take that risk to protect life, especially for someone with mental illness.

Imagine the same incident, except that the woman holding the knife was a close relative of the deputy who fired his gun. Would he have been so quick to shoot? Probably not. If faced with a loved one wielding a knife, most of us would be more reluctant to use deadly force than was the deputy who shot Stephenson. In fact, we would understand ourselves as *obligated* to exercise greater restraint. For at least some aggressors to whom we have special relationships, we recognize our obligation to take on extra risks to save them. The fusion account suggests that the same is true for police interactions with VADCs, such as Stephenson and the mentally ill aggressor who wielded a machete at police in the UK.

This point does not necessarily imply criminal penalties for officers who fall short of their obligation to exercise greater restraint in interactions with VADCs. Criminal penalties do not make sense in every instance where police violate a moral obligation. While someone plausibly has an obligation to exercise greater restraint in the case of a loved one engaged in aggressive action, failing to take on extra risks in this scenario represents a moral failure that typically does not prompt legal penalties. Such penalties seem unduly harsh for someone whose fault is not taking on additional risks for a loved one and instead responding with force that would be morally justified against a stranger. That conclusion likely holds for individual officers responding to VADCs. If an officer in an encounter with a VADC fails to take on risks beyond what would be required in an encounter with a non-VADC posing a similar threat, it's a moral failure but probably not one that calls for criminal penalties. Less severe but still meaningful forms of accountability, like departmental discipline, may be more appropriate for such cases.

What if an officer encounters a VADC threatening an innocent civilian? Though much depends on the details, generally there is a stronger intuition in favor of police deadly force when an innocent civilian is at risk. That intuition aligns with the fusion account's view of necessity, which takes into account the significant harm of killing an innocent civilian. We should be wary, though, of jumping to the conclusion that any small but nontrivial risk to an innocent civilian by a VADC justifies deadly force. In the example that opened this chapter, the police shooting of Walter Wallace Jr., his mother rushed into the street to try to stop her son from threatening police with a knife (Dale 2020). Some might justify police deadly force on the ground that, even if officers had an obligation to take on extra risks to protect an aggressor with mental illness like Wallace, shooting him was necessary to protect his mother. That justification is morally dubious, though. His mother willingly put herself in harm's way to save her son, suggesting that she would not want that risk treated as a justification for killing her son. If someone willingly takes a risk to protect a VADC and that risk remains mostly limited to the person choosing it, officers should avoid treating it as a justification for deadly force.

The focus here and throughout the chapter has been on clarifying police obligations in cases where it is relatively clear that the aggressor has mental illness. Sometimes, though, officers find themselves in a situation where it is unclear whether an aggressor's erratic and combative behavior stems from a mental health crisis or another factor like drug use. Under such uncertainty, should police still exercise greater restraint?

This is a tough case. Potential guidance for dealing with it comes from a distinction that Jake Monaghan makes in his book *Just Policing*. In uncertain scenarios, he notes, policing can be either harsh or lenient (Monaghan 2023, 90–92). Harsh strategies look to minimize false negatives: failing to take enforcement action—like stopping, arresting, or using force against someone—where such action is merited from an objective point of view with full knowledge of the crime or threat in question. Not stopping someone who just robbed a store because police mistakenly believe them to be innocent counts as a false negative. While reducing the risk of false negatives, harsh strategies raise the risk of false positives: mistakenly taking enforcement action where it isn't merited from an objective point of view. A classic example of a false positive is police arresting someone for a crime they didn't commit.

For our question here, a harsh policing strategy means that officers exercise greater restraint only if they have a high degree of certainty that an aggressor has mental illness or some other feature that significantly diminishes culpability. By setting a high bar for using greater restraint, a harsh strategy makes it less likely that officers distribute this benefit to aggressors who are not VADCs. But it raises the risk of withholding that benefit from aggressors who are in fact VADCs. A lenient strategy takes the opposite approach. Where there is uncertainty, it errs on the side of greater restraint. As a result, VADCs are less likely to miss out on a benefit they should receive, while less culpable aggressors are more likely to receive a benefit that police are not obligated to provide them.

Two factors, I believe, favor a lenient strategy in this context. First, creating a world hospitable for individuals with mental illness (as well as other forms of disability) requires making accessible the benefits and protections they should enjoy. Even if we recognize in theory that persons with mental illness are a vulnerable group that should receive priority in the distribution of certain benefits and protections, stringent barriers to accessing benefits and protections frustrates that goal in practice. Adopting a lenient strategy in cases where police are uncertain whether an aggressor has mental illness represents a step officers can take to make the world less threatening and more welcoming to persons with mental illness (see Thacher 2024).

Second, there are well-established links between mental illness and drug use, so it would be a mistake to develop police strategies that treat those with mental illness and those who use drugs as distinct populations. Mental illness is a recognized risk factor for substance abuse. Survey data consistently find that persons with mental illness use drugs at higher rates (National Institute on Drug Abuse 2020). Even if we understand mental illness as a more compelling exculpatory factor than drug use, it is not uncommon for an aggressor impaired by drugs to also have mental illness and qualify as a VADC. A lenient strategy reflects awareness of that reality. It recognizes the overlap between aggressors impaired by drugs and VADCs, given the comorbidity between substance abuse and mental illness.

So just as there are compelling reasons for leniency in other areas of criminal justice—such as the trial process, where it is better to acquit the guilty than convict the innocent—leniency should guide officers in encounters with aggressors whose status as a VADC is uncertain. Still, a thorny question remains: *how* lenient? It is difficult to specify where exactly to draw the line on what additional risks officers should bear in uncertain cases. But here is one plausible rule: for an aggressor who is unarmed or whose weapon is less lethal than a firearm, where it is unclear whether they are impaired by drugs or by mental illness, officers should commit to greater restraint. This proposal offers extra protections in precisely the circumstances where VADCs have the strongest claim to them. It also avoids placing excessive burdens on officers. The strategy imposes on officers some risks beyond what they would be required to bear with perfect information, but these risks remain relatively modest since encounters where a suspect lacks a firearm tend not to be the deadliest ones that police face.

When thinking about how to fulfill their obligations to VADCs, officers need to recognize that these obligations have implications beyond just the encounters themselves. Responding with restraint to a VADC is an unrealistic expectation if one has not prepared for it. In this and other contexts, we put ourselves in the best position to succeed through cultivating practices and habits that help us meet our moral obligations. Officers should seek out training grounded in evidence-based strategies for safely interacting with individuals experiencing a mental health crisis. If their department has failed to implement policies, training, and equipment that would help save the lives of persons with mental illness, they should lobby their superiors for such changes.

Encouragingly, policy changes that better protect vulnerable groups also can benefit officers. Consider a randomized controlled trial of de-escalation training that drew on practices from policing in the UK with the objective of reducing deadly force against suspects with mental illness and suspects without a firearm. It found that the training led to fewer injuries for suspects *and* officers (Engel et al. 2022). Slowing things down and not rushing to resolve an encounter tend to make it safer for all parties involved. These findings suggest that officers need not view efforts to better protect the vulnerable as a zero-sum game. In some scenarios, exercising greater restraint to protect the vulnerable may unavoidably lead to additional risks. But overall, an emphasis on de-escalation coupled with effective training appears to promote officer safety.

Implications for the Law

Police administrators and officers have obligations to make extra efforts to protect VADCs and, ideally, would willingly fulfill those obligations. But seeing that they do is a responsibility that, in the US and elsewhere, ultimately falls to democratic institutions. They have both the power and responsibility to implement laws and mechanisms of accountability for police that prioritize protecting vulnerable populations.

This issue came before the US Supreme Court in *City and County of San Francisco v. Sheehan* (2015). In 2008, San Francisco officers shot Teresa Sheehan multiple times in a group home for individuals with mental illness. Sheehan had threatened two officers with a knife after they entered her private room, where she was alone. The officers retreated but then shot her after taking the questionable step of reentering her room before the arrival of more officers, who could have helped avoid the need for deadly force. The Supreme Court granted the officers qualified immunity on the ground that they did not violate "clearly established" law. It also refused to rule on a question that lower courts had split on: does the Americans with Disabilities Act's (ADA) requirement that public entities provide reasonable accommodations to those with disability—including psychiatric disability or mental illness—apply to police responding to persons with mental illness who are armed and violent?

Here I am interested in the moral question of whether the law generally should require police to make accommodations to protect the lives of aggressors with mental illness, rather than the interpretive question of how to read the ADA. On the moral question, the fusion account makes clear that the answer is yes. Police have an obligation to take extra steps to protect the lives of VADCs. Given the state's interest in protecting life, it has strong reason to put in place laws that promote this obligation and hold police accountable when they fail to fulfill it.

If such laws were in place, police could have faced penalties for many of the incidents discussed above—the shootings of Walter Wallace Jr., Adrean Stephenson, and Teresa Sheehan. Police were ill-prepared to resolve these encounters through less lethal means, though training in those methods was available. Democratic institutions can and should push police to address such failures, while providing the resources to do so.

The fusion account's implications for the law intersect with its implications for police administrators and officers. Rather than being a barrier to reform, police should support legislation to better protect persons with mental illness and other vulnerable individuals (see Monaghan 2017, 229–30). Police professionals who use their influence in this way would demonstrate their commitment to protecting the vulnerable.

Clearly, much needs to change given the alarming rate at which police in the US kill individuals with mental illness. Various factors are to blame, including inadequate mental health services that put police in a difficult spot. Current police practices exacerbate the problem, however. Many departments lack policies, training, and equipment that would reduce harm to those with mental illness and other vulnerable populations. Aggressors with mental illness have two features—vulnerability and diminished culpability—that together call for them to receive more extensive protections from deadly force. The dearth of such protections in law and practice represents a moral failure, which police and democratic institutions must remedy if they are to fulfill their obligations to those with mental illness.

5

Racial Disparities in Police Deadly Force

For some incidents of police violence, it is hard not to come away with the impression that racial bias impacted officers' actions. Take one of the most high-profile examples, the 2020 murder of George Floyd in Minneapolis, Minnesota. Floyd was unarmed and defenseless on the ground while a White police officer knelt on his neck for over nine minutes, suffocating the life out of him. Bystanders pleaded with the officer to get off Floyd as he cried for help, to no avail (Willis et al. 2021). Video of the murder shocked much of the country. What Floyd as a Black American suffered seemed entirely foreign to many White Americans' experiences with the police. Even if only briefly in the summer of 2020, Floyd's murder prompted more people to accept that racial bias influences policing and puts Black Americans at greater risk of harm.

Several years later in 2023, another Black American, Tyre Nichols, died in an incident every bit as brutal as Floyd's murder. Like Floyd, Nichols was unarmed when Memphis police officers beat him to death following a traffic stop. There were differences, though, in how the media and public reacted to the incident. The killing less clearly fit the mold of one motivated by racial bias since the officers who brutalized Nichols were also Black (McGrady 2023). Certainly, individuals can exhibit bias against members of their own racial group. Nonetheless, the details in the case raise the possibility that other factors—like where police patrol and focus enforcement activities—contribute to racial disparities in police deadly force.

When we shift from looking at individual cases to aggregate data, we consistently find racial disparities in who is killed by police. Historically marginalized groups, particularly Black Americans, make up a disproportionate share of those killed by police (*Washington Post* 2024; Campaign Zero 2026). Though few dispute this basic fact, there is less agreement on what explains these disparities and what policy conclusions to draw from them.

Social science research offers three leading explanations for the racial disparities in police killings in the US.

(1) *Individual bias*: implicit or explicit bias affects officers' deadly force decisions.

Protecting Life. Ben Jones, Oxford University Press. © Ben Jones 2026.
DOI: 10.1093/9780197823316.003.0008

(2) *Disparate enforcement*: police focus patrols and enforcement activities in marginalized neighborhoods, which expose certain racial groups to more police contacts and a greater risk of being killed by them.

(3) *Differential involvement hypothesis*: certain racial groups engage in more violent crime, which puts them at greater risk of being confronted and killed by police. (see Tregle, Nix, and Alpert 2019; Unnever, Owusu-Bempah, and Deryol 2019; Knox, Lowe, and Mummolo 2020; Ross, Winterhalder, and McElreath 2021)

Those who see racial disparities in police killings as a pressing injustice, which demands policy solutions, primarily point to (1) individual bias or (2) disparate enforcement to explain the disparities. In contrast, those who defend the police against charges of discriminatory behavior tend to explain the disparities by appealing to the (3) differential involvement hypothesis.

It is unsurprising that the debate breaks down along these lines. If (1), (2), or both explain racial disparities in police killings, factors beyond the control of marginalized racial groups make them more vulnerable to police violence. Such factors make for a world that is fundamentally unfair for marginalized groups by forcing them to live with a heightened risk of police violence. If that view is right, basic notions of fairness and justice (covered in Chapter 3) suggest that the state must take steps to reduce the risks these groups face from the police. But most people who point to (3) as the primary reason for racial disparities in police killings draw a different conclusion. In their view, it is a mistake to see certain racial groups as vulnerable in the sense of facing a higher risk of police violence due to factors *beyond their control*. Rather, something within their control—criminal activity—increases their risk of being killed by police. In other words, some groups are at fault for the higher risk of police violence they face (see Mac Donald 2016).

It is beyond this study's scope to resolve whether (1), (2), or (3) best explains racial disparities in police killings. Debates over this question among social scientists have failed to yield a consensus view. Importantly, (1), (2), and (3) are not mutually exclusive explanations. All three factors likely contribute to some extent to racial disparities in police killings. This chapter reviews the evidence for each explanation and considers the moral and policy implications that follow from each. Regardless of *which* explanation is true, *all* imply injustice by the state that demands policy interventions to address it. That point holds even for the (3) differential involvement hypothesis.

We can turn to Martin Luther King Jr.'s thought to better understand why. When responding to riots in US cities during the late 1960s, King (2015) identified and condemned the conditions that led to the riots: inequality and lack of economic opportunity, giving way to despair. There are parallels between then and now. Patterns of crime and violence are not an accident but closely linked to societal structures that unfairly disadvantage marginalized groups.

Perhaps unexpectedly, then, the differential involvement hypothesis ends up having the most dramatic implications for policy. If racial disparities are due to officer bias or how police deploy resources, police reform is the best way to address the problem. The differential involvement hypothesis implies instead the need to change society more broadly. In societies marked by structural racism, factors outside policing often contribute to racial disparities in police killings. Given the problem's complexity, we cannot expect police reforms alone to fix it.

What the Data Say

Government records of police killings, like those maintained by the Federal Bureau of Investigation (FBI) and National Vital Statistics System, suffer from underreporting and missing data, which lead to dramatic underestimates (Zimring 2017, 23–40; GBD 2019 Police Violence US Subnational Collaborators 2021). In the 2010s, the widely recognized shortcomings of government sources, combined with growing public interest, prompted media and nonprofit organizations to begin tracking police killings in the US. Some like the *Guardian* (2016) recorded police killings for a few years before stopping. The *Washington Post*'s (2024) "Fatal Force" database collected data for a decade, recording all fatal shootings by on-duty police between 2015 and 2024. The "Mapping Police Violence" database maintained by Campaign Zero (2026), an organization that advocates for police reform, goes back to 2013 and remains current as of 2026. It includes all incidents of lethal force by on- or off-duty police leading to a civilian's death. Given their different methodologies, there are some discrepancies between databases. George Floyd's murder, for instance, shows up in Campaign Zero's but not the *Washington Post*'s database. The latter excludes Floyd's murder because his death did not result from an officer shooting.

Though exact numbers and percentages differ depending on the source one consults, a similar picture emerges from the various databases. From the 2010s through to the present, police have killed over a thousand people annually. Black Americans make up more than a quarter of those killed by police, which is double their share of the US population (Campaign Zero 2026; *Washington Post* 2024). Studies find that Black, Hispanic, and Native Americans all face a greater risk of being killed by police than do White Americans, with the risk being particularly high for Black men. Estimates put Black men's risk of being killed by police at two to three times higher than it is for White men (Edwards, Esposito, and Lee 2018; Edwards, Lee, and Esposito 2019). Concretely, that heightened risk means one out of every thousand Black men in the US will die from police violence (Edwards, Lee, and Esposito 2019). Data on police deadly force that proves nonfatal—such as a police shooting that injures rather than kills—are harder to come by. But for states that make such data available, the disparities are even starker than for police killings. In some states, Black Americans are over five times more likely than White Americans to be injured by a police shooting (Nix and Shjarback 2021, 5–6).

Together, the evidence makes clear that police use deadly force against Black Americans at higher rates than what we would expect given their share of the population. This finding is troubling on its face. Black Americans are a historically marginalized group. They have been subjected to slavery, Jim Crow, and other forms of oppression. Racial disparities in police deadly force continue the legacy of the state inflicting disproportionate harm on Black Americans. It is difficult, though, to diagnose the exact nature of this injustice and identify the appropriate policy responses without first understanding the causes of the disparities. Let's turn now to potential causes.

Explanation 1: Individual Bias

Racial bias comes in both explicit and implicit forms. Explicit bias openly endorses that certain racial groups are inferior. Explicit avowals of White supremacy appear throughout policing's history in the US. During Jim Crow as well as after, we find examples of local police departments made up largely of Ku Klux Klan (KKK) members (Rothstein 2017, 150; Burnham 2022, 103). In certain states and counties, police cooperation emboldened the KKK to threaten and brutalize Black residents with impunity (e.g., Burnham 2022, 222–29). In one case from South Carolina, an officer died while participating in an attack on a Black-owned business. Afterward, he was found wearing a Klan robe over his police uniform (Ward 2018, 173). It is a mistake to think that explicit bias is a problem that only existed in the past. Acting on evidence that it uncovered, the FBI has warned about efforts by White supremacist groups to infiltrate law enforcement. In a variety of recent incidents, police officers' membership in the KKK or other hate groups has come to light (Johnson 2022, 563–69). Such explicit bias has the potential to motivate officers to brutalize Black Americans and other groups. Those targeted find themselves placed outside the law's protections by the very agents charged to uphold it (see Donelson 2017).

Today researchers, police administrators, and policymakers concerned about bias primarily focus on implicit rather than explicit bias (Glaser 2014; Spencer, Charbonneau, and Glaser 2016). For most police killings in recent years, it is rare to find evidence of explicit bias. Nonetheless, the worry remains that implicit bias may have played a role. Implicit bias is more subtle and operates automatically, often without awareness of its effects (Onyeador, Hudson, and Lewis Jr., 2021, 20). For some officers, sight of a Black individual may automatically evoke certain stereotypes, prejudice, and suspicion. That risk proves especially acute for interactions with young Black men, who have long been saddled with perceptions of being dangerous (Stevenson 2017, 4). When implicit bias prompts such reactions, it may make officers more likely to use deadly force than they would against someone of a different race.

The most common way to measure implicit bias is with the Implicit Association Test (IAT). The version of the IAT that measures racial bias shows White and Black faces and asks test-takers to click on either positive or negative words in association with those faces, like "spectacular" or "horrible." The speed with which test-takers accomplish these tasks indicates whether their automatic associations to a particular race tends to be more positive or negative (Project Implicit 2024). We have reason, though, to be wary of taking an officer's IAT score as evidence that implicit bias would affect how they use deadly force. Studies find that IAT scores tend to be poor predictors of discriminatory behavior (Oswald et al. 2013).

Psychologists have developed other tests of implicit bias, inspired by the decisions police face on whether to use deadly force. In the first-person shooter task (FPST), participants are instructed to press "shoot" in response to images of an armed individual and "don't shoot" in response to images of an unarmed individual. They are asked to respond quickly to a series of images in which the individual's race varies, as does what is in their hand—sometimes a gun, other times a harmless object like a cell phone. In the original FPST experiment, participants exhibited anti-Black bias. When shown Black subjects, they were both quicker to shoot and more likely to shoot an unarmed individual (Correll et al. 2002, 1325).

One could interpret the FPST experiments as evidence that implicit bias influences deadly force decisions like those police officers face. But we have reasons to be cautious about drawing strong conclusions about policing from these experiments. First, in FPST experiments with both police officers and lay people, officers make fewer errors and exhibit less racial bias (Correll et al. 2007; Correll et al. 2014). In fact, across most FPST experiments involving officers, they do not "shoot" unarmed Black subjects at a higher rate (Cesario 2022, 9; Cesario and Carrillo 2024, 537–40). Second, there is also little evidence of anti-Black bias from experiments where officers make shoot/don't shoot decisions in a simulator under more realistic conditions than the FPST (Cesario and Carrillo 2024, 530–32). Third, FPST studies do not consistently find anti-Black bias in shooting errors. A meta-analysis of such studies failed to find that race has a significant effect on the false alarm rate. In other words, an unarmed subject's race did not appear to affect participants' likelihood to shoot (Mekawi and Bresin 2015, 123).

Overall, the FPST and related experiments offer somewhat tenuous evidence for a link between implicit bias and racial disparities in police killings. The artificial nature of the FPST makes it difficult to generalize its lab-based results to police behavior in the field. Plus, FPST experiments—especially those involving police officers—do not consistently yield outcomes suggesting racial bias.

Those points do not mean that concerns about implicit bias in policing lack any basis. It is just that other evidence proves more compelling than the FPST studies. Findings particularly worth looking at are measures of implicit bias in the aggregate.

While *individual* measures of implicit bias often vary across tests and are poor predictors of discriminatory behavior, *aggregate* measures of implicit bias in a population prove to be more stable and better predictors of discrimination (Payne and Hannay 2021, 928). For example, implicit bias against women among a nation's population predicts gender gaps in math and science scores for the nation's schoolchildren (Nosek et al. 2009). Such findings suggest that we can understand aggregate implicit bias as an indicator of sexism or racism broadly in society. On this model, implicit bias and entrenched forms of disadvantage reinforce one another. People's exposure to persistent inequality strengthens implicit bias against marginalized groups at the population level. Such bias, in turn, influences patterns of behavior in society that further contribute to the disadvantage experienced by marginalized groups (Payne and Hannay 2021).

Notably, researchers find that regional measures of implicit bias predict racial disparities in police killings. In areas with higher scores of implicit racial bias among White residents, police kill Black Americans at higher rates (Hehman, Flake, and Calanchini 2018). This research has limitations since it establishes correlation rather than causation (Hehman, Flake, and Calanchini 2018, 398). Nonetheless, it shows a close link between implicit bias and racial disparities. It is plausible that forms of racial disadvantage and implicit bias mutually reinforce one another. In that case, there would be a causal relationship between the two. Implicit bias contributes to the societal disadvantages experienced by certain racial groups, and vice versa.

Racial disparities for a subset of police killings—those involving unarmed individuals—offer further potential evidence of implicit bias. If implicit bias impacts police decisions to use deadly force, it means that officers act differently than they would in the exact same circumstances with only the race of the suspect changed. Obviously, we cannot run that counterfactual in real life. Still, we can see whether race appears to play a role in officers' decisions by examining police killings that share similar features. Many of the most questionable killings involve officers taking the life of an unarmed individual. Racial disparities for this subset of cases are even more pronounced than for police killings generally. Police kill unarmed Black Americans at markedly higher rates than they kill unarmed White Americans (*Washington Post* 2024; DeAngelis 2024, 418–19). Such disparities suggests that race does influence officers' decisions. Even when facing similar circumstances and threats, officers are more likely to resort to deadly force against Black individuals.

Now perhaps a factor besides implicit bias explains the disparities. For instance, Black suspects might be more likely to resist. This alternative explanation lacks much evidence to support it, however. A study examining the racial make-up of unarmed victims killed by police found that Black individuals were not more likely than White individuals to be attacking officers when killed (Nix et al. 2017, 324–26). Together these findings suggest that implicit bias, which can distort officers' perceptions of danger, explains some of the racial disparities in police deadly force.

Explanation 2: Disparate Enforcement

Police lack the resources to be everywhere all at once, so they must make strategic decisions about where to deploy resources. Many proactive policing strategies to deter and prevent crime concentrate patrols and enforcement activities in high-crime areas (see Weisburd and Majmundar 2018). There is an obvious rationale for this approach. Given scarce resources, it makes sense to direct them where they are most needed and can have the biggest impact in reducing crime and violence. But proactive policing risks becoming a self-fulfilling prophecy that exacerbates racial disparities. If police spend most of their time enforcing the law in neighborhoods of color, that is where they will issue the most tickets and make the most arrests. Crime data then indicate that these neighborhoods have the highest crime rates. That finding, though, is partly a function of heightened enforcement. What can emerge is a gap between the true rate of criminal involvement for marginalized groups and the rate at which they are arrested or fined.

Disparate enforcement offers a potential explanation for racial disparities in police killings. Every police contact carries some risk of escalating and turning fatal. That risk is higher with certain enforcement practices, like no-knock raids (see Chapter 6). If police focus on neighborhoods of color when conducting stops aimed at finding drugs and other contraband, residents of those neighborhoods find themselves at greater risk of coming into contact with an armed officer. More contacts mean a higher overall chance of being killed by police.

Note that disparate enforcement can lead to racial disparities even if individual officers act free from bias. Imagine police officers who are equally likely to stop and ticket a White driver as a Black driver for the same traffic violations. If supervisors send these unbiased officers to a predominantly Black neighborhood to conduct traffic enforcement but do not send any units to the nearby White neighborhood, the officers will primarily encounter—as well as stop and ticket—Black drivers, leading to racial disparities.

Strong evidence suggests that disparate enforcement can explain at least some of the racial differences in police killings. Racial disparities have long characterized drug arrests, despite the fact that Black and White Americans use drugs at similar rates. Several factors contribute to these racial disparities, with disparate enforcement being among them. Black Americans are more likely to live in neighborhoods with a stronger police presence and emphasis on drug enforcement (Mitchell and Caudy 2015, 303, 307). Disparate enforcement notably shows up in some of the most aggressive forms of policing. A study found that police in Maryland are more likely to deploy SWAT teams to areas with a higher percentage of Black residents, even after controlling for local crime rates (Mummolo 2018a, 9183). It is hardly surprising that police violence harms Blacks Americans at higher rates than White Americans when the most aggressive enforcement practices occur disproportionately in Black neighborhoods.

As with implicit bias, it is difficult to say how much of the racial disparities in police killings can be attributed to disparate enforcement. At a minimum, we can safely say that enforcement practices contribute to the problem. Consider the incident discussed earlier, the police killing of Tyre Nichols in Memphis. What did Nichols do to prompt police to pull him over? Something that drivers do all the time: speeding up to avoid a red light (Cochrane and Stanley 2025). If he had been driving in an area without aggressive enforcement of crime hot spots, he likely never would have been forced out of his car and beaten. There is a good chance he wouldn't have been stopped at all for such a minor violation and would have made it home that night unscathed. As this case shows, disparate enforcement can impose substantial and deadly harm on marginalized groups.

Explanation 3: Differential Involvement Hypothesis

Not all disparities in who is killed by police necessarily raise concerns. We expect police to be more likely to kill those who violently attack and threaten others than peaceful individuals. From an ethical and legal perspective, the former are more appropriate targets for deadly force than the latter. That point informs one explanation for racial disparities in police deadly force: it is a product of correlations between race and who commits violence. According to the differential involvement hypothesis, certain racial groups commit crimes—particularly violent crimes—at higher rates. Since those groups are more like to engage in action justifying deadly force, it follows that they make up a disproportionate share of those killed by police.

Defenders of the police often make this argument. In her book *The War on Cops*, Heather Mac Donald (2016, 30) takes issue with the "relentless effort to demonize the police" for purported racial bias. As she puts it in a later article, systemic racism in policing is a "myth." In her view, "Crime and suspect behavior, not race, determine most police actions." Police shootings in particular are "a function of how often officers encounter armed and violent suspects" (Mac Donald 2020). Because Black Americans commit a disproportionate share of homicides and other violent crimes, she reasons, it makes sense that they are killed by police at higher rates than other racial groups.

Even critics of the police concede the racial disparities in crime rates that Mac Donald highlights. For instance, the legal theorist Paul Butler is highly critical of racist practices in policing and praises Black Lives Matter. At the same time, he stresses, antiracist movements need to confront that "African American men commit a disproportionate share of certain serious crimes, including homicide, assault, robbery, and are disproportionately victims of those same crimes" (Butler 2017, 121). In his view, ignoring those data leaves us with an incomplete picture. As a result, we end up poorly positioned to identify the causes of current racial disparities and the best strategies to address them.

Given how differential criminal involvement could impact police killings, some researchers caution against using population data as a benchmark for whether there is evidence of racial discrimination (Tregle, Nix, and Alpert 2019; Cesario, Johnson, and Terrill 2019). If population is the benchmark, when a racial group makes up a higher percentage of those killed by police than their percentage of the population, that counts as evidence of racial discrimination. An alternative approach relies on a measure of criminal involvement, like arrest rates for violent crime, as its benchmark. This approach sets a higher bar for evidence of racial discrimination: a group's share of those killed by police must exceed their share of those arrested for certain crimes. Studies adopting this approach generally do not find that Black Americans' share of those killed by police exceeds what we would expect based on their arrest rates (Cesario, Johnson, and Terrill 2019; Fryer 2019; Tregle, Nix, and Alpert 2019; Mentch 2020).

Adopting crime rates as a benchmark raises its own concerns, however. If factors like implicit bias or disparate enforcement influence arrest rates, our benchmark for measuring racial discrimination is itself the result of racial discrimination. Such a benchmark overstates the criminal involvement of groups whose arrest rates are, at least in part, a function of racially discriminatory policing. It can have the effect of obscuring discrimination's role in police killings (see Knox, Lowe, and Mummolo 2020). In addition, even if we rely on arrest rates as a benchmark, it still proves difficult to explain the stark racial disparities in police killings of unarmed individuals (Ross, Winterhalder, and McElreath 2021, 327–29).

So what should we make of the differential involvement hypothesis as an explanation for racial disparities in police killings? Given the limitations discussed, the hypothesis likely cannot explain all the disparities observed. It appears more plausible that the differential involvement hypothesis explains *some* of the disparities. As Butler notes, racially discriminatory police practices affect some arrest rates more than others. Survey data and how police have conducted the war on drugs give us strong reason to conclude that drug arrests overstate the rate at which Black Americans use drugs compared with other groups. Such gaps in actual criminal involvement and arrests are likely to be less pronounced for more serious crimes like murder, which are reported more consistently and tend to be intraracial, meaning that the victim and perpetrator are the same race (Butler 2017, 121–24). Persistent racial disparities in both victimization and arrests for homicide offer some support for the differential involvement hypothesis, which in turn could impact disparities in police killings.

The Moral Issues at Stake in the Debate over Racial Disparities

On the surface, competing explanations for racial disparities in police killings are a social scientific debate. What *causes* these disparities? Some who study police killings stress that this is an empirical rather than a moral question. Joseph Cesario (2022, 7–8) writes: "It is necessary to keep causal analysis distinct from 'blaming the victim' . . . . Whatever the causal factors that lead an individual to one or another outcome, such factors can be described without the language of blame and responsibility." He makes this remark in the context of questioning bias by individual officers as an explanation for racial disparities in police killings, while suggesting that differential criminal involvement may be a more compelling explanation.

Causal explanations need not involve assigning blame, as Cesario points out. But by itself his remark gives an incomplete picture of the relationship between causal and moral reasoning. The two often interact. If social science reveals that one factor rather than another causes an outcome that we regard as morally bad, that finding helps answer the moral question of what policies we *should* adopt. For instance, if an environmental toxin rather than poor diet is the primary cause of extraordinarily high cancer rates in several neighborhoods, our policy response should focus on cleaning up the environment rather than trying to change how people eat. Causal explanations also help in determining whether individuals contribute to an outcome or whether it is outside their control. In this way, causal explanations inform moral judgments about blame and vulnerability. We need to understand causal relationships in the world to figure out if someone is vulnerable in the sense that factors beyond their control make them more susceptible to harm. Someone vulnerable in this sense is unfairly disadvantaged and not to blame for the heightened risk they face.

Those points all apply when evaluating racial disparities in police killings. If groups are at higher risk of being killed due to factors outside their control, it makes little sense to blame them for their predicament. They qualify as vulnerable, a condition that is fundamentally unfair for them. As we saw in Chapter 3, the state and its institutions have obligations to the vulnerable. When groups are unfairly disadvantaged due to a heightened risk of suffering police violence through no fault of their own, the state should address that vulnerability—specifically, by taking steps to reduce the unjust risks they face.

It is possible to imagine a different causal story that fails to trigger the same institutional obligations. Sometimes culpable action within individuals' control puts them at greater risk of suffering harm from defensive force. If culpable action by certain racial groups fully explains why they face a greater risk of police deadly force, these groups no longer appear vulnerable in the sense of being more susceptible to harm for reasons *outside* their control. It also becomes harder to blame the state and its institutions for these disparities. Different causal explanations have the potential to alter our moral conclusions.

That is partly why the debate over the causes of racial disparities in police killings can be so contentious. If the cause of the disparities is individual bias by officers or disparate enforcement, a clear injustice explains the disparities. In the case of racial bias, it increases officers' likelihood of using deadly force. As a result, they unjustly subject marginalized racial groups to a heightened risk of grave harm, which wrongs these groups. The same is true when police engage in disparate enforcement. Over-policing of marginalized groups subjects them to a higher risk of police contact and suffering various harms, including death, which cannot be explained by their crime rates. If racial disparities in police killings are due to either of these two factors, we have good reason to blame the police for the disparities.

But the differential involvement hypothesis, if correct, paints the police in a different light. According to this explanation, police are just doing their job by responding to crime and violence. They cannot be blamed for the underlying racial disparities in criminal activity. That is Mac Donald's (2016) position in *The War on Cops*. She takes criticism of the police, in response to racial disparities, as mistaken on two fronts. First, this line of criticism misidentifies the cause of racial disparities. Second, it directs blame at police who don't deserve it.

Given the empirical research discussed in this chapter, Mac Donald likely overstates her case. The available evidence suggests that individual bias and disparate enforcement in policing also contribute to racial disparities in police killings. But for the sake of argument, assume that differential criminal involvement explains all the disparities in police killings. This explanation does shift blame away from the police today. But contrary to what some proponents of the differential involvement hypothesis suggest (Mac Donald 2020), it does not necessarily exclude structural racism as a cause of racial disparities in police killings.

Let's step back and explain what is meant by structural or systemic racism (terms that I use here interchangeably). Structural racism captures the idea that features in society unjustly disadvantage certain racial groups, closing them off to benefits and subjecting them to harms. In other words, structural racism stacks the deck against marginalized groups. They don't have the same shot at succeeding in life as do groups living under more favorable circumstances. Take the policy of redlining, which denied low-interest, government-backed mortgages to Black Americans during the 20th century. The policy limited Black Americans' access to affordable and desirable housing. As a result, many Black families found themselves cut off from one of the primary paths for building wealth in the US—owning a home, whose value tends to grow over time (Rothstein 2017). Well after redlining was outlawed, its ramifications persist. The ability to purchase a home decades ago has helped many White families build wealth and pass it down to their children and grandchildren, giving them opportunities like going to college, starting a small business, and building further wealth. The stark racial wealth gap in the US due to policies like redlining limits the opportunities and resources available to Black Americans across many spheres, from housing to education (Hamilton and Darity 2017; Addo, Darity, and Myers 2024).

We can define structural or systemic racism as follows.

Structural/systemic racism: the unjust disadvantage experienced by marginalized groups resulting from institutions, laws, policies, norms, and practices with racially disparate harms—sometimes intentional, sometimes unintentional—that often reinforce one another. (see Carmichael and Hamilton 1967, 3–4; Bonilla-Silva 1997, 2021; Grant-Thomas and powell 2006; Haslanger 2012; Shelby 2016, 22–29)

This concept is relevant for debates over racial disparities in police deadly force because of how social conditions influence crime and violence. Say differential criminal involvement explains racial disparities in police deadly force. We also can ask what explains differential criminal involvement. If structural racism partly explains differential criminal involvement, structural racism becomes part of the causal story for why there are racial disparities in police killings. Ultimately, differential criminal involvement and structural racism are not mutually exclusive explanations.

We see this insight in King's (2015, 239) famous quote that "the riot is the language of the unheard." The quote comes from his speech "The Other America," given shortly before his assassination in 1968. The events prompting the speech—urban upheaval in response to police brutality, deprivation, and persistent lack of opportunity in Black neighborhoods—have parallels to the mass protests after George Floyd's murder in 2020 (Hinton 2021). The speech offers a damning indictment of structural racism and America's complacency toward it.

That message comes through in King's explanation of the root causes behind the riots.

> [T]he great tragedy is that the nation continues in its national policy to ignore the conditions that brought the riots or the rebellions into being. For in the final analysis, the riot is the language of the unheard. And what is it that America's failed to hear? It's failed to hear that the plight of the Negro poor has worsened over the last few years. It has failed to hear that the promises of justice and freedom have not been met. It has failed to hear that large segments of white society are more concerned about tranquility and the status quo than about justice, humanity, and equality. (King 2015, 239)

In effect, riots are a symptom of structural racism. Here King makes a social science claim. Conditions of unjust disadvantage marked by poverty, unemployment, substandard housing, and inferior education—how King (2015, 236–37) describes life in the "other America"—make riots more likely. Such conditions severely constrain people's prospects in life, resulting in despair, anger, and resentment. These attitudes can push people to rebel against a social system hostile to their well-being and aspirations.

Notably, King avoids condoning the riots. Structural racism represents an injustice but doesn't give individuals a blank moral check to engage in violence. Victims of injustice still have moral obligations, in his view, to commit themselves to nonviolence in efforts to advance justice (King 2015, 239–40). But King doesn't stop there. Simply "condemning the rioters" gives us an incomplete picture, which conveniently leaves out larger societal failures (King 2015, 240). As King (2015, 239) stresses, the nation and its institutions bear responsibility for subjecting Black Americans to conditions of deprivation. He puts institutions front and center when thinking about the moral issues at stake in a society marked by structural racism. America's institutions have allowed, furthered, and entrenched structural racism. By contributing to this wrong, our institutions have obligations to work toward remedying it. Without institutional action, it is difficult if not impossible to make meaningful progress on the daunting problems posed by structural racism.

In "The Other America," King deftly moves between an ethical and social scientific perspective, with lessons for thinking about racial disparities in police killings today. When Mac Donald and others point to higher rates of criminal involvement by some racial groups to explain racial disparities in police killings, often the implication is that these groups are to blame for the disparities. To be sure, individuals can bear culpability for violent acts that increase their risk of experiencing police deadly force. But if our analysis stops there, we fail to consider structural racism's potential effects on crime and violence. Structural racism changes the moral picture, signaling that the state is failing to meet its obligations to vulnerable groups. To better understand this failure, let's look more closely at the evidence for structural racism's link to violent crime.

Structural Racism's Link to Violent Crime

Sociology and criminology have long examined how social conditions such as poverty, unemployment, economic inequality, and segregation influence crime and violence. From this research has emerged what is known as the "racial invariance thesis." As explained by its proponents, it is the view that "racial disparities in rates of violent crime ultimately stem from the very different social ecological contexts in which Blacks and Whites reside, and that concentrated disadvantage predicts crime similarly across racial groups" (Sampson, Wilson, and Katz 2018, 14). This view accepts racial disparities in violent crime rates. But it goes on to argue that the different levels of social disadvantage experienced by racial groups explain these disparities. The racial invariance thesis makes the prediction that, if rates of poverty, unemployment, and other forms of social disadvantage were equal across racial groups, so too would be their rates of violent crime. In a society free of structural racism where racial groups had the same opportunities and advantages, there wouldn't be racial disparities in violent crime.

The racial invariance thesis can help explain why, even if the differential involvement hypothesis is correct, the state ultimately bears responsibility for racial disparities in police killings. Differential criminal involvement may be the proximate cause for these disparities. But the racial invariance thesis identifies structural racism as the root cause, which the state contributes to through its policies and actions. The thesis proves attractive for those who see racial disparities in police killings as a pressing injustice.

We need to evaluate the evidence for this theory. After all, if the evidence fails to back it up, it's a shaky basis for making policy recommendations for policing. Proponents of the racial invariance thesis point to various findings supporting it. Extensive research shows a strong link between higher violent crime and conditions of social disadvantage like poverty and lack of economic opportunity.

That general link shows up across racial groups. As Ruth Peterson and Lauren Krivo (2005, 337) put it in a review of this research, "One consistent pattern emerges from race-specific studies irrespective of the outcomes, predictors, and units under consideration: Structural disadvantage contributes significantly to violence for both blacks and whites" (see also Pratt and Cullen 2005). More recent studies lend further support for this conclusion (e.g., Light and Ulmer 2016; Mann, Edin, and Shaefer 2024).

Some research, though, challenges the racial invariance thesis. In a number of studies, structural disadvantage explains some but not all the disparities in violence between racial groups. Furthermore, factors like poverty and unemployment have effects of varying magnitude on violent crime, depending on the racial group. For some groups, high poverty increases crime rates, while for others it appears to have little impact on their rates of criminal involvement (see, e.g., Ousey 1999; Phillips 2002; Steffensmeier et al. 2010). Such findings seem at odds with the racial invariance thesis. It is difficult for the thesis's proponents to deny these findings, which show up in some of their own research. For instance, in one study purportedly confirming the thesis, structural factors still fail to explain around 40 percent of the variance in violence between racial groups (Sampson, Morenoff, and Raudenbush 2005, 231). In response, a critic of the thesis calls for looking elsewhere "to account theoretically and empirically for the variance that remains unexplained" (Unnever 2018, 93).

Unexplained racial disparities in criminal violence do not necessarily invalidate the racial invariance thesis. As the thesis's proponents point out, researchers have imperfect data and must rely on incomplete measures of structural disadvantage in society when trying to estimate its effect on violence. In all likelihood, such analyses leave out other variables that also contribute to forms of structural disadvantage. Recent work suggests that there may be something to this claim. One study examines at the county level the relationship in the US between violence and economic mobility—that is, the likelihood that children born to low-income parents would move up the income ladder as adults. It finds that a community's economic "mobility is a more consistent predictor of violent crime and homicide rates than more commonly tested factors like poverty, inequality, unemployment, and law enforcement presence" (Mann, Edin, and Shaefer 2024, 1). Incorporating this measure of economic opportunity helps account for variance in violence across racial groups that had been unexplained. Where economic opportunity is low, violence tends to be higher.

Further factors may also contribute to disparities in violence across racial groups. One proposal suggests that experiences of racial subordination make some groups more likely to engage in violence (Unnever, Barnes, and Cullen 2016; Unnever 2018). Whether that claim, if correct, counts for or against the racial invariance thesis is debatable. One could argue that the claim is compatible with the racial invariance thesis in the sense that, if White Americans experienced the same subordination as Black Americans, it would have the same effect on their likelihood to engage in violence. Yet skeptics of the thesis point out that it is impossible to ever test that claim, given the reality of racism in America (Unnever 2018).

Let's sum up the current research. It remains unclear whether structural disadvantage *fully* explains the variance in violence across racial groups. But clearly, research on the racial invariance thesis reveals that structural disadvantage explains a *significant portion* of the variance. Even skeptics of the racial invariance thesis accept this point (Unnever 2018).

We have strong reason to conclude, then, that in societies like the US—where much of the research on the racial invariance thesis has occurred—structural racism contributes to racial disparities in criminal involvement. Indeed, it is likely not a coincidence that areas with high violent crime today are often the same ones once subjected to racially discriminatory policies, like redlining (Jacoby et al. 2018). These policies' effects reverberate into the present.

Once we recognize that reality, the moral and policy implications of the differential involvement hypothesis look different than the conclusion drawn by Mac Donald, who blames certain racial groups for being at higher risk of suffering police violence. Conditions of structural racism—which are beyond the control of vulnerable groups—contribute to differential criminal involvement today. In other words, differential criminal involvement is a symptom of structural racism, which the state bears responsibility for. As a result, the state has obligations to work toward remedying structural racism's effects, such as racial disparities in police deadly force. Even if the differential involvement hypothesis explains racial disparities in police deadly force, the state remains morally on the hook for reducing those disparities.

Implications for Police Reform

We have considered different explanations for racial disparities in police killings: individual bias, disparate enforcement, and the differential involvement hypothesis. Evidence suggests that all likely contribute to these disparities. Each explanation points to features in society that unfairly disadvantage certain racial groups, particularly Black Americans. The first two explanations focus on features in policing—bias by individual officers and disparate enforcement—that heighten marginalized groups' vulnerability. In this way, police wrong such groups. Here we consider potential ways for police to fulfill their institutional obligations to reduce marginalized groups' exposure to a higher risk of deadly force.

Let's start with reforms to reduce individual bias. One popular intervention is implicit bias training, which many police departments have adopted (CBS News 2019). In other sectors, like business and education, implicit bias training has had mixed results, with often limited effectiveness in changing behavior (Dobbin and Kalev 2018; Forscher et al. 2019; Paluck et al. 2021). That's also true for policing. Though several studies find that implicit bias training improves officers' understanding of the concept (Kochel 2022; Kochel and Nouri 2024), studies measuring behavior find little evidence that the training changes how officers do their jobs or reduces racial disparities (Miller et al. 2020; Lai and Lisnek 2023; Worden et al. 2024). We see such mixed results in a randomized controlled trial of over fourteen thousand New York City police officers. Researchers concluded from the trial that "positive short-lived impacts of [implicit bias] training on knowledge and awareness of bias do not appear to have affected officers' enforcement decisions" (Worden et al. 2024, 350). Such outcomes are disappointing but perhaps unsurprising. Implicit bias training tries to reverse associations and attitudes that form over years and decades. Short, one-off interventions—as is typically the case for implicit bias trainings—may simply be insufficient for such an entrenched problem. More sustained interventions to reduce bias may be more effective in changing behavior (see James, James, and Mitchell 2023; Dube, MacArthur, and Shah 2025).

Implicit bias training's largely lackluster track record suggests the need for additional or alternative strategies in policing to reduce individual bias. One option is to increase the share of officers from underrepresented and historically marginalized groups. The rationale for this reform is that these officers have greater familiarity with, and therefore may exhibit less bias toward, marginalized groups who bear the brunt of policing's harms, including deadly force. Furthermore, through mechanisms like intergroup contact, greater representation of marginalized groups within police departments can help reduce bias among other officers.

It is important to be realistic about what increased diversity in policing can achieve. This reform is not a panacea for policing's ills. Members of historically marginalized groups can still engage in biased and brutal actions, as the killing of Tyre Nichols by Black officers in Memphis reminds us. One worry is that police culture has such a strong influence on officers that it prevents greater diversity from making a meaningful difference (Forman 2017, 106–11). Some research backs up that skepticism, finding for instance that Black officers use deadly force with similar frequency as White officers (Menifield, Shin, and Strother 2019).

That research, though, may be comparing apples to oranges if Black officers tend to be assigned to higher crime areas with a greater likelihood of dangerous encounters requiring force. In recent years, access to more fine-grained data has allowed researchers to compare the enforcement actions—stops, arrests, and uses of force—of officers in similar shifts and circumstances. This more recent strand of research indicates that officers' race and gender appear to influence police behavior.

A study of one US city with a high homicide rate (left unidentified due to a confidentiality agreement with the participating police department) finds that Black officers are significantly less likely than White officers to use force, including deadly force. Though Black and White officers use their guns at around the same rate in the city's White and racially mixed neighborhoods, White officers are five times more likely to shoot their guns in neighborhoods that are 80 percent or more Black (Hoekstra and Sloan 2022, 829). Due to Black officers' greater restraint in such contexts, the study estimates that having Black officers respond to all 911 calls in predominantly Black neighborhoods would entirely eliminate racial disparities in shootings by police in the city (Hoekstra and Sloan 2022, 858).

In Chicago, analysis of nearly three million shifts shows that, compared with White officers, Black and Hispanic officers stop people less often, make fewer arrests, and resort to force less frequently. These differences are most dramatic in interactions with Black civilians. Similarly, female officers arrest and use force less often than do male officers, particularly with Black civilians (Ba et al. 2021, 698–700). Other research looking at the same data highlights diversity's role in individual police units. In the Chicago Police Department, Black officers are underrepresented compared with the city's racial composition. But in units with a greater percentage of Black officers and a racial composition closer to the neighborhoods they serve, officers stop Black civilians at significantly lower rates. Notably, White officers stop Black civilians less often when they are part of shifts with a higher number of Black officers (Risi and Graif 2024, 469–76).

A plausible interpretation of this research is that greater diversity counteracts not just one but two sources of racial disparities in police deadly force: individual bias and disparate enforcement. To begin with individual bias, the life experiences of officers from marginalized groups can give them perspectives different than those of many of their colleagues. Officers from marginalized groups appear less prone to automatically see members of such groups as dangerous. That trait may help officers exercise greater restraint in using deadly force under uncertain and ambiguous circumstances.

Greater diversity in policing likewise offers solutions for disparate enforcement. The presence of officers from marginalized groups changes police behavior, reducing racial disparities in stops and arrests. Encounters with police always carry some risk of escalating and turning deadly. By reducing marginalized groups' contacts with police, racial and gender diversity among officers lowers these groups' risk of being victimized by police violence.

Another strategy for reducing disparate enforcement makes targeted changes to police practices characterized by stark racial disparities. Consider two such practices: pretextual traffic stops for minor infractions—like a broken taillight or failing to signal—and stop and frisk. For both, officers typically have broad discretion to stop individuals with the ultimate aim of recovering weapons, drugs, and other contraband. Studies show that Black and Hispanic Americans are significantly more likely to be subject to such stops, while at the same time less likely to have contraband on them when stopped (e.g., MacDonald and Braga 2019, 971–73; Pierson et al. 2020, 738–39; Gaebler and Goel 2025, 5–6). This evidence suggests that police have a lower bar for stopping marginalized racial groups. As a result, members of these groups—including those carrying no contraband—face a greater risk of being stopped than other Americans. Since some police stops escalate and turn deadly, reforms that reduce racial disparities for this enforcement practice can, in turn, help reduce racial disparities in police killings.

Encouragingly, some reforms do meaningfully change how police carry out stops. In the early 2010s, New York City's stop and frisk program surpassed over a half million stops of pedestrians annually, with Blacks and Hispanics comprising more than 80 percent of those stopped. Those stark racial disparities prompted a successful lawsuit against the city (MacDonald and Braga 2019, 957, 964). In response, the New York City Police Department adopted a combination of voluntary and court-mandated reforms, such as requiring officers to submit justifications for stops made. A precipitous decline in stops followed. In the year after the reforms, stops had dropped to under fifty thousand annually (Mummolo 2018b, 3–4; Kramer and Remster 2018, 969; MacDonald and Braga 2019, 958, 964). Since marginalized racial groups had made up the bulk of those stopped, they benefited the most from the decrease. In addition to the overall number of stops going down, racial disparities in stops declined (MacDonald and Braga 2019, 968–76), even if they did not end entirely (Kramer and Remster 2018, 984–85). The reforms also reduced collateral harms from stops—in particular, police use of force. Because of the reforms and decline in stops, researchers estimate that there were fifty thousand fewer incidents each year of police force against Black civilians in New York City (Kramer and Remster 2018, 985).

Reforms to limit pretextual traffic stops also have had success. Between 2013 and 2016, the police chief in Fayetteville, North Carolina, Harold Medlock, responded to community concerns over racial disparities by prioritizing traffic stops directly related to road safety and de-emphasizing pretextual stops. This shift meant that his department's officers dedicated more energy to stopping people for dangerous driving, like speeding or drunk driving, than for less consequential matters like having something hanging from the rearview mirror. A study of the intervention found that stops focused on road safety rose from 30 to over 80 percent of the department's overall number of traffic stops. With this intervention, racial disparities in traffic stops declined—and so did traffic fatalities and injuries. Notably, crime did not increase (Fliss et al. 2020, 6–7). In the years since, other municipalities have taken steps to limit pretextual stops. Though these reforms' full effects continue to be studied, the preliminary results are positive. Generally, restrictions on pretextual stops appear to reduce racial disparities in enforcement without undermining public safety, as measured by crime and traffic accidents (Raim 2024). The reform represents a win-win for both racial justice and public safety.

So police have options to reduce individual bias and disparate enforcement, two likely sources of racial disparities in police deadly force. By adopting such reforms, police departments can take concrete steps toward fulfilling their obligations to reduce the disproportionate harms that vulnerable groups face. But as we'll see, the state likely has obligations to take steps beyond just police reforms to lower policing's lethal risks to vulnerable groups.

The Limits of Police Reform

Our review of what causes racial disparities in police deadly force reveals a complex picture. Part of the problem lies in individual bias and discriminatory practices in policing, both of which treat certain racial groups unfairly. Police reforms make sense as remedies for these problems. But factors outside policing likely also contribute to racial disparities in who is killed by police. As King pointed out during the social unrest of the 1960s, structural racism shapes patterns of crime and violence in society. Marginalized groups live under conditions of poverty and deprivation, due in no small part to years of discriminatory policies and their long-term legacy. Such conditions foster crime and violence. Since police go where crime and violence are high, marginalized neighborhoods are more likely to be the sites of police killings. These links show how structural racism can contribute to racial disparities in police deadly force. To state the obvious, structural racism is a much bigger problem than what police reforms alone can solve.

For this reason, to reduce racial disparities in police deadly force, we must look beyond merely police reforms (Bonilla-Silva 2021, 524). Policing interacts with structural racism in society to exacerbate harms to marginalized racial groups. Such dynamics require a holistic approach: police reforms in conjunction with policies tackling the root causes of crime and violence. The latter could include interventions to improve education, healthcare access, and employment opportunities in marginalized communities. A number of interventions in these areas have proven effective in reducing crime and violence (e.g., Heckman et al. 2010; Wen, Hockenberry, and Cummings 2017; Heller 2022).

The conclusion that police reforms can mitigate racial disparities in police killings but are unlikely to eliminate them is understandably discouraging for some policymakers. Police reforms are tough enough to pass and implement. It is even more challenging to enact policies that redistribute resources and improve opportunities for marginalized racial groups. Whenever the US has taken steps in that direction—during Reconstruction, the civil rights movement, and most recently the Black Lives Matter movement—fierce backlash has followed. Some policymakers may conclude that, in trying to reduce racial disparities in police deadly force, the best they can do is get the police to adopt certain evidence-based reforms.

It is unclear whether the US can or ever will free itself of structures that unfairly disadvantage certain racial groups. At least one point, though, is clear: this moral failure inflicts considerable costs across society, policing being just one example. We need to be honest about that reality when thinking about racial disparities in police deadly force. As long as we tolerate a society marked by structural injustice, such disparities are likely to persist.

6

Police-Generated Killings

Because video evidence and key details are missing for many police killings, it is impossible to know exactly how many are justified. But some clearly are not. Consider the 2015 shooting of Walter Scott in South Carolina. Video shows Officer Michael Slager shooting a plainly unarmed Scott in the back as he fled a traffic stop (*New York Times* 2015). Slager's actions provoke a combination of anger, disgust, and horror—and rightly so. At the time he was shot, Scott presented a threat to no one. There was no need to use deadly force to protect life, yet the officer shot anyway. In this case, the law backs up our moral intuitions. The law in the US prohibits police from shooting nondangerous suspects who flee (*Tennessee v. Garner* 1985).

The law, though, does not always match our intuitions on police killings. That is especially true for some of the most controversial incidents, what I call *police-generated killings*. In these cases, bad police tactics create a situation where deadly force becomes necessary, becomes perceived as necessary, or occurs unintentionally. Since current law in the US fails to ban many bad tactics, police-generated killings often are treated as "lawful but awful" (Cournoyer 2016). Several high-profile incidents fall into this category, like the 2014 shooting of Tamir Rice, a Black child of only twelve years old. An officer shot Rice after perceiving him make a threatening movement with a gun that turned out to be fake. The shooting occurred after the officer and his partner confronted Rice at close range with his firearm drawn. This abrupt escalation of force appeared unnecessary since Rice presented no immediate threat (Park and Lindsay 2015). Many use-of-force experts criticized the officers' tactics for contributing to an avoidable death (Kindy 2016; Pickering and Klinger 2016, 28).

The standard defense of officers' actions in such cases focuses on the moment they use deadly force. At that moment, some argue, officers had grounds to reasonably believe that deadly force was necessary to stop a threat to life, which makes incidents like the police shooting of Rice justified (Holloway 2015). This line of defense frequently proves successful in shielding officers from legal penalties (e.g., Williams and Smith 2015). But as protests in recent years show, many strongly disagree with that outcome.

This chapter looks at the causes of police-generated killings and what to do about them. Such killings sometimes stem from officers violating departmental

Protecting Life. Ben Jones, Oxford University Press. © Ben Jones 2026.
DOI: 10.1093/9780197823316.003.0009

policy. But the problem goes deeper than a few bad apples who fail to follow policy. Flaws in departmental training and policy also are to blame. Police-generated killings ultimately reveal failures at the individual and institutional level.

In these incidents, officers choose tactics that foreseeably and unnecessarily raise the risk of deadly force, which violates their professional obligation to prioritize the protection of life. Because they violate that obligation, officers responsible for police-generated killings merit moral blame. But what about legal penalties? I conclude that they are appropriate after considering the analogy of self-generated self-defense—someone engaging in self-defense after starting the trouble—for which the law typically outlines penalties (Leverick 2006, 109–29).

The analysis suggests greater emphasis on ensuring that "lawful but awful" killings by police *cease to be lawful*. Some have been reluctant to pursue this approach (for exceptions, see Garrett and Stoughton 2017; Stoughton 2021). Even among those recognizing the need to change police practices, much of the focus has been on reforms that do not require changes to the law, such as new departmental policies implemented by police administrators and reparations to victims paid by municipalities (Mummolo 2018b; Police Executive Research Forum 2016; Zimring 2017; Page 2019). Though these proposals have merit, they are inadequate on their own. Unless the law mandates change, many police departments continue to teach bad tactics (Gilbert 2017). As a result, the law often proves unable to provide meaningful accountability for questionable killings, which further erodes trust in government—especially among groups most harmed by police violence, such as Black Americans (Jones 2020; Weitzer 2002).

In sum, police-generated killings threaten both life and government's legitimacy, which together provide compelling reason to change laws and tactics that contribute to such killings. The chapter closes with specific policy recommendations to reduce police-generated killings and ensure greater accountability when they occur.

Obligation to Reduce the Risk of Deadly Force

As discussed in Chapter 2, police have an obligation to prioritize the protection of life in their jobs. This obligation has implications for police tactics. Perhaps most obviously, if deadly force is unnecessary because police could use nonlethal tactics to stop a grave threat, nonlethal tactics are the option most consistent with prioritizing the protection of life. In those circumstances, nonlethal tactics protect both the aggressor's and victim's life, while deadly force protects only the latter. So the obligation to prioritize the protection of life has the following implication.

> *Obligation to choose nonlethal tactics*: Police have an ethical obligation to use nonlethal tactics, unless deadly force is necessary to stop an unjust threat to life or other grave threat (serious bodily injury, being raped, or being kidnapped).

This obligation provides valuable guidance and prohibits a range of actions, like shooting a thief just because they are elusive and might get away.

But such guidance, though valuable, is limited. Officers often have multiple nonlethal options. The above obligation offers little guidance on which option to choose. Officers' overarching obligation to prioritize the protection of life has implications that can guide those decisions. It specifically requires police to favor nonlethal tactics known to reduce the risk of deadly force since they are most consistent with the goal of protecting life. We can express this principle as follows.

> *Obligation to reduce the risk of deadly force*: If there is no grave threat requiring deadly force and nonlethal tactic X is available to police, known to reduce the risk of deadly force compared with other tactics, and generally as effective as other tactics in achieving a legitimate objective, then police have an ethical obligation to choose X.

This principle shows how a commitment to protecting life influences earlier stages of police work, not just split-second decisions on whether to shoot. Police have an obligation to choose tactics that avoid needlessly creating situations that make deadly force more likely.

Notably, this obligation concerns reducing the risk for all parties in an interaction. Tactics that raise the risk of deadly force for suspects often raise that same risk for officers. If a suspect who is likely armed poses no imminent threat and an officer confronts them at close range, that tactical decision makes escalation of force more likely and puts both in greater danger. There is little margin for error, as any false move or misperception can precipitate deadly force (Pickering and Klinger 2016, 27–28). In comparison, use of distance and cover by police during the interaction (when feasible) reduces the risk of deadly force for one or more parties without raising that risk for others. The tactic represents a Pareto improvement, in that it makes at least one party better off without making anyone worse off. Such Pareto improvements are what the *obligation to reduce the risk of deadly force* most clearly demands.

This obligation places a modest constraint on law enforcement. It only requires police to choose the less risky tactic when it is *generally as effective* as other nonlethal options in achieving a legitimate objective, such as promoting public safety or enforcing the law. That caveat is important. If effectiveness were no concern, the *obligation to reduce the risk of deadly force* could be interpreted as ruling out almost all police activities in favor of doing nothing. Just about every time police go into the world, whether it is to make an arrest or conduct patrol, their action comes with some lethal risks. For the vast majority of police actions, the risk is slight. If police had to abandon all tactics that introduce a risk of deadly force, no matter how small, they would be subject to a constraint seen as unduly restrictive in other contexts. Driving, cooking, playing sports, and a host of other permissible activities introduce small fatal risks. Pursuing aims we value almost always comes with risk, and the mere presence of risk is an insufficient reason to close off such pursuits. The above obligation avoids suggesting that outcome for policing. It rather advises police, when choosing among tactics that would be effective in achieving a legitimate objective, to select the one that would minimize the risk of deadly force.

Saying that police have an obligation to choose a tactic *generally* as effective as a riskier option suggests that police sometime may need to forgo small gains in effectiveness for more substantial gains in reducing deadly risks. One potential example is how police serve warrants and conduct searches. A common justification for no-knock warrants is that they allow police to enter a residence quickly and prevent the destruction of evidence, especially drugs (*Richards v. Wisconsin* 1997). Perhaps in some cases, no-knock raids are marginally more effective in recovering drugs than knocking, announcing, and waiting a brief period (15–30 seconds) before entering. No-knock raids, however, come with significant risks for both officers and occupants of residences raided. The latter sometimes mistake police for a criminal intruder and reach for a weapon, leading to an escalation of violence. Such outcomes remind us to weigh small gains in effectiveness against deadly risks that sometimes come with them.

When police fail to choose tactics that reduce the risk of deadly force, that failure tends to hurt some groups more than others. As we saw in Chapter 5, disparate enforcement likely explains part of why Black Americans make up a disproportionate share of those killed by police. Data on stop and frisk, traffic stops, SWAT team deployments, and arrests show that Black Americans come in contact more frequently with police. Many of these disparities cannot be explained by differences in crime rates (Gelman, Fagan, and Kiss 2007, 818–21; Mitchell and Caudy 2015, 309–10; Mummolo 2018a, 9183; Pierson et al. 2020, 738–39; Weaver, Papachristos, and Zanger-Tishler 2019, 109). If police are using bad tactics in enforcement practices marked by racial disparities, we should expect the resulting harms to fall disproportionately on groups targeted by those practices. Indeed, police kill Black Americans at higher rates, especially in questionable circumstances—like the suspect being unarmed—where bad tactics are more likely to be at play (Nix et al. 2017, 324–26; *Washington Post* 2024). Clearly, there are compelling racial justice reasons to end bad tactics.

Now what if we lived in a hypothetical society where police enforced the law free from racial bias? Even there, it would remain a moral imperative to rein in bad tactics for the simple reason that they undermine the protection of life. If the protection of life is truly a priority, bad police tactics deserve our attention.

The Problem of Police-Generated Killings

Some killings by police are both lawful and morally justified, like when deadly force is necessary to stop an unjust threat to life. Other killings by police violate the law and officers' ethical obligations, like shooting an unarmed fleeing suspect. Here the focus is on a third category: lawful but morally wrong killings. These killings involve police actions that, though legal, run afoul of our ethical intuitions because they take life unnecessarily and violate the obligation to prioritize the protection of life.

What I call police-generated killings often fall in this category of lawful but wrong. As understood here, a police-generated killing does not refer to any killing where police play a causal role in the outcome. Rather, it refers to a narrower category: killings that result from bad tactics known to raise the risk of deadly force during a police interaction. Tactics that lead to police-generated killings deserve moral blame not because they fall short of perfection, but because they are *obviously bad*. Such tactics are negligent or reckless. Police know—or at least should know—that the tactics raise the risk of avoidable harm. Those responsible for police-generated killings choose risky tactics despite having safer options to achieve their objectives.

Police-generated killings come in two varieties. In the first, deadly force is intentional.

> *Police-generated killing involving intentional deadly force*: A killing by police in which an officer's or officers' bad tactics create a situation where deadly force becomes necessary or perceived as necessary.

Scholarship on policing sometimes uses the term "officer-created jeopardy" to refer to incidents in this category (Stoughton, Noble, and Alpert 2020, 155–58). The category does not include killings that accidentally result from morally justified tactics. If an officer engages in sound tactics when using deadly force necessary to stop an imminent threat to life, their action carries a small risk to bystanders and in rare cases may cause accidental death. Though the officer causes the death, bad tactics do not. My focus is instead on cases where bad tactics are to blame. In such cases, deadly force may appear justified if we look just at the moment it is used. But that perspective proves incomplete, for it fails to account for prior police actions that unnecessarily escalated an encounter and created a situation requiring deadly force. Such poor tactical decisions violate police obligations to reduce the risk of deadly force.

The 2014 shooting of Tamir Rice represents an example of a police-generated killing involving intentional deadly force. Only twelve years old, Rice was playing in a Cleveland park with a pellet gun when someone called 911, worried the gun might be real while noting it was "probably fake." In the first of several errors, the dispatcher failed to tell officers the gun might be a toy. Officers Frank Garmback and Timothy Loehmann rushed to the scene, with Garmback pulling their car directly in front of Rice. Loehmann jumped out and, perceiving a movement by Rice as a threat, shot him within two seconds of exiting the vehicle (Dewan and Oppel 2015).

Pulling the car so close to Rice was a tactical blunder criticized by use-of-force experts. Even if there were reasonable grounds to justify deadly force at the moment of the shooting, officers made critical mistakes beforehand, which created a situation where deadly force was perceived as necessary. When a potentially armed suspect is not an imminent threat, as in this case, best practice is for officers to maintain distance, talk to the suspect with the benefit of cover, and use de-escalation strategies to resolve the situation. Instead, officers pulled only a few feet from Rice, predictably increasing the risk of deadly force (Pickering and Klinger 2016, 28). It was almost certainly an avoidable killing, which occurred because of bad tactics.

Other police-generated killings involve officers using bad tactics that, though not intended to be deadly, have that effect. These incidents comprise a second category.

Police-generated killing involving unintentional deadly force: A killing by police in which an officer's or officers' bad tactics have unintentionally deadly effects.

Not all unintentional deaths by officers are police-generated killings, as defined here. Sometimes officers exercise diligence and engage in best practices, yet by accident their actions prove fatal—as when a well-maintained police cruiser blows a tire and, as a result, strikes and kills a pedestrian. Police instead deserve blame for tactics known to increase the risk of deadly force and unnecessary to achieve their objective.

One of the most notorious examples of a police-generated killing involving unintentional deadly force is the incident that took Eric Garner's life in 2014. Officers confronted Garner for allegedly selling untaxed cigarettes on the street in New York City. Video shows Garner resisting arrest but without being violent. Officer Daniel Pantaleo used a chokehold to take down Garner, keeping his arm compressed around Garner's neck for approximately fifteen seconds. While restrained, Garner told officers "I can't breathe" numerous times (*Guardian* 2014). Shortly after, Garner lost consciousness and was taken to the hospital, where he was pronounced dead. The medical examiner ruled the death a homicide, identifying the chokehold and pressure to Garner's chest as causes of death (Goldstein and Santora 2014).

There is no evidence that Pantaleo *intended* to kill Garner, which would have been excessive, given that Garner posed no imminent threat. Still, Pantaleo erred in choosing a tactic less safe than other options and known to carry lethal risks. There was no state law at the time banning chokeholds, which would not come until 2020 (Ferré-Sadurní and McKinley 2020). The New York City Police Department (NYPD), however, had a longstanding policy prohibiting the tactic. This policy stated: "members of the New York City Police Department will NOT use chokeholds. A chokehold shall include, but is not limited to, any pressure to the throat or windpipe, which may prevent or hinder breathing or reduce intake of air" (New York City Civilian Complaint Review Board 2014, 11). Pantaleo's action clearly fits the NYPD's definition of a chokehold, as video shows him applying pressure to Garner's throat with his arms. At the time of Garner's death, the NYPD had been lax in enforcing its prohibition on chokeholds, so the department deserves blame for fostering conditions that made such a death more likely (New York City Civilian Complaint Review Board 2014, 57–84). But Pantaleo also deserves blame for choosing a prohibited tactic that posed unnecessary risks.

The deaths of Rice and Garner highlight bad tactics associated with police-generated killings. Though not meant to be exhaustive, the following list identifies police tactics for which there is growing evidence that they unnecessarily endanger life.

(1) *Chokeholds and other neck restraints.* Neck restraints are especially risky tactics that can have fatal consequences, as Garner's death illustrates. Chokeholds or air chokes apply pressure to the throat and interfere with breathing. Carotid holds or blood chokes apply pressure to the side of the neck and cut off blood to the brain (Matteis 2015, 106–9; Gardner and Al-Shareffi 2022, 115; Beck, Antonelli, and LaScala-Gruenewald 2024, 666). Both restraints have potentially deadly effects and should be treated as deadly force, only justified if necessary to stop a grave threat (Kleinig 1996, 106). Research examining US municipal police departments finds that a ban on neck restraints—or near ban, with an exception for the tactic when it is the only way to stop a grave threat—reduces killings by police without undermining officer safety. In fact, assaults and killings of officers as well as violent crime tend to be lower in cities with a ban (Beck, Antonelli,

and LaScala-Gruenewald 2024, 675–79). Together this evidence suggests that, outside of narrowly defined exigent circumstances, neck restraints unnecessarily endanger life.

(2) *Failure to use distance and cover.* When officers confront at close range a suspect believed to be armed and potentially dangerous but not an imminent threat, they make the encounter more hazardous for all involved. Those hazards were on display in the fatal shooting of Rice. Maintaining distance and cover gives officers more time to react while keeping nonlethal options available, which sometimes includes allowing more officers and specialized units to arrive (Pickering and Klinger 2016, 28; Stoughton, Noble, and Alpert 2020, 167–74). Notably, unarmed suspects are more likely to be killed by an officer who is alone, data from the US suggest. This finding makes sense: a single officer is more vulnerable and more likely to have to rely on deadly force against an actual or perceived threat (Zimring 2017, 59–61). So it is especially risky to rush in alone to confront a dangerous suspect and often better to wait for backup, if the suspect poses no immediate threat. Encouragingly, in a randomized controlled trial, de-escalation training with an emphasis on distance, cover, and creating time led to fewer injuries for both officers and suspects (Engel et al. 2022, 214–17; see also Goh 2021).

(3) *No-knock warrants and raids.* The 2022 killing of Amir Locke in Minneapolis, Minnesota, while executing a no-knock warrant reveals the tactic's inherent dangers. Not named in the warrant, Locke was at the wrong place at the wrong time—shot by police seconds after a SWAT team in the early morning burst into the apartment where he slept. Police were searching for another person but instead encountered Locke, who had with him a gun that he was licensed to carry. In the heat of the moment, police took his gun as a deadly threat and justification to fire (Karnowski 2022). No-knock warrants and raids began in the 1970s as part of the war on drugs and involve police forcibly entering a premise without knocking and announcing. Fearing a home intruder, some surprised residents respond with deadly force. Such chaotic circumstances have resulted in avoidable deaths to suspects, bystanders, and officers (Dolan 2019, 211, 216–22). We need more comprehensive data on no-knock raids, but the available data show police using the tactic (and closely related ones) in cases where its risks are disproportionate to the underlying offense. In the vast majority of killings in the US from forcible entries by police—a category that encompasses no-knock raids as well as forcible entries after quickly announcing—the basis for the warrant was a nonviolent offense (Perez and Whitehouse 2024, 6).

(4) *21-foot rule.* This rule, developed in the 1980s, advises officers to shoot aggressors who have an edged or blunt weapon and get within twenty-one feet of an officer. More recent experiments do find that many individuals can cover

twenty-one feet in about the time it takes an officer to draw their firearm. But experiments also find that moving and creating distance help officers avoid the reach of a rushing attacker (Sandel, Martaindale, and Blair 2021, 1316–17, 1320–24). That finding aligns with the experiences of police agencies in the United Kingdom, which have developed effective nonlethal tactics to disarm aggressors with an edged or blunt weapon (discussed earlier in Chapter 4). Despite the availability of alternative approaches that reduce the need for deadly force, the 21-foot rule continues to be influential among US police (Stoughton, Noble, and Alpert 2020, 168–71; Zimring 2017, 100–2).

(5) *Vehicle pursuits.* Estimates suggest that 30 percent of police pursuits of fleeing vehicles end in accidents (Alpert and Lum 2014, 40). An investigation by the *San Francisco Chronicle* found that police chases in the US killed over three thousand people, while injuring nearly another fifty-three thousand between 2017 and 2022 (Gollan and Neilson 2024). Given other alternatives to apprehend suspects—like tracking them via helicopter or obtaining a warrant to arrest them later—many vehicle pursuits unnecessarily increase the risk of fatal outcomes. Such a risky tactic proves difficult to justify unless it is necessary to stop a suspect posing a grave threat. Some departments restrict vehicle pursuits to those circumstances (e.g., Metropolitan Police Department of the District of Columbia 2023), but many do not.

(6) *Shooting at moving vehicles.* Most big city police departments in the US place prohibitions on shooting at moving vehicles (Obasogie and Newman 2017, 288). A recent analysis found such policies to be associated with fewer vehicle shootings (Shjarback and Ward 2025). The NYPD initially adopted prohibitions on shooting at moving vehicles in the 1970s, which led to a reduction in shootings by police (Police Executive Research Forum 2016, 45–46). Notably, these policies also have officers' safety in mind. Due to simple physics, shooting a driver rarely brings a moving vehicle to an immediate stop, so it is almost always safer for an officer, where feasible, to step out of a vehicle's way instead (Jones 2026). Still, we continue see incidents like the 2023 killing of Ta'Kiya Young in a suburb of Columbus, Ohio. In this case, two officers questioned Young in a supermarket parking lot about shoplifting as she was about to leave. One officer positioned himself in front of her car. As the pregnant mother tried to slowly pull away, her car bumped the officer, who responded by shooting and killing her (Levenson 2023). Here the officer's actions—placing himself in the vehicle's path and treating his vulnerable position as reason to shoot—put himself and the suspect at risk of grave harm that could have been avoided with better tactical decisions.

What makes the six tactics listed above bad? It's not that they lead to grave harm in every or even most cases. It is easy to imagine examples where, say, a high-speed pursuit ends without injuries while achieving the law enforcement goal of arresting the suspect. Defenders of these tactics often point to such counterexamples. But a counterexample in which police achieve their objective without grave harm is an insufficient reason for allowing a tactic. After all, by that rationale, we could defend drunk driving. There are plenty of examples of intoxicated drivers making it to their destination without harming others, as the vast majority of drunk driving does not result in accidents (Jones 2021, 136). An action that sometimes has beneficial outcomes can still be morally impermissible because of its risks and its harms in the aggregate.

That is what makes certain police tactics bad: they pose morally impermissible risks. We can identify bad tactics because their foreseeable risks have three notable features:

(1) A bad tactic's risks are *exceptionally high* compared with the risks of relevant alternatives.
(2) A bad tactic's risks are *unnecessary* because there are less risky alternatives that are generally as or more effective in achieving a legitimate objective.
(3) A bad tactic's risks are *grave* and endanger other people.

In other areas, we are quick to recognize that actions posing risks with these three features are morally impermissible. Most support bans on reckless high-speed driving because it imposes *exceptionally high*, *unnecessary*, and *grave* risks on others (Jones 2021, 136). Bad police tactics impose similar risks on a community.

Risky action that would otherwise be impermissible, most agree, can be acceptable when it is necessary to prevent death or other grave harm. Such an exception makes moral sense. People should avoid action with exceptionally high, unnecessary, and grave risks because of the heightened threat it poses to others' lives. But if risky action represents one's best chance in an emergency to protect life, there is a stronger moral basis for the action. For instance, the law bans high-speed driving but makes an exception for ambulance drivers who engage in this risky activity to provide urgent, life-saving care. Likewise, some bans on risky police tactics permit them in narrow circumstances, when necessary to prevent grave harm. That approach would ban chokeholds in almost all instances but allow the tactic in a struggle where a chokehold is the officer's only way to stop a suspect's deadly threat. In the case of no-knock raids, such an exception still would allow police to enter a residence without knocking and announcing to disrupt a deadly attack and stop an imminent threat of harm. Bans with these narrow exceptions essentially treat risky tactics like deadly force, only permitting them in emergency circumstances where they are necessary to protect individuals from grave threats.

Accountability for Bad Tactics

For some police-generated killings, it may seem unfair to impose penalties on officers. Simply because an officer engages in bad tactics does not automatically justify any response by a suspect. Sometimes suspects respond to bad tactics by unjustly threatening an officer's life, making deadly force necessary to avert the threat. For instance, officers *should* use distance and cover when engaging armed suspects who are not imminent threats. But if officers instead confront a suspect at close distance, command him to drop his weapon, and the suspect responds by threatening deadly force, officers face an unjust threat to their life. Officers who do not use deadly force in this scenario jeopardize their lives and possibly the lives of others, too. These are tough cases. If legal penalties are appropriate even in such cases, it is safe to conclude that they also are appropriate for other police-generated killings where the exculpatory factors are weaker.

One source of insight for this question comes from ethical and legal thinking on self-generated self-defense, in which the person who engages in self-defense started the trouble (Leverick 2006, 109–29). Here is an example.

> *Bar fight*: At a bar, Sam provokes Hank by punching him once in the jaw. Hank responds disproportionately by pulling a deadly weapon. Faced with an imminent threat to his life that appears to require deadly force to stop it, Sam shoots and kills Hank. Though Sam ends the fight by resorting to intentional deadly force, he did not intend to kill Hank at the start of the fight.

Sam intentionally uses deadly force *only after* Hank makes an imminent and unjust threat against his life. Normally, that threat would justify deadly force, but Sam's initial assault puts his self-defense claim in doubt. After all, had Sam never punched Hank, he likely would have never ended up in a situation requiring deadly force. Similarly, in police-generated killings, deadly force likely would not have occurred if officers had avoided tactics that escalated force unnecessarily.

Some may object to the analogy between self-generated self-defense and police-generated killings on the following grounds: police often respond to disturbances caused by others. They're not the ones who start the trouble, as Sam does in the bar fight. But even if someone else starts the trouble, an officer intervening still has an obligation to choose tactics that reduce the risk of deadly force (assuming deadly force is unnecessary). An officer violates this obligation when they choose bad tactics with morally impermissible risks. They act wrongly and, like Sam, merit moral blame. Both the officer's and Sam's actions share the feature of escalating force unnecessarily and playing a causal role in the resulting death.

Cases of self-generated self-defense, like the bar fight, raise thorny questions about culpability (Leverick 2006, 109–29; Robinson 1985; Sangero 2006, 310–39). Broadly speaking, there are three different ways to treat this case:

(1) *Not justified self-defense*: Initial aggressor is fully liable for the victim's death due to provoking the conditions that made deadly force necessary (Sam is guilty of murder).
(2) *Justified self-defense*: Initial aggressor is only liable for the provocation considered in isolation (Sam is guilty of battery).
(3) *Imperfect self-defense*: Initial aggressor is partially liable for the victim's death (Sam is guilty of manslaughter).

None of these approaches enjoys a clear consensus, which is evident in the different state laws on self-generated self-defense (Robinson 1985). The rationale behind (1) is straightforward: a common criterion for justified self-defense is that the person making the claim did not provoke the trouble requiring defensive force, and failing to meet that criterion precludes a claim to self-defense (e.g., *State v. Moore* 1975, 276). Arizona's statute on self-defense reflects that approach. It only allows an initial aggressor to regain a self-defense justification by withdrawing or communicating their desire to end the conflict (Arizona State Legislature 2025).

Other states like Iowa opt for (2). Its statute treats deadly force by an initial aggressor as justified when in response to force "grossly disproportionate to the provocation" that puts the initial aggressor in "imminent danger of death or serious injury," based on their reasonable belief. In line with the Model Penal Code, Iowa's statute denies a self-defense justification to those who provoke an attack with the *intention* of having an excuse to kill (Dubber 2015, 164–65; Iowa Legislature 2024).

Option (3), imperfect self-defense, emerged as a compromise position in the common law (Moreland 1952, 87–92). The Supreme Court of North Carolina as well as other courts recognize this doctrine. Under its compromise approach, a manslaughter conviction is appropriate for someone who kills another person under conditions where deadly force is necessary but whose unlawful action provoked those conditions (*State v. Bush* 1982, 158–59).

The goal here is not to resolve longstanding debates over whether (1), (2), or (3) is correct. Still, from these approaches, we can draw two important conclusions for police-generated killings.

First, the most lenient option still imposes penalties for self-generated self-defense. Most readily recognize that Sam acts wrongly and deserves some penalty for starting the fight that leads to Hank's death. Similarly, police-generated killings involve a clear wrong: police choosing tactics with exceptionally high, unnecessary, and grave risks. Such action violates police's ethical obligation to prioritize the protection of life. Of course, not all ethical violations merit legal penalties. In some cases, such penalties fail to advance a legitimate state interest. Take adultery. Even if we believe that being unfaithful to one's spouse is wrong, it is hard to make the case that responding to this wrong with legal penalties advances a legitimate state interest (at least in a liberal democratic state). But for police-generated-killings, a legitimate state interest is at stake: protecting life. Policymaking has as one of its core purposes guarding against action that imposes morally impermissible risks on others. Since bad police tactics pose such risks, the state has compelling grounds to impose penalties on officers whose bad tactics prove deadly.

Second, penalties for self-generated self-defense apply to civilians who often lack any training in use of force or de-escalation. Such laws communicate the moral expectation that everyone should avoid actions that unnecessarily risk precipitating deadly force. That expectation should be *even stronger* for professionals trained in use of force and de-escalation. For this reason, democratic institutions have strong reason to prohibit bad tactics and impose meaningful penalties on officers who use them—especially when they cause an avoidable death.

Some may object to individual sanctions, arguing that police-generated killings stem from system failures, not just errors by particular officers. Typically, in these incidents, various factors are to blame—like breakdowns in communication, inadequate training, and institutional pressures—similar to how plane crashes stem from multiple errors (Sherman 2018; Armacost 2019). This objection conveys an important point. But it also can minimize officers' roles. For instance, Lawrence Sherman (2018, 439) identifies several factors leading to Tamir Rice's death: the 911 dispatcher's miscommunication, the Cleveland Division of Police's failure to contact the department where the newly hired officer who shot Rice had previously worked, and Rice's pellet gun lacking the standard orange mark to identify it as a toy. Those observations are all true but omit a crucial point. Even *with* all those factors, Rice likely would still be alive if officers at the scene chose better tactics. Officers should have known not to pull their cruiser so close to Rice, which violated a departmental rule (Calamur 2017). Many factors can contribute to an outcome without eliminating individual actors' moral responsibility (see Miller 2016, 138–57).

But the systems approach does point out something critical: greater individual accountability must be paired with broader institutional change. Many police-generated killings result from bad tactics consistent with departmental training and policies, which shows the shortcomings with the status quo. Ideally, we want law, policy, norms, and practices to be aligned in guarding against police-generated killings. A well-functioning system offers clear rules in law and policy on bad police tactics to avoid, regular training on alternative tactics that reduce the risk of deadly force, resources to employ those alternatives, and incentives to encourage their use. This approach gives officers resources to avoid police-generated killings, and with those resources come higher expectations for officers. Greater accountability also reinforces institutional change. When the law has in place penalties for bad police tactics, it incentivizes police administrators to implement training and policies aimed at avoiding those tactics and penalties.

How should we hold officers accountable? The law offers several options: (1) criminal penalties, (2) decertification, and (3) civil damages. All have a role, with their own strengths and weaknesses. When responding to police killings involving bad tactics, the public often focuses on (1), for understandable reasons. Of the three, criminal penalties represent the most severe option and communicate most directly the gravity of the offense.

Criminal penalties serve an important role. But it would be a mistake to rely only on them to ensure accountability. A high bar must be met to impose criminal penalties. Criminal law is set up to err on the side of acquitting the guilty rather than convicting the innocent. This principle applies across the board—including to officers whose bad tactics jeopardize life. Even in a fair and well-functioning criminal justice system, the high burden of proof needed to convict an officer of a crime would frustrate advocates of police accountability on occasion.

For this reason, pairing criminal penalties with other measures that require a lower burden of proof can provide a meaningful floor of accountability for police-generated killings. Police decertification, which revokes an officer's law enforcement license, is the most natural option to serve that function. Officers responsible for police-generated killings commit serious violations of their professional obligations. License revocation imposes a severe professional penalty in response. If an officer is merely fired, some find employment in other law enforcement agencies (Grunwald and Rappaport 2020). In contrast, decertification prevents officers from serving in law enforcement elsewhere. And since administrative law frequently relies on a lower standard of proof than criminal law—like preponderance of the evidence—it faces less formidable hurdles for ensuring accountability (Goldman 2003, 139).

Admittedly, lowering the burden of proof raises the risk of imposing penalties on officers who were justified in using deadly force. Such increased risk is intolerable in the criminal context, where mistakes mean imprisoning the innocent. But it is less problematic for license revocation. Unlike criminal penalties, mistakenly revoking a license—though regrettable—does not deprive an officer of a basic right like liberty. Such mistakes are justified if an unavoidable part of an overall system that improves police accountability and conducts reliably accurate (though not foolproof) investigations of alleged misconduct.

In addition, professional penalties for police-generated killings can have indirect effects that improve accountability in the criminal system. If administrative law bans specific tactics, it becomes easier to show that officers *should have known* to avoid such tactics. Professional penalties are thus relevant for criminal convictions that require showing an officer acted recklessly or negligently (e.g., manslaughter).

Like police decertification, civil suits against officers require a lower burden of proof than does criminal law. When courts award civil damages to victims of police misconduct, local governments pay these damages (Schwartz 2014). In this way, civil suits hold democratic institutions accountable for failing to prevent police misconduct. Such suits also serve an important function that criminal penalties and decertification do not: providing restitution to those harmed most directly by bad police tactics.

Criminal penalties, decertification, and civil damages together have the *potential* to provide meaningful accountability for bad police tactics. Current law, however, often falls short of that goal, as the next section explains.

Where the Law Falls Short

This chapter opened by discussing the fatal shooting of Walter Scott, an unarmed fleeing suspect who presented no immediate danger. Deadly force by police in such circumstances violates the law and can result in the sanctions listed above: criminal penalties, decertification, and civil damages. But that was not always true. Had the shooting occurred in the 1970s, in many jurisdictions it would have been "lawful but awful." The category of lawful but awful police force can shift, which reminds us that current failures to legally prohibit bad tactics are far from inevitable.

Tennessee v. Garner (1985) illustrates this point. Here the Supreme Court intervened, resulting in perhaps its greatest success in restricting excessive force by police. *Garner* prohibits police from shooting a fleeing suspect unless they have probable cause that the suspect poses "a significant threat of death or serious physical injury" to others (*Tennessee v. Garner* 1985, 1). Outside those circumstances, it deems deadly force by police an unreasonable seizure, which the Fourth Amendment bans. Prior to the decision, numerous police departments had already scrapped the fleeing felon rule, which allowed officers to use deadly force to prevent the escape of felony suspects, regardless of whether they were dangerous. As more departments banned deadly force against nondangerous fleeing suspects, killings by police decreased without officer deaths increasing (Sherman 2018, 425–28). These findings contributed to a growing consensus that the fleeing felon rule was inconsistent with best practices and unnecessary to enforce the law. The court cited this shift as a reason for its ruling (*Tennessee v. Garner* 1985, 10–11, 18–19). The result was a specific rule on police deadly force. Evidence suggests that the ruling helped to further reduce killings by police (Tennenbaum 1994, 254).

Garner gives police concrete guidance to avoid a specific bad tactic. But the same reason for why *Garner* is effective—its specificity—also limits it as a panacea for bad tactics. Many police tactics beyond what *Garner* addresses also endanger life unnecessarily. Before deciding whether to shoot, police make various tactical decisions that can have lethal consequences. For those decisions, *Garner* offers limited guidance.

In *Graham v. Connor* (1989), the Supreme Court put forth a more general rule for evaluating police force. According to *Graham*'s "objective reasonableness" standard, the constitutionality of police force is determined not by an officer's intentions, but by whether the force in question would be justified from the perspective of a reasonable officer in the same situation. This principle has the virtue of offering guidance for a broader range of action than *Garner* does. Yet that apparent advantage comes with a downside: *Graham* offers a principle whose guidance is far less clear. How exactly a "reasonable" officer would act has sparked much disagreement since *Graham* (Alpert and Smith 1994; Harmon 2008). That is especially true in the decentralized context of US policing, which consists of nearly eighteen thousand different law enforcement agencies that lack uniform policies and training (Gardner and Scott 2022, 1).

Graham's lack of specificity limits its ability to meaningfully change police behavior, as suggested by data on police killings. Whereas the evidence suggests that *Garner* did reduce police killings, at least against fleeing suspects and those resisting arrest, *Graham* does not appear to have had a similar effect (Powell and Wu 2025, 6–7).

Language from *Graham* contributes to the confusion over how to apply its objective reasonableness standard. An oft-quoted passage from *Graham* reads:

> The "reasonableness" of a particular use of force must be judged from the perspective of a reasonable officer on the scene, rather than with the 20/20 vision of hindsight. . . . The calculus of reasonableness must embody allowance for the fact that police officers are often forced to make split-second judgments—in circumstances that are tense, uncertain, and rapidly evolving—about the amount of force that is necessary in a particular situation. (*Graham v. Connor* 1989, 396–97)

Notably, this passage echoes language from Justice Sandra Day O'Connor's dissent in *Tennessee v. Garner* (1985, 23) and has become a common justification by the court for bad police tactics—a development that complicates *Garner*'s legacy (Obasogie and Newman 2018, 1476). By incorporating concerns from O'Connor's earlier dissent, *Graham* signaled the court's reluctance to second-guess tactical decisions by police. Certainly, any evaluation of police force must consider the stress and uncertainty that officers experienced at the time. The problem with *Graham*, however, is that its emphasis on split-second decisions can discourage analysis of deliberate tactical planning that often comes prior.

For decades lower courts split on how to apply *Graham*. Some considered prior tactics when evaluating the reasonableness of police force. Others restricted their focus to the final frame when force was used (Noble and Alpert 2010, 486–87; Lee 2021, 1398–406). In its 2025 decision *Barnes v. Felix*, the Supreme Court finally clarified that evaluating the reasonableness of police deadly force requires looking at the totality of the circumstances. No longer could courts limit their analysis to the moment in which a threat prompted an officer to use force. This decision broadens the analysis of reasonableness, which many proponents of police reform support (Policing Project 2025). Still, the ruling has major limitations. It explicitly refuses to address whether foreseeably creating a dangerous situation, which then leads to force by police, should factor into the analysis of whether force was reasonable (*Barnes v. Felix* 2025, 9)—a question the court also punted on in a past decision (*County of Los Angeles v. Mendez* 2017, 8). Leaving that question unaddressed likely means continued disagreement and uncertainty among lower courts on how to evaluate the reasonableness of police force precipitated by bad tactics.

Generally, the courts have been inconsistent in incorporating the latest research on best police practices into their analyses of reasonable action (Garrett and Stoughton 2017). With the exception of *Garner*, the Supreme Court has shown little appetite for declaring specific tactics unreasonable. Rather, it has doubled down on *Graham*'s approach of eschewing specific rules against bad tactics. We see that in *Scott v. Harris* (2007). Here the court deemed it constitutional for an officer to end a high-speed chase by ramming the suspect's car, which left him paralyzed. The ruling rejects the idea that *Garner* prohibits deadly force against a suspect fleeing after only a minor traffic offense. More generally, it rejects attempts to formulate "an easy-to-apply legal test" for specific police tactics (*Scott v. Harris* 2007, 383).

The Supreme Court's embrace of the doctrine of qualified immunity creates another barrier to reining in bad police tactics. This doctrine says that police officers and other government officials are protected from civil damages for violations of constitutional rights unless "clearly established" law prohibited their actions. *Pearson v. Callahan* (2009) even allows courts to skip their analysis of whether an officer's actions violated another's constitutional rights and go straight to deciding whether the officer broke clearly established law. That wrinkle stunts the law's development. If courts do not analyze whether police tactics violated someone's rights, plaintiffs have no opportunity to establish that egregious actions are in fact unconstitutional. As result, bad tactics continue without penalties (Schwartz 2017, 65–66).

So despite *Garner's* success in prohibiting a bad tactic and reducing police killings, the Supreme Court has resisted taking that approach in other cases. When confronted with many of the bad police tactics discussed above, the court has avoided banning them. In *City of Los Angeles v. Lyons* (1983), the court sidestepped the question of whether chokeholds were unconstitutional, allowing them to remain police practice throughout much of the country. In *Richards v. Wisconsin* (1997), the court ruled that no-knock entries by police were constitutional. In *Scott v. Harris* (2007), the court gave police a green light to engage in high-speed pursuits and ram fleeing vehicles, even when the underlying offense is a minor traffic violation. In *Mullenix v. Luna* (2015), the court granted qualified immunity to an officer who disobeyed a superior's order and fired at a moving vehicle, killing the driver. Likewise, as discussed in Chapter 4, the court in *City and County of San Francisco v. Sheehan* (2015) granted qualified immunity to officers who confronted and shot a woman with mental illness holding a knife, who was alone in her room, rather than waiting for backup to arrive.

These and other cases suggest a troubling conclusion: instead of serving as a bulwark against bad tactics, constitutional law too often empowers police to use them—especially against the most vulnerable and marginalized (Butler 2016).

There are, of course, tools beyond constitutional law to promote accountability for bad tactics. Constitutional law sets minimum standards that police nationwide must uphold. States can go further by prohibiting additional tactics that unnecessarily endanger life. Many states, though, fail to pursue that option. In fact, an analysis of state criminal statutes on police deadly force finds that some outline standards less restrictive than what *Garner* requires (Stoughton, Noble, and Alpert 2020, 81–82). Such statutes represent more than just dead laws superseded by federal rulings. Outdated laws make it difficult to convict officers responsible for avoidable killings if the action in question did not violate state law (Stoughton, Noble, and Alpert 2020, 68). State administrative law also has deficiencies. It could be a tool to revoke the licenses of officers who engage in bad tactics, but too often it closes off that option (Goldman 2016).

All these factors hinder meaningful accountability for police-generated killings. Consider the shooting of Tamir Rice. In this case, the prosecutor argued against criminal charges and commissioned two reports that drew heavily on *Graham* to claim that the officer's deadly force was objectively reasonable (Crawford 2015; Sims 2015). The grand jury then followed the prosecutor's recommendation to not charge the officers (Williams and Smith 2015). Having escaped legal penalties, the officer who made the critical error of driving immediately in front of Rice received only a five-day suspension (Associated Press 2018a). The officer who shot Rice was fired but for a reason unrelated to the shooting—providing false information on his job application (Calamur 2017). Since his license was not revoked, another department was able to hire him (Associated Press 2018b). Without clear case law or statutes prohibiting the tactics that led to Rice's death, accountability proved elusive.

The Case and Tools for Reform

Police-generated killings needlessly cut lives short. That is clearly a bad outcome we should want to avoid. Still, some may see police-generated killings as rare events and doubt that they merit policymakers' attention. I think this skepticism is mistaken for a couple reasons.

First, police-generated killings may occur more often than many assume. Each year in the US, police kill dozens and sometimes hundreds of suspects who either are unarmed or have a weapon less lethal than a firearm, like a knife or club (*Washington Post* 2024). Evidence from other countries suggests that many of these killings can be avoided. In the UK, police kill individuals at a far lower rate. That is partly due to fewer guns in circulation among the population, but police tactics also play a role. Since many officers do not carry firearms, UK police have had to develop nonlethal tactics to disarm suspects with knives and clubs, such as repositioning, use of protective shields, and not rushing to resolve incidents (Police Executive Research Forum 2016, 88–105). These tactics do not appear to sacrifice officer safety, given the low proportion of police in the UK who are killed (Zimring 2017, 85–87).

Second, regardless of their frequency, police-generated killings can have outsized effects because bad tactics were involved. Killings that involve questionable force are more likely to generate protests, erode community trust in and cooperation with the police, and hinder public safety. Indeed, public trust in the police tends to drop after high-profile and controversial incidents of police violence, especially among those groups most directly affected (Weitzer 2002; Jones 2020). Distrust of the police and government institutions more broadly only compounds when there is a lack of accountability for police-generated killings.

So we have compelling reasons to pursue reforms that could reduce police-generated killings. If successful, such reforms can save lives and foster greater trust between police and communities. Democratic institutions have several tools to advance those goals.

(1) *Laws that explicitly ban bad tactics.* To combat bad tactics, some emphasize that police administrators should lead through making changes to departmental policy (Zimring 2017, 219–38). Certainly, that strategy is worth pursuing. Police administrators *should* do everything in their power to prevent unnecessary killings. But the reality is that, unless lawmakers take action, many

agencies never adopt reforms (Gilbert 2017). Criminal law serves as a tool for implementing stronger and more uniform accountability for bad tactics. Many states fail to prohibit bad tactics like chokeholds, no-knock raids, and vehicle pursuits prompted by minor infractions. Such broad permissions make it difficult to obtain convictions after police-generated killings. Following the 2020 Black Lives Matter protests, some states did enact criminal laws banning bad tactics responsible for recent high-profile killings by police (Subramanian and Arzy 2021). More states should do the same.

(2) *License revocation for officers who engage in bad tactics.* State administrative law has the potential to define and ban bad police tactics that unnecessarily risk life, as well as impose penalties for their use. Though some states list unjustified deadly force as a reason for license revocation (Goldman 2012, 152), that provision alone offers limited guidance. Ideally, administrative law should outline specific bad tactics that would result in losing one's license, especially in cases of repeat violations or police-generated killings. For decertification to be a meaningful floor of accountability even when other mechanisms fail, states should be able to pursue it independent of whether an officer is criminally convicted or terminated following arbitration (Goldman 2012, 150–51; Rushin 2019, 586–87). Such measures would incentivize Peace Officer Standards and Training (POST) commissions—which in most states have authority over police training requirements and revoking licenses (Goldman 2003, 122)—to train officers to avoid bad tactics banned by law. States also can pass laws requiring training that cautions against such tactics and provides officers with alternative approaches for protecting life.

(3) *Constitutional protections against bad tactics.* In *Garner*, the Supreme Court banned a bad tactic by ending police's blanket permission to shoot fleeing felons to prevent their escape. This ruling came after numerous states and police agencies already had abandoned the fleeing felon rule. Looking forward, if more states and police agencies abandon other tactics that unnecessarily threaten life, future litigation can make the case that these tactics no longer are reasonable and thus unconstitutional. This long-term strategy can bolster protections against bad police tactics and ensure that they apply nationally (see Garrett and Stoughton 2017). Currently, the doctrine of qualified immunity hinders courts from recognizing force tied to bad tactics as unreasonable. Both Congress and the Supreme Court have the power to end this judicial invention. Encouragingly, in recent years, the idea of ending qualified immunity has garnered greater support across the political spectrum (Baude 2018; Sonmez, Kane, and Colvin 2020).

(4) *Experiment with some officers not carrying a firearm.* The US has more guns than people, heightening the dangers for police. In this environment, many officers are resistant to the idea of not carrying a firearm. Even reform-minded voices in policing deem the idea a "non-starter" (del Pozo 2019; see also del

Pozo and Friedman 2023). The abundant supply of guns in circulation makes it unlikely that police forces in the US could look like those in the UK, where most officers do not carry a gun. But do all patrols and police activities require a gun? Though it doesn't make sense to send unarmed police to serve a warrant, it may make sense for officers not to carry a gun on certain low-risk foot and bike patrols focused on community relations and soft deterrence. Other public safety workers do their jobs unarmed, such as civilian school guards and civilian crisis responders who handle calls for service related to mental illness, substance use, and homelessness that previously fell to police (McMillen, Sarmiento-Barbieri, and Singh 2019; Midgette and Reuter 2024). Worries that it would be too dangerous to send such workers unarmed into neighborhoods have proved largely unfounded. In the rare instances where there is violence or a firearm, civilian crisis responders call armed police to handle the threat (Midgette and Reuter 2024, 790, 793–94). A similar rule could apply to officers not carrying a firearm. It would be particularly important for these officers to master nonlethal tactics on responding to aggressors who are unarmed or have a weapon less lethal than a firearm. That impetus for more robust de-escalation tactics, like those found in the UK, could help spur training in such tactics within US policing.

Together, the above recommendations give officers more detailed guidance on using force and responding to a range of different threats. As the sociologist Egon Bittner (1970, 38) noted over a half century ago, it "smacks of . . . perversity" to empower police to use force without also providing clear guidelines on how to use it (see also Friedman 2017). The recommendations proposed here represent a more proactive approach to using the law—complemented by departmental policy and training—to identify and prohibit bad tactics.

Some may balk at this approach since any list of legal prohibitions will prove incomplete, in need of revision as new research emerges. To be sure, it sometimes will be necessary to update the law, especially when evidence builds that specific tactics unnecessarily raise the risk of deadly force. But that work is the inevitable price of meaningful police oversight in a democratic society. Democratic oversight of the police is an ongoing project, not something we can check off and be done with.

Others may have concerns that bans on bad tactics would limit police discretion to choose the right tactic for the right situation. For certain tactics, however, we have growing evidence that discretion has backfired in the form of avoidable deaths, injuries, and loss of public trust. In short, when there is a clear pattern of discretion being abused and undermining key police objectives, like protecting life, it makes sense to limit officers' discretion to use the tactics at fault. As history illustrates through examples like the ban on the fleeing felon rule, laws and policies that restrict bad tactics can save lives without hindering police work or endangering officers (Fyfe 1979, 313–21; Nowacki 2015, 657).

Now it would be a mistake to conclude that tackling the problem of bad tactics is *just* about limiting police discretion. The most effective policy responses entail not just instructions on what tactics to avoid, but also guidance on what alternatives to employ, along with training and resources to facilitate their adoption (which is reflected in the above recommendations). Such a comprehensive approach puts police in the best position to uphold the ethical obligation that should always be at the forefront of their mind—prioritizing the protection of life.

7

Fleeing "Dangerous" Suspects

Saddened and outraged, people took to the streets in 2018 after video came out of an East Pittsburgh officer killing Antwon Rose II, a Black 17-year-old. The bystander's video showed Rose jumping out of a car stopped by police and fleeing the scene unarmed until Officer Michael Rosfeld shot him multiple times. Rose posed no imminent threat when he was killed. Rose's mother Michelle Kenney expressed what many felt: "You can never explain, to me or to any rational person, how three shots to the back is acceptable force" (Bradbury 2019).

Though prosecutors charged the officer with criminal homicide, he was found not guilty. That outcome disappointed many but was unsurprising given existing law. In Pennsylvania, officers have legal justification to use deadly force when they believe it is necessary to prevent the escape of an individual suspected of a violent felony (Pennsylvania General Assembly 2023, 18 Pa. Code §508). Police stopped Rose and those with him because they were suspected of a drive-by shooting. Video and other evidence later released showed another occupant in the car other than Rose firing the gun in the drive-by shooting (Ward 2019). But police did not have those details when Rose fled. The officer could claim he reasonably believed that Rose had committed a violent felony, and that deadly force was necessary to prevent his escape. Those two factors combined give an officer legal justification to use deadly force.

Rosfeld's acquittal highlights how the law permits police to use deadly force even against suspects who pose no imminent threat. In this respect, Pennsylvania is hardly alone. Most state statutes permit police to use deadly force in circumstances involving no imminent threat. Many statutes specifically authorize officers to use deadly force when they perceive it as necessary to prevent the escape of someone suspected of a violent crime or possessing a deadly weapon (Stoughton, Noble, and Alpert 2020, 81–84). A close reading of the US Supreme Court decision *Tennessee v. Garner* (1985) shows a similar approach. Constitutional law allows police deadly force against "dangerous" fleeing suspects—a broader category than fleeing suspects who pose an imminent threat.

That feature of the law permits police to use deadly force in situations where civilians may not. Criminal law often places what is known as the *imminence requirement* on civilians (see Ferzan 2004; Leverick 2006, 87–108; Harmon 2008;

Baron 2011; Allhoff 2019). This requirement imposes the following constraint on the use of deadly force.

> *Imminence requirement*: a necessary condition to justify deadly force is reasonable belief that oneself or another innocent person faces imminent threat of grave harm, such as death or serious bodily injury

Most state laws place no such requirement on police (Lee 2018, 656). Rather, the law treats an imminent threat of grave harm as one, but not the only, justification for police deadly force.

Discussion of the imminence requirement's role in policing sometimes gets muddled due to the mistaken claim that *Tennessee v. Garner* imposes this constraint on officers (Smith 1997, 2022; Marcus 2016; Stoughton, Noble, and Alpert 2020). This chapter explains the problems with that interpretation and why extending the imminence requirement to police typically requires new law rather than appeals to existing law. It also brings attention to efforts by policymakers to incorporate the imminence requirement into policing. Unlike many of the policies discussed in Chapter 6, there is little empirical research comparing the imminence requirement with the status quo. The lack of research presents challenges for morally evaluating the policy. After all, the policy's merit depends in no small part on whether it is effective in minimizing grave harm and protecting life.

Some observers see the imminence requirement as fundamentally at odds with officers' responsibilities and conclude that we can reject it in policing on a priori grounds (Ford 2022, 2–5). This chapter points out problems with that view. Two core principles from law and ethics support the imminence requirement in policing: (1) the doing/allowing distinction—the idea that causing harm is worse than allowing it—and (2) equality before the law. Both represent presumptions against exempting police from the imminence requirement. The legal status quo makes that exemption, which puts it on morally shaky ground. That's especially true given the lack of empirical evidence that the status quo helps protect life. We would need such evidence to overcome the presumptions against exempting police from the imminence requirement.

What does this all mean for policymakers? In short, the imminence requirement is not inherently at odds with police responsibilities, so policymakers should not have moral qualms about adopting and experimenting with the policy, keeping in mind the need for ongoing evaluation. Key to advancing the ethical and policy debate over whether police should be subject to the imminence requirement is careful study of its effects on police shootings, officer injuries, and violent crime. Gathering such data would give us a clearer sense of whether the imminence requirement helps police prioritize the protection of life.

The Imminence Requirement

If a threat has passed, civilians lack permission to kill whoever caused it. In that context, force is retaliation, not defensive action to prevent harm. Merely potential threats also fail to justify defensive force since such threats are everywhere and many never come to fruition. Given those considerations, the law often specifies that a threat must be imminent to justify defensive force.

The concept of imminence conveys that something is clearly at hand and will occur at once, absent intervention to prevent it. In policing and law, an imminent threat is commonly understood as referring to suspects who possess three features: present (1) ability, (2) opportunity, and (3) apparent intent to cause harm (e.g., Association of State Criminal Investigative Agencies et al. 2020, 11; California Legislative Information 2024, §835a; Illinois General Assembly 2024, 720 ILSC 5/7-5).

That definition has the advantage of offering practical guidance to officers. It specifies three criteria—ability, opportunity, and intent—that officers should look for when determining if a suspect poses an imminent threat. The definition does require a few tweaks. Some suspects, like drunk drivers, can lack intent to cause harm yet still pose an imminent threat due to recklessness or negligence. It also is possible to pose an imminent threat absent bad intent, recklessness, or negligence—in other words, without doing anything wrong. A conscientious driver fulfilling their ethical and legal responsibilities on the road could pose an imminent threat when a freak event causes their brakes to malfunction, leaving them powerless to stop their vehicle as it careers toward a pedestrian.

The following definition makes room for these other ways imminent threats can manifest themselves, while still preserving the principal criteria from the conception of imminence commonly found in policing.

> *Imminent threat*: danger clearly at hand that will cause harm at once absent intervention; someone posing such danger has the present (1) ability, (2) opportunity, and (3) intent to cause harm (or whose reckless, negligent, or blameless action is about to cause harm)

In the ethical and legal literature, the terms imminent and immediate are often used interchangeably (e.g., Leverick 2006, 87; Association of State Criminal Investigative Agencies et al. 2020, 11). That same convention is adopted here.

The imminence requirement appears in many criminal codes, meaning that they treat reasonable belief of an imminent threat as a *necessary* rather than merely *sufficient* condition to justify deadly force by civilians (Ferzan 2004; Leverick 2006, 87–108; Harmon 2008; Baron 2011; Allhoff 2019). Just because a law or policy mentions imminent threats as a justification for defensive force does not automatically imply the imminence requirement. It could list imminent threats as one of several justifications, which is different from requiring that a threat be imminent. When imminence is required, deadly defensive force lacks justification absent reasonable belief of a grave and imminent threat. Wisconsin's statute on self-defense serves as an example: "[An] actor may not intentionally use force which is intended or likely to cause death or great bodily harm unless the actor reasonably believes that such force is necessary to prevent imminent death or great bodily harm to himself or herself" (Wisconsin State Legislature 2024, §939.48). Though not universal, the imminence requirement represents the prevailing approach in US law on what justifies deadly force by civilians (Allhoff 2019, 1530).

It is important to avoid reducing the concept of imminence to something else, like being armed. A person armed with a knife could be too far from anyone else to pose an imminent threat. Similarly, someone with a gun could pose no imminent threat as long as it remains in its holster. Indeed, given concealed and open carry laws in many states—regardless of their wisdom—it would be absurd to treat everyone with a gun as an imminent threat. Questions of imminence are related to but distinct from whether someone is armed.

Imminence also is distinct from necessity. Necessity says that force is justified only if one reasonably believes that it is required to stop an unjust threat and the least harmful way to do so (see Chapter 1). In theory, force could satisfy necessity but not the imminence requirement. Such a hypothetical imagines a threat that, despite posing no imminent danger, will inflict future harm that only force can prevent (we take a closer look at such hypotheticals in the later section "Objection 2: The Imminence Requirement Undermines the Protection of Life"). With those scenarios in mind, justificatory criteria sometimes require that force satisfy necessity while leaving out the imminence requirement. The Model Penal Code, for instance, takes that approach (Dubber 2015, 149–50, 159). When justificatory frameworks include the imminence requirement, it functions as an *additional* restriction on force beyond necessity.

Though imminence and necessity are separate concepts, there are important links between them. The primary motivation behind the imminence requirement is to serve as a proxy for necessity. It often is difficult to know what level of force, if any, is necessary to stop a threat. The imminence requirement offers guidance when there is uncertainty, serving as a check against gratuitous force. It supplements the principle of necessity by indicating that defensive force is only needed for threats at hand and therefore most likely to occur. As Fiona Leverick (2006, 89) notes, "If a threat of harm is not imminent, it is more difficult to know with any degree of certainty whether the harm would have occurred and whether the accused could have saved her life simply by doing nothing (and thus preserving the life of the potential aggressor)."

We can illustrate this point by breaking imminence down into its three components—present (1) ability, (2) opportunity, and (3) intent to cause harm—and considering the implications for necessity if any condition is not met. Consider someone with the present opportunity and intent to cause harm but not the ability (say, they lack a weapon). That feature of the scenario makes it less certain that force is necessary. The individual in question could acquire a weapon, gaining the ability to carry out their intent, but the future does not guarantee it. If it turns out that they never gain the ability to act on their intention, using force against them would be unnecessary. The same follows for someone who has the ability and intent to cause harm but lacks access to their target. Their lack of opportunity casts doubts on the need for force, since it is unclear whether their intended harm will come to fruition. That is even more true for someone with the ability and opportunity to cause harm—a description that applies, for instance, to about everyone driving a car—but without any intent to cause harm.

If the imminence requirement is not satisfied, one of the components for causing *present* harm is missing, which introduces uncertainty on whether the harm will occur and, relatedly, whether force is necessary. Uncertainty about threats that are not imminent, as we will see later, proves especially relevant when considering objections to the imminence requirement.

Police's Exemption from the Imminence Requirement

The imminence requirement for civilians traces back to the common law (Ferzan 2004, 257–59), but it has long exempted police. This asymmetry partly stems from the distinct path that the common law took in how it justified deadly force by law enforcement. The common law included the *fleeing felon rule*, which authorized officials to use deadly force when necessary to prevent the escape of any felony suspect. Since most felonies used to be capital offenses, the common law treated deadly force as a proportionate response to a fleeing felony suspect (Dubber 2015, 171). This principle later became part of criminal statutes and police policy, with the effect of authorizing deadly force against suspects who, at the time of their flight, posed no danger to others (Stoughton, Noble, and Alpert 2020, 81–82).

The fleeing felon rule is no longer constitutional in the US, since the Supreme Court struck it down in *Tennessee v. Garner* (1985). But current state and federal laws still permit police to use deadly force against certain non-imminent threats.

Notably, this permission shows up in the law that provided justification for shooting Antwon Rose, discussed earlier. Pennsylvania's statute on police deadly force reads:

> A peace officer ... is justified in using deadly force only when he believes that
> such force is necessary to prevent death or serious bodily injury to himself
> or ... [an]other person, or when he believes both that:
> (i)　such force is necessary to prevent the arrest from being defeated by re-
> sistance or escape; and
> (ii)　the person to be arrested has committed or attempted a forcible felony
> or is attempting to escape and possesses a deadly weapon, or otherwise
> indicates that he will endanger human life or inflict serious bodily in-
> jury unless arrested without delay. (Pennsylvania General Assembly
> 2025, 18 Pa. Code §508)

Though not exactly a model of clarity—the disjunctions in subsection (ii) are difficult to follow and have been the subject of litigation (Palmer 2019)—the Pennsylvania statute still proves informative because it features justifications common in other state statutes (Stoughton, Noble, and Alpert 2020, 82–84). It divides these justifications into two categories: (1) defense against grave harm and (2) stopping the escape of a dangerous fleeing suspect. Subsection (ii) lists which fleeing suspects fall into this second category: those who have committed or attempted a forcible felony (i.e., a felony involving actual or threatened violence like murder or robbery), those with a deadly weapon, and those who otherwise indicate that they will cause grave harm.

Under Pennsylvania's law and those similar to it, police have a justification for deadly force that civilians lack—preventing the escape of individuals deemed dangerous. The law reflects the idea that, to fulfill their responsibilities, police need broader permissions to use deadly force. Exempting police from the imminence requirement opens the door, however, to deadly force across a wider range of circumstances, including cases where such force appears inconsistent with prioritizing the protection of life.

Take the following case.

Gas station robbery: Someone robs a gas station by threatening the cashier with a knife but hurts no one. When fleeing, the robber poses no imminent danger to anyone—in fact, they even toss the knife away. Police recognize that the robber poses no imminent threat but reasonably believe that deadly force is necessary to prevent their escape.

In those circumstances, officers would be legally justified in shooting the suspect, according to the Pennsylvania statute. It explicitly permits police deadly force if (1) necessary to prevent the escape of a suspect who (2) committed a forcible felony, like robbery. Both conditions are met.

Yet deadly force in this scenario seems wrong. There is little reason to believe that it is necessary to prevent grave harm. Pennsylvania's forcible felony category is overly broad and a flawed proxy for threats warranting deadly force. This problem shows up in the law beyond just Pennsylvania. Without the imminence requirement, existing law often relies on the less stringent criterion of dangerousness, which can yield dubious justifications for police deadly force.

By itself, *gas station robbery* is not decisive evidence against the approach found in Pennsylvania's and other states' statutes. Just about every policy comes with drawbacks and tradeoffs. *Gas station robbery* does, though, clearly reveal the drawbacks of exempting police from the imminence requirement. It gives us reason to scrutinize the policy more closely and consider whether any alternatives do a better job in striking a balance between the moral benefits and drawbacks they entail.

Garner's Limitations

Though attempts to rein in police violence often fail, *Garner* has been a rare success in many respects. The ruling made national a reform that a growing number of police departments and jurisdictions had adopted, ending the fleeing felon rule. Before *Garner*, many officers in the US had a blanket permission to shoot fleeing felony suspects when officers had reason to believe that such force was necessary to prevent their escape. That rule allowed force disproportionate to the underlying offense and threat, as we can see in the incident considered in *Garner*: the fatal police shooting of a visibly unarmed Black 15-year-old, Edward Garner, as he fled over a fence after a burglary (*Tennessee v. Garner* 1985, 3–4). By declaring the fleeing felon rule a violation of the Fourth Amendment's ban on unreasonable seizures, the Supreme Court prohibited a police practice that needlessly took lives. This tactical guidance at the level of constitutional law—don't shoot nondangerous suspects—proved effective in reducing police violence. Data suggest that the ruling led to a decrease in police killings without sacrificing officer or public safety (Tennenbaum 1994; Sherman 2018, 425–28).

The goal here is not to deny *Garner's* benefits but to note that it also has limitations. *Garner* prohibits police deadly force against *nondangerous* suspects, while still allowing such force against *dangerous* suspects to prevent their escape. That rule raises the question: who counts as dangerous? One proposal from the philosopher Seumas Miller (2016, 127) understands dangerous as "a *standing* threat to life and limb," which "cannot be removed by leaving [the offender] alone." As we have seen, this is not the prevailing view in US law, where the category of dangerous encompasses a broader range of suspects. The result is that police have legal justification to kill individuals who pose little threat to public safety.

Some use-of-force of scholars rightly criticize this aspect of state statutes yet fail to recognize that *Garner* suffers from a similar defect. An oft-repeated claim in the police use-of-force literature is that *Garner,* in effect, imposed the imminence requirement on police. Michael Smith (1997, 109) writes: "*Garner* held that a police officer may not use deadly force to apprehend a fleeing felon who does not pose an immediate risk of death or serious injury to the officer or others" (see also Smith 2022). Similarly, Nancy Marcus (2016, 57) claims that *Garner* prohibits "deadly police force against fleeing, unarmed suspects and others who do not pose an imminent threat of physical harm to others." In *Evaluating Police Uses of Force*, Seth Stoughton, Jeffrey Noble, and Geoffrey Alpert (2020, 82) characterize "the *Garner* rule" as requiring "an imminent threat of death or great bodily harm" to justify police deadly force. This same view shows up in the US Department of Justice's report on the Cleveland Division of Police. It interprets *Garner* as only permitting deadly force "when an officer has probable cause to believe that a suspect poses an immediate threat of serious physical harm to the officer or another person" (US Department of Justice 2014, 13).

This common interpretation misrepresents *Garner.* The words imminent or immediate never appear in its holding, which in its entirety reads:

> The Tennessee statute is unconstitutional insofar as it authorizes the use of deadly force against, as in this case, an apparently unarmed, nondangerous fleeing suspect; such force may not be used unless necessary to prevent the escape and the officer has probable cause to believe that the suspect poses a significant threat of death or serious physical injury to the officer or others. (*Tennessee v. Garner* 1985, 1)

The ruling's most critical part notably avoids specifying probable cause of an *imminent* threat as a necessary condition to justify deadly force.

Those who claim that *Garner* imposes the imminence requirement on police largely base their interpretation on the following passage: "Where the suspect poses no immediate threat to the officer and no threat to others, the harm resulting from failing to apprehend him does not justify the use of deadly force" (*Tennessee v. Garner* 1985, 11). The problem with appealing to this passage as evidence of the imminence requirement is that the wording carefully avoids implying such a requirement. The term "immediate" only modifies "threat to the officer," not "threat to others." If immediate were meant to modify both sorts of threats, it instead would read "no immediate threat to the officer or others." The passage's actual wording implies that officers, like civilians, are justified in using deadly force if necessary to stop imminent threats to themselves. But officers have an additional justification to use deadly force necessary to stop a broader range of threats to others, which need not be imminent.

Further textual evidence supports this view. When explaining what constitutes probable cause that a suspect poses a significant threat of death or serious physical injury, *Garner* outlines conditions beyond just the presence of an imminent threat.

> Where the officer has probable cause to believe that the suspect poses a threat of serious physical harm, either to the officer or to others, it is not constitutionally unreasonable to prevent escape by using deadly force. Thus, if the suspect threatens the officer with a weapon or there is probable cause to believe that he has committed a crime involving the infliction or threatened infliction of serious physical harm, deadly force may be used if necessary to prevent escape, and if, where feasible, some warning has been given. (*Tennessee v. Garner* 1985, 11–12)

This passage outlines circumstances, like individuals fleeing police suspected of violent felonies, where officers would be legally justified in using deadly force even absent an imminent threat.

Some recognize that this passage poses a problem for the claim that *Garner* imposes the imminence requirement on police, but they try to get around it by interpreting the passage's remarks as incidental with "no precedential value" (Smith 1997, 100). This understanding of precedent is overly narrow, however. *Garner* held that to justify police use of deadly force, an officer must have "probable cause to believe that the suspect poses a significant threat of death or serious physical injury." The holding itself does not explain what constitutes probable cause for such a threat, but the passage some try to dismiss does exactly that. For legislatures, lower courts, and law enforcement agencies looking to follow *Garner*, its explanation of probable cause is naturally and appropriately one of the first places to turn to understand how the decision does and does not constrain officers.

Garner's explanation of when police deadly force is permitted draws on state statutes like Pennsylvania's adopted before the decision. In fact, when describing the statutes of Pennsylvania and seventeen other states, *Garner* uses language that mirrors the criteria permitting deadly force found in Pennsylvania law: "Eighteen [states] allow, in slightly varying language, the use of deadly force only if the suspect has committed a felony involving the use or threat of physical or deadly force, or is escaping with a deadly weapon, or is likely to endanger life or inflict serious physical injury if not arrested" (*Tennessee v. Garner* 1985,

17). Importantly, the decision distinguishes these statutes—which permit police deadly force against certain non-imminent threats—from those struck down as unconstitutional for embracing the fleeing felon rule.

It is understandable why the majority in *Garner* avoided extending the imminence requirement to police. Doing so would have been dramatically out of line with existing law. Whereas numerous states and departments had scrapped the fleeing felon rule in the years prior to *Garner*, there was no similar movement at the time to impose the imminence requirement on police. By striking down the fleeing felon rule, the court took a more modest step in line with then-existing trends (see *Tennessee v. Garner* 1985, 10–11, 18–19).

So though the court's ruling has saved lives, it still has many of the same flaws that show up in state statutes today, which use-of-force scholarship sometimes fails to acknowledge. That oversight encourages reliance on a Supreme Court precedent that, despite its benefits, remains saddled with an overly permissive standard for police deadly force (e.g., Marcus 2016, 77–84). Recognizing *Garner*'s limitations helps clarify the minimum standards in current constitutional law—and what further policies may be needed to curb unnecessary police force.

Gesturing at the Imminence Requirement

Several prominent proposals suggest that laws governing police force could benefit from moving closer to the imminence requirement without fully adopting it. In her influential article "When Is Police Violence Justified?" Rachel Harmon argues that criminal law on policing should draw on legal principles from civilian self-defense like the imminence requirement. "On balance," she writes, "it seems that police uses of force should be governed by something very similar to the imminence standard that applies to self-defenders" (Harmon 2008, 1169–70).

Despite making this connection, Harmon alters the imminence requirement when applying it to police. Officers, in her view, have a broader range of legitimate ends for using force. Self-defense is a legitimate aim of force for both police and civilians. But maintaining order and preventing suspects' escape are legitimate aims of force only for police (Harmon 2008, 1158). Within this framework, a suspect's imminent threat of escape can justify police force, even if the suspect poses no imminent threat of physical harm (Harmon 2008, 1171). In sum, Harmon's imminence requirement for police recognizes a greater variety of threats that justify force than does the standard imminence requirement.

This point applies to deadly force, which Harmon sees as justified when necessary to stop the escape of a suspect whose underlying offense predicts future violence. So police deadly force would be justified against a suspected serial killer posing no imminent threat of physical harm, if such force were necessary to prevent their escape. To be sure, Harmon is uncomfortable extending justifications for deadly force to a broad range of suspects. Still, her proposal makes room for a category—people who pose no imminent threat of grave harm but are legally liable to deadly force—that the standard imminence requirement precludes (Harmon 2008, 1160–61).

The National Consensus Policy on Use of Force, developed by nearly a dozen law enforcement organizations like the Fraternal Order of Police and International Association of Chiefs of Police, offers another proposal that flirts with adopting the imminence requirement. The Consensus Policy's section on deadly force states:

> Use of deadly force is justified when one or both of the following apply:
> a. to protect the officer or others from what is reasonably believed to be an immediate threat of death or serious bodily injury
> b. to prevent the escape of a fleeing subject when the officer has probable cause to believe that the person has committed, or intends to commit a felony involving serious bodily injury or death, and the officer reasonably believes that there is an imminent risk of serious bodily injury or death to the officer or another if the subject is not immediately apprehended (Association of State Criminal Investigative Agencies et al. 2020, 3–4)

According to the Consensus Policy, police are justified in using deadly force if either the conditions in subsection a or subsection b are met. The conditions outlined in subsection a match those that typically must be met to justify deadly force by civilians. Like civilians, police are justified in using deadly force when they reasonably believe that it is necessary to prevent an immediate or imminent threat of grave harm. (The policy uses the terms "immediate" and "imminent" synonymously. See Association of State Criminal Investigative Agencies et al. 2020, 11.) Importantly, though, subsection a provides *sufficient* conditions to justify deadly force, not *necessary* conditions. After all, subsection b outlines an additional justification for deadly force only available to police.

Subsection b engages in verbal gymnastics to stake out a standard just short of the imminence requirement—and it is doubtful that it sticks the landing. This subsection avoids directly saying that the fleeing suspect poses an imminent threat. Instead, it uses the circumlocution "there is an imminent risk of serious bodily injury or death . . . if the subject is not immediately apprehended." Though this section of the Consensus Policy does not describe the fleeing suspect as posing an imminent threat, such a threat exists based on the officer's reasonable belief. Yet *someone* must be the source of the threat. In this context, the only plausible candidate is the fleeing suspect. But when subsection b is read with subsection a, it seems clear that part of the motivation for b is to outline conditions where deadly force would be justified against suspects who do *not* pose an immediate or imminent threat. Otherwise, subsection b would be redundant, since subsection a already outlines a justification for deadly force against such threats.

The Consensus Policy defines an *"immediate, or imminent, threat"* of grave harm as a danger posed by someone with the apparent intent, ability, and opportunity to inflict serious bodily injury or death (Association of State Criminal Investigative Agencies et al. 2020, 11). Based on that definition, if a fleeing suspect lacks the apparent intent, ability, and opportunity to inflict grave harm, there is no imminent threat. The language in subsection b obscures that basic point by describing an imminent threat disconnected from any agent who causes it.

Move Toward the Imminence Requirement in Policing

In recent years, some lawmakers have proposed applying the imminence requirement to police. The Pennsylvania Legislative Black Caucus made such a proposal in legislation introduced in response to the police shooting of Antwon Rose (Lee and Gainey 2019). The legislation reads: "A peace officer . . . is justified in using deadly force only when he reasonably believes that such force is necessary to protect himself or another from imminent death, serious bodily injury, kidnapping or sexual intercourse compelled by force or threat" (Pennsylvania General Assembly 2019). This bill leaves no room for justifying deadly force based on speculation about a suspect's future danger. Rather, police are justified in using deadly force only against what they reasonably believe is an imminent threat of grave harm.

The bill did not pass the Pennsylvania legislature. But after the 2020 Black Lives Matter protests, other states did pass legislation restricting police deadly force (Subramanian and Arzy 2021). Massachusetts arguably went the furthest by adopting the imminence requirement:

A law enforcement officer shall not use deadly force upon a person unless de-escalation tactics have been attempted and failed or are not feasible based on the totality of the circumstances and such force is necessary to prevent imminent harm to a person and the amount of force used is proportionate to the threat of imminent harm. (General Court of the Commonwealth of Massachusetts 2020, 6E §14)

This measure clearly prohibits officers from using deadly force against suspects who pose no imminent threat of grave harm. Colorado also passed a statute restricting deadly force by police against fleeing suspects, allowing it only against those posing an "immediate threat" (unlike the Massachusetts law, the Colorado statute fails to specify that the suspect must pose a threat for which deadly force is a proportionate response) (Colorado General Assembly 2020, §5).

In 2022, another important shift occurred: the US Department of Justice (DOJ) revised its deadly force policy. The updated policy stated: "Law enforcement officers and correctional officers of the Department of Justice may use deadly force only when necessary, that is, when the officer has a reasonable belief that the subject of such force poses an imminent danger of death or serious physical injury to the officer or to another person" (US Department of Justice 2022). This clear articulation of the imminence requirement applied to law enforcement officers in agencies under the DOJ, like the Federal Bureau of Investigation (FBI).

The DOJ's previous policy had permitted deadly force against a fleeing suspect whose escape would pose an imminent threat of grave harm without specifying that the suspect must pose such a threat (US Department of Justice 1995b). In this way, it resembled the Consensus Policy developed by different law enforcement groups and discussed earlier. A commentary accompanying the DOJ's previous policy further loosened restrictions on using deadly force. It explained imminent as "having a broader meaning than 'immediate' or 'instantaneous'" (US Department of Justice 1995a). This language no longer appeared in the 2022 revision.

Before the DOJ revised its policy, several big city police departments already incorporated the imminence requirement into their deadly force policies (Obasogie and Newman 2017). Examples include the Chicago Police Department (2023, 5), Houston Police Department (2022, 3), and Dallas Police Department (2024, 906.02) (see Table 7.1).

The Chicago Police Department (2023, 1) policy notes that it satisfies the use-of-force standards outlined by the Commission on Accreditation for Law Enforcement Agencies (CALEA). CALEA includes the imminence requirement in its deadly force standard for agencies seeking accreditation. CALEA advises agencies to have a policy stating: "deadly force may only be used when an officer reasonably believes the action is in defense of any human life in imminent danger of death or serious bodily injury" (Commission on Accreditation for Law Enforcement Agencies 2021, §4.1.2). Though only a minority of the roughly eighteen thousand law enforcement agencies in the US have CALEA accreditation, its model policies remain influential. Many of the largest and most high-profile agencies participate in its accreditation program (Commission on Accreditation for Law Enforcement Agencies 2025).

Table 7.1. Examples of Police Department Policies with the Imminence Requirement

Agency/Organization	Deadly Force Policy
Chicago Police Department (2023)	*Last Resort.* The use of deadly force is a last resort that is permissible only when necessary to protect against an imminent threat to life or to prevent great bodily harm to the member or another person. Consistent with this requirement, a sworn Department member may use deadly force only when such force is necessary to prevent: 1. death or great bodily harm from an imminent threat posed to the sworn member or to another person. 2. an arrest from being defeated by resistance or escape, where the person to be arrested poses an imminent threat of death or great bodily harm to a sworn member or another person unless arrested without delay.
Houston Police Department (2022)	The use of deadly force shall be limited to those circumstances in which officers have an objectively reasonable belief that deadly force is necessary to protect themselves or others from the imminent threat of serious bodily injury or death.
Dallas Police Department (2024)	Authorization to Use Deadly Force—Officers will only use deadly force to protect themselves or another person from imminent death or serious bodily injury.

Note: Policies as of July 1, 2025

It appears that CALEA could have more influence in this area of policy. The organization has been lax in making the imminence requirement a prerequisite for accreditation. Consider the deadly force policy of the Atlanta Police Department (2022, §4.2), an agency with CALEA accreditation (Commission on Accreditation for Law Enforcement Agencies 2025). Its policy lacks the imminence requirement and instead resembles state law (LexisNexis 2025, §17-4-20). Compared with CALEA's policy, Georgia state law gives police broader permissions to use deadly force, allowing it to apprehend suspects who are not necessarily an imminent threat (see Table 7.2). Though Georgia law sets a floor, individual departments can adopt more restrictive standards. The Atlanta department could have adopted CALEA's standard but went with a less restrictive one, while still receiving CALEA accreditation.

At present, the imminence requirement in policing remains a minority practice among US law enforcement agencies and a legal novelty. Nonetheless,

Table 7.2. Comparing Deadly Force Policies: CALEA and the Atlanta Police Department (which has CALEA accreditation)

Agency/ Organization	Deadly Force Policy
Commission on Accreditation for Law Enforcement Agencies (2021)	A written directive states deadly force may only be used when an officer reasonably believes the action is in defense of any human life in imminent danger of death or serious bodily injury.
Atlanta Police Department (2022)	An employee may use deadly force to apprehend a suspected felon only when: 1. The officer reasonably believes that the suspect possesses a deadly weapon or any object, device, or instrument which, when used offensively against a person, is likely to or actually does result in serious bodily injury; when the officer reasonably believes that the suspect poses an immediate threat of physical violence to the officer or others; or when there is probable cause to believe that the suspect has committed a crime involving the infliction or threatened infliction of serious physical harm. [OCGA 17-4-20 (b)] 2. When there is probable cause to believe that the suspect has committed a crime involving the infliction or threatened infliction of serious physical harm (O.C.G.A. Section 17-4-20) and the employee reasonably believes that the suspect's escape would create a continuing danger of serious physical harm to any person. 3. Where feasible, some warning has been given [Tennessee v. Garner, 471 US 1 (1985)].

Note: Policies as of July 1, 2025

the DOJ's embrace of it, CALEA's endorsement of it, and recent bills in state legislatures to implement it—including some signed into law—suggest some movement toward this more stringent rule for police. The next sections examine the moral case for this shift.

Doing/Allowing Distinction

A key moral principle that favors the imminence requirement in policing over the status quo is the doing/allowing distinction. This principle captures that causing harm is worse than allowing harm and more difficult to justify, all else being equal (Quinn 1989; Hosein 2014; Woollard 2015). The doing/allowing distinction is grounded in the following idea: *negative duties* to avoid harming others are more stringent than *positive duties* to help others by preventing harm threatened against them. Both positive and negative duties are key components of morality. But negative duties are weightier, as Adam Hosein (2014, 238) notes, because "I must take special responsibility for what *I* do to other people as opposed to what merely befalls them or what other people inflict on them."

The doing/allowing distinction is fundamental to the ethics of defensive force. It shows up, for instance, in the structure of lesser evil justifications. Some actions that cause harm can be justified as a lesser evil. But because of the doing/allowing distinction, an action must prevent more harm than it causes to qualify for a lesser evil justification (Alexander 2005; Rodin 2011; Frowe 2018; Jones and Tian 2022, 2025; Gordon-Solmon 2023).

So the doing/allowing distinction does not rule out action that causes harm. Rather, it represents a presumption against actions and policies that cause harm. In some cases, other moral considerations override this presumption.

Aspects of the criminal justice system already reflect the doing/allowing distinction. For instance, most believe that it is better to acquit several guilty defendants than to convict one innocent person. When the latter occurs, the state inflicts harm on the innocent. When the former occurs, the state allows the guilty to go free and potentially cause harm to the innocent (or encourage others to cause harm due to lack of deterrence). Neither outcome is optimal. But since it is worse for the state to cause harm than to allow it, all else being equal, the criminal justice system often is structured to minimize false-positive errors (convicting the innocent) while accepting a greater risk of false-negative errors (acquitting the guilty). That policy choice aligns with what the doing/allowing distinction implies (Hosein 2014, 239–40).

The doing/allowing distinction offers similar guidance on what rules should govern police deadly force against fleeing suspects. Using deadly force against a suspect mistakenly identified as a future threat—but who in fact would have caused no grave harm had they escaped—would count as a false positive error. A false negative error would mean refraining from deadly force against a suspect who turns out to be a future threat and inflicts grave harm after their escape (see Bolinger 2021, 144). We want officers to avoid both errors. Ideally, officers' deadly force decisions would always fall in either the upper-left or lower-right quadrant of Table 7.3. That is, they use deadly force when necessary to stop suspects from causing future grave harm, and they avoid deadly force against suspects who will not cause grave harm, even if they escape. Since imperfect information and human fallibility are inevitable, neither the imminence requirement nor the prevailing status quo can entirely eliminate both errors. But which policy is in place affects which errors are more likely. Compared with the status quo, the imminence requirement places a more stringent restriction on deadly force, which brings a greater risk of false-negative errors. Conversely, the status quo brings a greater risk of false-positive errors. Since false-positive errors cause harm and false-negative errors allow harm, the doing/allowing distinction favors the latter over the former, all else being equal.

Table 7.3. Potential Errors from Police Deadly Force

	Suspect causes grave harm if they escape	Suspect causes no grave harm if they escape
Police use deadly force	Deadly Force that Protects Life	False-Positive Error
Police avoid deadly force	False-Negative Error	Restraint that Protects Life

Cases where: (1) suspect poses no imminent threat of grave harm, (2) suspect will escape absent deadly force, and (3) deadly force will stop their escape

Say that the less restrictive status quo prevented significantly more false-negative errors and resulted in only slightly more false-positive errors than the imminence requirement. In that case, there would be a moral case for the status quo even after accounting for the doing/allowing distinction. But we don't have evidence suggesting that the status quo does a better job at preventing grave harm than the imminence requirement. We therefore lack compelling grounds to overcome the doing/allowing distinction's presumption against the status quo.

Some may question the relevance of the doing/allowing distinction for policing, given officers' responsibility to protect the public from violence. The police do have more demanding obligations to intervene and prevent grave harm than do civilians (Fabre 2007, 371; del Pozo 2023, 25–46). That point, however, does not render the doing/allowing distinction irrelevant for policing. Consider which police actions are the most consistent catalyst for mass protests: deadly force and other violence perceived as unnecessary and avoidable (DiPasquale and Glaeser 1998; Hinton 2021). Consistent with that pattern, empirical research finds that people judge false-positive errors more negatively than false-negative errors when evaluating police use of force in different scenarios (Patil 2018, 380). It seems safe to say that the public generally assigns greater moral blame to officers who cause harm unnecessarily than to officers who fail to prevent it. We can understand how the public reacts to different errors by officers as reflecting underlying support for the doing/allowing distinction in policing. Policymakers can respond to that ethical judgment by adopting the imminence requirement for police, a policy consistent with the doing/allowing distinction.

Equality Before the Law

In most jurisdictions, the police have long been exempted from the imminence requirement, making it appear normal. But from another perspective, such an exemption represents a departure from the norm. The imminence requirement typically constrains the use of deadly force, just not for police. By creating an exception for police, the status quo stands in tension with a key principle from law and ethics: equality before the law.

This principle is foundational to legal systems throughout the world. Article 7 of the Universal Declaration of Human Rights states: "All are equal before the law and are entitled without any discrimination to equal protection of the law." Similarly, the 14th Amendment of the US Constitution guarantees "equal protection of the laws." This principle has relevance for police deadly force. When the law imposes the imminence requirement on civilians but not police, the result is that officers have more expansive rights to use deadly force. An officer and a civilian could use deadly force in the same circumstances—against someone believed to pose a future but non-imminent threat—and the former could be legally justified while the latter would face criminal penalties. Such differential treatment conflicts with the idea that the law should treat everyone equally.

Of course, the principle of equality before the law does not preclude different legal rights and obligations for different classes of people. Rather, it should be understood as a presumption in favor of equal treatment, which can only be overridden for compelling reasons. Doctors and lawyers have more extensive legal rights due to their specialized training and professional responsibilities. Similarly, one could argue that police should have more expansive permissions to use deadly force against non-imminent threats, given their training and responsibilities.

To evaluate that claim, we can start by identifying what exactly exempting police from the imminence requirement does. This exemption authorizes officers to determine whether someone, despite posing no imminent threat of grave harm, would cause such harm in the *future*, which requires deadly force *now* to prevent it. The imminence requirement prohibits civilians from acting on such judgments by limiting their justification for using deadly force to only imminent threats. The law places that restraint on civilians for understandable reasons. It is difficult to know whether someone will pose a threat of grave harm in the future when they pose no such threat now, let alone whether deadly force now is the only way to stop a future threat. Do we have reason to believe that police can reliably and accurately predict which fleeing suspects will prove dangerous in the future—a judgment the law does not trust civilians to make?

Though empirical research on policing has advanced our understanding of which rules help reduce unnecessary deadly force (e.g., Tennenbaum 1994; Zimring 2017; Shjarback, White, and Bishopp 2021), we lack research specifically on the accuracy of police judgments regarding non-imminent threats. At present, there has been little work to gather data on whether police can reliably identify which fleeing suspects pose a grave future threat, or whether they are more accurate in those judgments than civilians. No evidence-based training or practices are available to guide police in deadly force decisions against suspects who are purportedly dangerous but pose no imminent threat. As a result, officers make these decisions absent research, training, and ongoing evaluation to help ensure reliable accuracy.

Notably, in another criminal justice context with far more time for deliberation—capital sentencing—predictions of future dangerousness prove to be wholly unreliable (Edmondson 2016; Jones 2023b). Studies find that capital defendants deemed a future danger are no more violent than those not found to be a future danger, even when these two groups are incarcerated in similar conditions (Marquart, Ekland-Olson, and Sorensen 1989; Edens et al. 2005; Cunningham, Sorenson, and Reidy 2009; Cunningham et al. 2011; Reidy, Sorenson, and Cunningham 2013). The criminal justice system's poor track record of predicting future dangerousness casts doubts on police's ability to do so reliably, especially given that officers must make those predictions under duress with limited information.

To summarize, the principle of equality before the law favors applying the imminence requirement to both police and civilians, and we currently lack much evidence to override that presumption. This claim need not imply that the law governing deadly force by civilians and police must be equivalent in all respects. Consider the duty to retreat—the legal requirement to avoid defensive force and retreat when there is a safe opportunity to do so—which applies to civilians in some jurisdictions (Leverick 2006, 69–85). That requirement would conflict more fundamentally with police's ethical responsibility to respond to public safety threats than would the imminence requirement (del Pozo 2023, 39–43). The imminence requirement constrains what tactics police can use when pursuing suspects who resist, whereas the duty to retreat would preclude police from pursuing those suspects altogether (for more on this point, see Chapter 2). So there certainly could be reasons to override the presumption in favor of equal treatment and exempt police from some of the standard rules on deadly force. At present, however, such reasons appear to be absent in the case of the imminence requirement.

Objection 1: The Imminence Requirement Undermines Respect for the Law

We have identified two ethical considerations—the doing/allowing distinction and equality before the law—that support the imminence requirement in policing. Though most agencies have not adopted this policy, we notably do find its adoption in some of the largest and most influential agencies, like the FBI. For that reason, we can't dismiss the imminence requirement as a fringe idea only championed by policing's critics. But despite some support within policing for the imminence requirement, it has yet to attract much support in ethical or legal scholarship on policing. In fact, a number of ethicists and legal scholars oppose applying the imminence requirement as defined here to the police (Miller and Blackler 2005, 80–81; Miller 2016, 137; Ford 2022, 2–5; Leider 2018; Harmon 2008, 1160–61). This section and the next look at the leading objections to the imminence requirement in policing.

The first line of objection worries that restricting police's ability to shoot fleeing felons would undermine respect for the law. More stringent rules on police deadly force against fleeing felons would lower the immediate consequences of trying to elude police, potentially encouraging more to flee and flout the law. This concern suggests another reason, distinct from defense of life, for why police are justified in using deadly force against fleeing felons: to compel compliance with and uphold the law. The imminence requirement can frustrate police efforts to advance that goal. After all, some who violate the law and would elude police—absent a deadly response—pose no imminent threat. By prohibiting police deadly force in those scenarios, the imminence requirement can get in the way of the state's interest in upholding the law. According to this argument, the imminence requirement has no place in policing because officers should be authorized to use deadly force simply to uphold the law, even if there is no imminent threat of grave harm (Leider 2018).

That approach represents, to a certain extent, a return to the common law, which recognized justifications for deadly force by law enforcement beyond just defense of life. The approach's defenders argue that it would clarify the different grounds for authorizing deadly force by police. In their view, it also has the potential to limit police deadly force compared with the status quo, given how vague and broad the category of "dangerous" has become (Leider 2018).

Rejecting not just the imminence requirement but also the rule outlined in *Garner* runs into several problems. First, lofty talk of upholding respect for the law loses its appeal when we turn to its implications in actual cases. Robert Leider (2018, 974) speaks of the "fleeing criminal's stubborn refusal to submit to the rule of law" as a justification for police deadly force. If we embrace that position, we quickly end up with unpalatable conclusions. Edward Garner disobeyed police when he ignored an officer's command to halt and tried to escape over a fence (*Tennessee v. Garner* 1985, 3–4). For Garner, who was unarmed and posed no grave threat, does his "stubborn refusal" to obey the law constitute adequate justification for killing him? Responding with deadly force in this case seems unduly harsh and incompatible with prioritizing the protection of human life. Despite defending police's authority to shoot some fleeing felons regardless of whether they endanger life, Leider (2018, 1012–13) sidesteps specifying *which* fleeing felons should be liable to deadly force. It is understandable why. Those details bring into focus the implications of his argument for concrete cases, which are difficult to stomach (for a similar criticism, see Ferzan and Harmon 2023, 606–7).

Second, Leider (2018, 987) tries to have his cake and eat it, too, by suggesting that a return to the fleeing felon rule (or something similar) would more effectively limit police deadly force than the rule outlined in *Garner*. The empirical evidence shows the opposite: ending the fleeing felon rule saved lives (Sherman 2018, 425–28). It is estimated that, by restricting deadly force to only dangerous suspects, *Garner* prevented dozens of killings by police annually (Tennenbaum 1994). Earlier research similarly found reductions in both shootings by police and killings of officers when departments abandoned the fleeing felon rule in favor of policies that *Garner* would later endorse (Fyfe 1979, 1988; see also Nowacki 2015, 657). Even if other Supreme Court rulings like its endorsement of qualified immunity for officers have undermined *Garner*, as Leider suggests, that hardly seems like good reason to loosen *Garner*'s restrictions on deadly force, given their benefits. It makes more sense to directly address concerns with other rulings—for example, by ending qualified immunity.

Third, high-profile events show how counterproductive it can be when police use deadly force to compel compliance and respect for the law. In 2023, video emerged of a French officer shooting Nahel Merzouk, a 17-year-old of Algerian and Moroccan descent, as he drove away from a traffic stop, though he posed no danger to others at the time. Public outrage erupted into mass protests (Bubola and Breeden 2023). Many factors contributed to the nationwide upheaval, including France's colonial history and its enduring legacy today. Another factor was the details of the police stop caught on video. Shooting Merzouk for nothing more than failing to stop showed a callous indifference toward human life. If the law, either explicitly or in practice, countenances deadly force against fleeing suspects who pose little danger, it shocks the conscience and people lose respect for it. Law grounded in a commitment to protecting life may allow more fleeing suspects to elude police, at least for a time. But more importantly, it is a law worthy of people's respect and more likely to command it.

Objection 2: The Imminence Requirement
Undermines the Protection of Life

A second and more serious objection to the imminence requirement in policing is that it would undermine the protection of life. This critique emphasizes that imminence, though a proxy for necessity, is a distinct concept. As such, the two concepts can come apart (Baron 2011; Allhoff 2019). If deadly force is *necessary* to stop an unjust threat of grave harm, it seems that such force should be justified, regardless of whether the threat is imminent. By ruling out deadly force in those circumstances, the imminence requirement strikes some as misguided, especially in policing where officers have a responsibility to intervene and protect life from grave threats.

When might deadly force be necessary to stop a threat even though that threat is not imminent? Critics of the imminence requirement often illustrate such scenarios through thought experiments (Robinson 1982, 217; Allhoff 2019, 1544; Ford 2022, 3). They typically involve a causal chain that eventually leads to grave harm, in which the only opportunity to prevent the harm arises well before the harm would occur. Shannon Brandt Ford (2022, 3) offers one example (referred to here as *bombing threat* and lightly abridged).

> *Bombing threat*: Olivia has a bomb in a backpack that will explode only when her GPS indicates that she has reached the busy town square of Walterville. Police have reliable intelligence that Olivia has a bomb, that it will go off in Walterville, and that otherwise she is unarmed. A lone officer, Peter, at a rural checkpoint over a day from Walterville recognizes Olivia on her motorbike as the suspect and orders her to stop and surrender. Olivia refuses and speeds off toward Walterville. Peter has good reason to believe that no one will be able to stop Olivia before her target unless he shoots and kills her now.

For Ford, this scenario shows why the imminence requirement has no place in policing. The rule would hamper and prevent officers from fulfilling their responsibility to confront and prevent unjust threats when it is within their power to do so.

There are several reasons to be skeptical of drawing that conclusion from hypotheticals like *bombing threat*. Let's begin with the limitations of this thought experiment. Though Ford takes *bombing threat* as showing that the imminence requirement should not apply to police, it has broader implications. Consider a slightly altered version of the scenario: Peter is an armed civilian instead of an officer, yet the other relevant facts remain the same—he correctly believes that Olivia has a deadly bomb that will detonate in a crowded place and that shooting her is the only way to stop this grave threat. Though a civilian, Peter seems equally justified in using deadly force as in the version of *bombing threat* in which he is an officer. In both cases, under the circumstances stipulated, deadly force is necessary to prevent someone from inflicting grave future harm, even if they pose no imminent threat. At most, Ford's thought experiment calls into question the imminence requirement generally, for both police and civilians. Yet Ford never questions this requirement for civilians. He only rejects it for police. His thought experiment's broader implications, notably at odds with a popular rule for civilian use of force, cast doubts on the narrow conclusion that he tries to draw from it.

Of course, we could conclude that the imminence requirement should also not apply to civilians. But that is a big leap to make from a thought experiment that fails to reflect the uncertainty common in use-of-force decisions, especially against non-imminent threats. Such threats lack the present ability, opportunity, or intent to cause harm, which introduces greater uncertainty over whether the threatened harm will occur absent defensive force. There is good reason to hesitate about allowing civilians to use deadly force against non-imminent threats. In short, it is less clear whether deadly force is necessary in such scenarios.

This point speaks to a larger problem with relying on thought experiments to challenge policies like the imminence requirement. There is often a disconnect between the assumptions in the thought experiments and real-life conditions. One critic of the imminence requirement, Fritz Allhoff (2019, 1544), concedes that he appeals to thought experiments because actual "cases simply do not exist" in which defensive force is necessary despite the lack of an imminent threat.

In addition, a policy's less-than-ideal outcome in one scenario fails to count as decisive evidence against it. Every policy has tradeoffs, including the imminence requirement. As noted already, this policy brings a higher risk of false negatives and a lower risk of false positives than the status quo. For almost any policy, it generally is not difficult to come up with a scenario supporting or undermining it.

Consider the following thought experiment in favor of the fleeing felon rule.

> *Burglary leads to murder*: An unarmed burglar flees a house with stolen goods. While the burglar is climbing a fence to escape police, an officer has a chance to shoot and stop the burglar from getting away but doesn't because the law forbids it. The burglar's successful caper motivates them to commit a more serious crime, murder, the next day.

In these circumstances, there is a strong case that shooting the burglar rather than allowing them to escape would have been more consistent with prioritizing the protection of life, as it would have prevented the burglar from taking an innocent life the following day. It does not follow, however, that the fleeing felon rule is the best rule to promote this principle. To answer that question, we need to compare the rule's overall impact on protecting life—its effects on shootings by police, injuries to officers, and violent crime—with the impact that alternative policies would have. Research investigated exactly those issues and showed that the fleeing felon rule undermined the protection of life (Fyfe 1979, 1988; Tennenbaum 1994; Sherman 2018).

Critics of the imminence requirement do sometimes try to identify real-life incidents that support their case. Ford (2022, 4–5) cites the police shooting of Hussein Said in London in 1982 (Ford mistakenly says the incident occurred in 1983). Said attempted to assassinate Israel's ambassador to Britain, Shlomo Argov. Though Argov survived, he suffered a gunshot to the head that left him paralyzed (Joffe 2003). Argov's police bodyguard pursued and shot Said, who survived and was taken into custody. Ford (2022, 4) notes that Said's gun jammed before the bodyguard shot him to emphasize that Said was not an imminent threat but still someone police were justified in shooting (see also Miller and Blackler 2005, 76; Miller 2016, 129–30).

A closer look at this case reveals details left out by Ford, which suggests that Said in fact qualified as an imminent threat. Ford's account implies that Said's gun jammed from shooting the ambassador. But as the *Washington Post* reports, his gun jammed while fleeing and *after* getting a shot off at the pursuing officer, who then returned fire and struck Said (Williams 1984). A fleeing suspect who fires at an officer clearly represents an imminent threat. In the moment he fired, the officer had reasonable grounds for treating Said an imminent threat.

More generally, the imminence requirement allows deadly force against some fleeing suspects. Imminent threats and fleeing suspects are not mutually exclusive categories. Consider an active shooter scenario in which the gunman shoots indiscriminately into a crowd, kills several people, and flees with their weapon through an empty alley toward another crowded street. In the alley, police have a choice whether to use deadly force—their only available option to prevent the killer from entering the next street. Police bound by the imminence requirement still are justified in using deadly force in these circumstances. The suspect has shown the intent to kill, has the capacity to kill, and in moments will again have the opportunity to kill. Though the suspect threatens no one's life in the alley, they pose an imminent threat of grave harm given their proximity to and movement toward the crowded street. The imminence requirement does not render police powerless against such threats.

In some incidents, there can be ambiguity over whether the imminence requirement is met. Amid the chaos immediately following a public shooting, police have the challenge of discerning the shooter's intent, one of the conditions for a threat to be imminent. Is it an active shooter scenario where the suspect plans to fire further? If police *know* that a suspect no longer plans further harm, the imminence requirement prohibits deadly force—the instruction most consistent with protecting life. The purpose of deadly force in that context would be stopping an escape, not preventing grave harm. But police often have trouble inferring a suspect's intent, which makes for tough cases. We should expect tough cases—as with any rule on police deadly force—when it is unclear whether the imminence requirement's conditions are met.

Notably, the imminence requirement includes the qualification that one must have reasonable belief of a grave and imminent threat. It carries the expectation that, to use deadly force under imperfect information, police must have evidence to reasonably infer that each condition for an imminent threat is satisfied: present (1) ability, (2) opportunity, and (3) intent to cause grave harm. The imminence requirement avoids, then, making impossible epistemic demands on police. In fact, it eases these burdens by not asking officers to predict whether someone who currently poses no grave threat will pose such a threat in the future.

Some critics of the imminence requirement likely will remain unsatisfied. Even if willing to concede that the conception of dangerous found in current law is too expansive, they insist that some suspects are truly dangerous. The most cited examples are suspected serial killers and terrorists (Harmon 2008, 1161; Ford 2022, 3–4; Ferzan and Harmon 2023, 610). Perhaps against such suspects, police should have the authority to use deadly force when necessary to stop their escape, regardless of whether they pose an imminent threat. The problem with the imminence requirement, critics contend, is that it frustrates police efforts to protect life by limiting their ability to stop the most dangerous suspects.

This objection should be taken seriously given the magnitude of harm some suspects cause. But even when officers pursue suspected serial killers and terrorists, it is not obvious that police should be exempted from the imminence requirement.

The imminence requirement limits one police tactic—deadly force when there is no grave imminent threat—while leaving a range of other options available to pursue suspects. Given the surveillance tools that police in many jurisdictions have at their disposal, efforts to locate and apprehend dangerous suspects often are successful and concluded expeditiously.

There is the risk, as with all fleeing suspects, that they could cause grave harm while eluding police. But a false-negative error is not the only type of error to worry about it with a suspected serial killer or terrorist. There is also the risk of a false-positive error—killing someone who would cause no grave harm to others—when police resort to deadly force against a suspect believed to be dangerous but who poses no imminent threat.

Such errors do occur. In 2005, London police shot and killed Jean Charles de Menezes in the subway, believing he was a suicide bomber, which turned out to be false. De Menezes was unarmed with no terrorist ties. One point stands out in the investigations of the shooting. Once officers had concluded that de Menezes was a terrorist suspect, they resorted to deadly force without many of the standard indicators of an imminent threat, like evidence that the suspect had a weapon or made an aggressive movement (see Independent Police Complaints Commission 2007; CNN 2009). A false-positive error that takes life unnecessarily, as occurred in this case, causes irrevocable harm to the victim and their loved ones. It also undermines public trust in the police and hinders officers' ability to collaborate effectively with communities.

Despite the temptation to abandon the imminence requirement when a suspect is perceived as especially dangerous, these contexts may be where its guardrails are most needed. From Stonewall to Abu Ghraib, there is no shortage of examples illustrating the heightened risk of gratuitous force when the government acts against unpopular groups. The imminence requirement serves as a check against that moral hazard by applying to all suspects.

Clearer Guidance for Police

Taking a rule that has long applied to civilians, the imminence requirement, and applying it to police has garnered support among some policymakers but has also prompted resistance (Caruso 2019). This chapter's goal has not been to completely resolve this debate. We need more empirical research to get a fuller picture of this policy's impact on protecting life. But outlining the relevant moral considerations hopefully makes clear that we have little reason to see the imminence requirement as fundamentally at odds with policing. Two presumptions—the doing/allowing distinction and equality before the law—favor applying the imminence requirement to police. Without evidence that the status quo helps save lives and minimize harm, we lack compelling moral grounds to override these presumptions. Given the available evidence, adopting the imminence requirement rests on solid ethical footing. Policymakers who take this step should complement it with ongoing evaluation of the policy's effects.

Some worry that bringing ethics and philosophy into debates over police deadly force will result in rules so convoluted and nuanced that they prove useless in the field. But that outcome is hardly inevitable. In fact, the analysis here yields the opposite result: more straightforward and less cumbersome guidance than what most laws offer. The criminologist Lawrence Sherman made this point about the imminence requirement decades ago. His research showed reductions in police shootings, without greater risks to officer safety, in departments that had ended the fleeing felon rule (Sherman 1983)—findings that proved influential at the Supreme Court (*Tennessee v. Garner* 1985, 10). Beyond just pointing out the problems with the fleeing felon rule, he outlined what should replace it in a 1980 law review article prior to *Garner*. For both police and civilians, he argued, "eyewitnessing an immediate threat to life" should be necessary to justify deadly force (Sherman 1980, 98). In other words, the imminence requirement should apply to police just as it applies to civilians. This rule in his view had the advantage of giving clearer guidance to police.

Sherman emphasized the uncertainty facing officers when a threat is *not* imminent: "The police are not armed with a crystal ball. Predicting that a fleeing felon is likely to kill . . . places an undue burden on the police officer. When people commit overt threatening acts, however, there is much less ambiguity." Sherman (1980, 99) added that officers often struggled to understand which fleeing suspects they were permitted to shoot. This problem remains post-*Garner*. As we saw with the Pennsylvania statute, existing law on police deadly force is often complicated and hard to follow. Overly complex rules come with significant limitations, as they are difficult to communicate in training and carry out in the field.

The imminence requirement avoids that pitfall by providing a clear and concise rule for deadly force across contexts. To be sure, there still will be tough cases where it is debatable whether a threat qualifies as imminent. Tough cases cannot be avoided. But the imminence requirement has the virtue of offering a plausible standard that both raises the bar for police deadly force and provides clearer guidance to officers. As such, it represents a policy with the potential to save lives that merits more experimentation and study.

Conclusion

Studying police ethics involves confronting failure. In cases where police use deadly force that is unnecessary to protect life, we need to ask: What went wrong at the individual level? What went wrong at the institutional level? What steps would reduce the likelihood of police using deadly force in such circumstances in the future? In the example that opened this book—the police killing of a young Black man with mental illness, Osaze Osagie—the state took a vulnerable person's life, an outcome that likely could have been avoided. Police failed to employ de-escalation tactics specifically designed to avoid fatal outcomes in this type of scenario—someone wielding a weapon less lethal than a firearm while experiencing a mental health crisis (Police Executive Research Forum 2016). As avoidable killings like this mount, it can give way to anger, frustration, and pessimism about the prospects of realizing police institutions that truly value life.

Encouragingly, some tools and strategies reduce police killings. Part II of this book showed that a number of interventions, from banning bad tactics to robust de-escalation training, do work. Yet progress on identifying which principles and policies should guide police won't do much good if institutions of policing are hostile to their adoption. As past and present illustrate, many effective reforms prompt opposition from within policing.

Before the landmark US Supreme Court ruling *Tennessee v. Garner* (1985), which struck down the fleeing felon rule, there was growing evidence that departmental bans on shooting at nondangerous fleeing suspects reduced police killings without undermining officer safety (Fyfe 1979). Despite that encouraging evidence, leading voices in law enforcement opposed the change. In 1980, by a four-to-one margin, membership of the International Association of Chiefs of Police (IACP) passed a resolution in support of the fleeing felon rule. The IACP later came to reverse its position (Fyfe 1988, 200).

More recently, the Police Executive Research Forum (PERF) (2016) recommended that police agencies take steps beyond the minimum requirements in constitutional law to reduce deadly force—especially against the mentally ill, the unarmed, and those with a weapon less lethal than a firearm. The proposal caused an uproar across policing (Jackman 2016). The Fraternal Order of Police (FOP) and IACP went so far as to issue a joint statement denouncing PERF's proposal. "[B]oth of our organizations," they stressed, "reject any call to require

Protecting Life. Ben Jones, Oxford University Press. © Ben Jones 2026.
DOI: 10.1093/9780197823316.003.0011

law enforcement agencies to unilaterally, and haphazardly, establish use-of-force guidelines that exceed the 'objectively reasonable' standard set forth by the U.S. Supreme Court" (Fraternal Order of Police and International Association of Chiefs of Police 2016).

This reaction portrayed use-of-force guidelines that go beyond what the courts require as radical and reckless. Yet various police agencies across the country have put in place restrictions on force not mandated by the courts—like the imminence requirement and bans on chokeholds—without catastrophic consequences. And it should not come as a surprise that agencies see the value of and need for such policies. The vagueness that has bedeviled the "objective reasonableness" standard proposed by the Supreme Court in *Graham v. Connor* (1989) severely limits it as a source of guidance for police.

Research supported by the IACP further revealed how its criticism of PERF's proposal had been off base. A randomized controlled trial showed that de-escalation training designed by PERF reduced injuries to both suspects and officers (Engel et al. 2022). Tactics criticized for endangering officers in fact made them safer. What PERF had championed turned out to be a win-win for officers and the communities they serve.

The joint FOP and IACP statement reflects a strand of resistance common in policing. Officers generally don't want further restrictions on what tactics and force they can use. Additional restrictions, they fear, would limit their discretion, endanger them, and put them at greater risk of criminal and civil penalties. Together, these worries can morph into a zero-sum mindset: more use-of-force restrictions hurt police and help the bad guys.

This mindset gets a few things wrong. First, the most effective interventions don't just tell police what force to avoid. They also equip police with additional tools for responding to threats. If police think a gun is their only reliable tool for staying alive, it's no surprise that some are so quick to use it. But officers trained in robust de-escalation tactics and equipped with defensive tools like shields are better prepared to resolve encounters without having to resort to deadly force. Having additional nonlethal options on hand makes it less likely that deadly force will be necessary to avert a threat. Training and equipment that provide such options put officers in a stronger position to fulfill their ethical obligation to prioritize the protection of life.

Second, police can undermine their own interests by opposing measures that would prevent avoidable killings. Police can only do their jobs effectively with cooperation from the community. It is in their interest to have the community's trust and support. But dubious uses of force by police erode that trust and support—a problem that only gets worse when police resist calls to take steps to rein in such force. It ultimately is short-sighted of police to oppose measures shown to reduce deadly force without undermining public safety.

Police have a potent voice in policy debates. When police come out against proposed reforms, that can be enough to derail them. Policymakers give significant deference to the police given their frontline role in efforts to promote public safety. But the police's influence can distort policy debates when they portray evidence-based reforms as endangering cops and the public. Here the principle of prioritizing the protection of life proves relevant, as it has implications for how police should use their political influence. Committing to this ethical principle means seeing the task of reducing avoidable killings as an urgent priority, which in turn means being open to police reforms focused on that goal.

Immigration enforcement during the Trump administration put on stark display the disastrous consequences of doubling down on policies and tactics shown to unnecessarily put lives at risk. Facing political pressure to ramp up deportations, Immigration and Customs Enforcement (ICE) cut training for its officers from thirteen to six weeks, with the goal of getting new recruits into the field faster. ICE also reduced staff responsible for oversight and monitoring misconduct within the agency (Bennett 2026). Such changes at federal agencies unleashed on American cities aggressive tactics that appeared to be a feature rather than a bug of a broader policy of mass deportation. Viral videos showed federal officers breaking windshields, shooting at moving vehicles, using banned chokeholds, and beating and pepper spraying protesters who posed no immediate threat (Foy and Funk 2026; Jones 2026; Shao et al. 2026). The harms from bad tactics fell on citizens and non-citizens alike, proving deadly in some cases. In January of 2026, federal immigration officers fatally shot two US citizens in Minneapolis (Stein et al. 2026; Lum et al. 2026).

Federal officials' response to the killings further betrayed a lack of commitment to prioritizing the protection of life. Officials misrepresented the events that precipitated the shootings, calling one person killed—Alex Pretti, a nurse at a Veterans Affairs hospital—a "domestic terrorist" and "would-be assassin" who had brandished a gun (Bishop 2026; Rogers and Aleaziz 2026). Video directly contradicted that account and instead showed Pretti holding a phone (Lum et al. 2026). Such narratives contributed to an overall strategy of trying to hamper efforts to hold federal officers accountable for bad tactics (Savage 2026).

There was, however, one silver lining: some leaders in law enforcement spoke out and condemned the tactics of federal agencies carrying out immigration enforcement (O'Hara 2026; Womack and Johnson 2026; Dewan 2026). They saw in the tactics employed by federal agencies policing at its worst. Not only did harsh immigration enforcement actions cause avoidable deaths, injuries, and trauma, but they also eroded public trust. Regaining legitimacy is incredibly difficult after it has been lost. Simply more force and harsher tactics will not restore it. These debates over immigration enforcement operations in Minneapolis and other US cities brought to light fractures within policing over what path it should take.

Members of law enforcement have an important role in determining the future of policing, but the task does not fall exclusively to them. Democratic institutions ultimately bear responsibility for overseeing institutions of policing. Elected officials can use the law to promote police practices that reduce the risk of deadly force, from prohibiting bad tactics to requiring more robust de-escalation training. Such reforms are the most direct—but far from the only—steps that policymakers can take to reduce police killings. As we have seen, factors outside policing also contribute to avoidable police killings. We put police in a difficult spot by asking them to do their jobs in conditions marked by poverty, racism, and homelessness. It's no coincidence that groups at the greatest risk of being killed by police, such as Black Americans and persons with mental illness, find themselves unjustly disadvantaged in other spheres of life, too. Unjust disadvantage tends to compound, with one outcome being that it leaves certain groups more vulnerable to police violence.

Since police killings are interconnected to broader injustices in society, it complicates the task of reducing them. A more holistic approach to public safety policy offers promising strategies to deal with this complexity (see Jones and Martin forthcoming). It can reduce structural injustice through tackling the root causes of crime and violence, such as limited access to mental health and substance abuse treatment (Bondurant, Lindo, and Swensen 2018; Deza, Maclean, and Solomon 2022), lack of economic opportunity (Mann, Edin, and Shaefer 2024), and poor schooling (Heckman et al. 2010). This approach provides needed services and resources to marginalized groups, decreasing their vulnerability to a range of harms including violence. It also benefits police, who often feel called to deal with challenges they don't have the tools to solve (e.g., McNamara, Crawford, and Burns 2013; Dennis, Berman, and Izadi 2016; Watson and Wood 2017; Wood, Watson, and Barber 2021). A more holistic approach to public safety has the important benefit of lightening the burdens on police, with the effect of making their ethical responsibilities less daunting.

So the police have much to gain from policies that prioritize the protection of life, giving them strong reason to embrace and champion such policies. That future proves far more attractive than our current reality: a seemingly endless cycle of avoidable killings that erode public trust, where no one wins. A commitment to protecting life and the vulnerable calls on police, policymakers, and the public alike to make that more just future a reality.

Model Deadly Force Policy

This model deadly force policy offers a concise overview of policy recommendations developed throughout the book. There are three points to note about the policy.

First, the model policy outlines rules and principles to guide police officers in their decisions regarding deadly force. Its purpose is not to offer a comprehensive account of all the policy suggestions from the preceding chapters. Chapter 5, in particular, emphasizes the need for policy interventions beyond policing to address structural injustices that contribute to disparities in who is harmed by police deadly force. Those recommendations fall outside the narrow scope of a deadly force policy. The provisions below represent concrete steps that police administrators can take to reduce avoidable deadly force and better protect life, but more policy work remains even if those steps are all taken. The provisions also offer potential guidance to lawmakers. As Chapter 6 notes, it often is insufficient to rely on police to adopt policies that prohibit bad tactics. Many departments fail to implement such policies and, even among those that do, some are lax in enforcing them. To better ensure that officers avoid bad tactics and are held accountable when they fail to, there often are benefits to prohibiting such tactics in law.

Second, though many of the provisions outlined in the model policy do not enjoy wide adoption, they do appear in some existing departmental policies and law. The citations in the model policy point to examples where the rules suggested have already been implemented.

Third, the provisions below, especially those prohibiting specific tactics, reflect current research on which police tactics are especially risky. It would be a mistake to view the list of prohibited tactics as set in stone. The list should evolve over time as evidence emerges that additional tactics pose unnecessary risks.

Model Policy

1. *Prioritize the protection of life.* A core principle of just policing is valuing human life and making its protection a priority. Officers must uphold this principle in all aspects of their work, including their decisions related to deadly force.

2. *This agency's responsibility to its officers.* Whether to use deadly force is the weightiest decision officers can face. This agency has the responsibility to ensure its officers are prepared to respond ethically and effectively when facing that decision. Officers will receive evidence-based training in de-escalation and use of force consistent with prioritizing the protection of life and minimizing harm, as well as equipment designed to reduce the need for deadly force.

3. *When deadly force is justified.* An officer is justified in using deadly force only if they reasonably believe that such force is *necessary* to prevent *imminent, wrongful,* and *grave* harm—death, serious bodily injury, being raped, or being kidnapped—to themself or another person.

Note: this rule specifies four conditions that must be met to justify deadly force.

(1) Deadly force has a just aim (prevent wrongful harm that would violate someone's rights).
(2) Deadly force is proportionate (the harm that it aims to prevent is grave).
(3) Deadly force is necessary (there are no less harmful options likely to stop the harm threatened).
(4) Deadly force confronts an imminent threat of harm (e.g., General Court of the Commonwealth of Massachusetts 2020, 6E §14; US Department of Justice 2022).

4. *Fleeing suspects.* Preventing a fleeing suspect from escaping is insufficient reason to use deadly force (e.g., US Department of Justice 2022). The same conditions must be met to justify deadly force against fleeing suspects as must be met for other suspects (see §3 above).

5. *De-escalation.* An officer shall exhaust de-escalation tactics, such as communication and tactical repositioning, before resorting to deadly force to avert a threat of grave harm, provided that de-escalation tactics are feasible and do not significantly raise the risk of grave harm (e.g., General Court of the Commonwealth of Massachusetts 2020, 6E §14). If de-escalation tactics fail to avert a threat of grave harm, an officer shall issue a warning before using deadly force where feasible (see *Tennessee v. Garner 1985*, 11–12).

6. *Unnecessary risks.* An officer shall avoid overly aggressive action that can precipitate deadly force and unnecessarily endanger others. Sometimes the best tactical option for reducing the risk of harm to all parties is to withdraw, take cover, or reposition rather than to advance or hold a position (see Philadelphia Police Department 2024, 6). A suspect with a knife or other weapon getting within twenty-one feet of an officer is, by itself, insufficient reason to justify deadly force.

7. *Moving vehicles*. An officer shall not fire their gun at a moving vehicle except when necessary to prevent an imminent threat from a deadly weapon, such as gunfire from someone inside the vehicle or use of the vehicle to ram other people. An officer shall not put themself in jeopardy by stepping into or remaining in a vehicle's path when there is an opportunity to get out of its way. In such circumstances, being in the vehicle's path fails to justify firing at the vehicle (e.g., Metropolitan Police Department of the District of Columbia 2024, 6).

8. *Prohibited tactics*. The following risky tactics are prohibited unless the conditions permitting deadly force are met (see §3 above):

(1) Chokeholds and other neck restraints (e.g., Houston Police Department 2022, 7)
(2) Forcible entry into a residence without knocking and announcing (e.g., Virginia General Assembly 2025, §19.2-56)

An officer should treat these tactics like deadly force—only allowed in circumstances where they are necessary to protect the officer or others from grave imminent harm.

9. *Suspects with diminished culpability*. Though circumstances may arise where deadly force is the only way to avert a threat of grave harm posed by a child, person with mental illness, or person with intellectual disability, an officer shall make special efforts to try to avoid deadly force against these populations. In such cases, they shall request assistance from the agency's de-escalation unit, unless the timing and nature of the threat prevents the unit from being able to assist and reduce the risk of grave harm. Deadly force is prohibited against suspects who are only a threat to themselves or property (e.g., Houston Police Department 2022, 3).

10. *Definitions*.

(1) *Deadly force*: force involving significant risk of death or serious bodily injury
(2) *De-escalation*: communication, tactical repositioning, or both with the goal of reducing a threat's immediacy by creating additional time and options to resolve a potentially dangerous encounter without force, especially deadly force
(3) *Grave harm*: death, serious bodily injury, being raped, or being kidnapped
(4) *Imminent threat*: danger clearly at hand that will cause harm at once absent intervention; someone posing such danger has the present (i) ability, (ii) opportunity, and (iii) intent to cause harm (or whose reckless, negligent, or blameless action is about to cause harm)

(5) *Necessary*: refers to force that does not inflict harm beyond what is required to avert a threat

(6) *Proportionate*: refers to force whose harm does not greatly exceed the harm that it seeks to prevent

(7) *Reasonable belief*: the facts, circumstances, and permissible tactics that an officer trained in agency policy and in the same situation would be expected to know

(8) *Wrongful*: action that violates or threatens to violate rights guaranteed by law

Acknowledgments

Work on this book spanned three presidencies and dramatic swings in the public debate over policing. There have been calls to abolish the police, mobilization of the military for domestic law enforcement, and about everything in between. In uncertain times, I have had the good fortune of having friends, family, and colleagues close by to encourage and remind me that this book was worth writing. Their kindness has helped get the project across the finish line.

The Rock Ethics Institute at Penn State and its director, Ted Toadvine, deserve special recognition for supporting this project, from seed grant funding to hosting events on police ethics. The Institute offers a rich intellectual home for interdisciplinary research on ethics, which this book aims to embody. I also am grateful to two friends and colleagues at the Institute, Désirée Lim and David Sollenberger. Both were exceptionally generous with their time and insights, helping me think through the book's arguments often on walks and hikes.

Several years into this project, I joined Penn State's School of Public Policy. Few public policy schools have a faculty member focused on ethics and normative theory. Though my research looks different than theirs, my colleagues all have been warm and welcoming. I am thankful to the school's director, Lilliard Richardson, for supporting this project and valuing the tools that ethics brings to the study of public policy. I likewise am indebted to Tony Bertelli, who has been an incredible mentor on developing research at the intersection of ethics and policy.

I was fortunate to receive both internal and external funding for this book. A fellowship with the Humanities Institute at Penn State in 2025 included a course release, which allowed me dedicated time to refine and submit the final manuscript. Earlier that same year, when it looked like I might have to cancel a book manuscript workshop due to a last-minute change in funding, the Institute for Humane Studies provided a grant on short notice to make sure the event went forward (grant no. IHS018757). I thank the workshop's participants—Brandon del Pozo, Raff Donelson, Désirée Lim, Christopher Moore, Jennifer Page, and Seth Stoughton—for their extensive comments on a draft manuscript. Their diverse perspectives spanning law, philosophy, and policing yielded immensely rich and valuable feedback, which I tried my best to incorporate.

I had the opportunity to present chapters from the book at several conferences and workshops: the Association for Political Theory Conference (2018, 2020, 2023), Association for Practical and Professional Ethics Conference (2019), Penn

State Law Faculty Workshop (2019, 2021), Penn State School of International Affairs (2020), Rocky Mountain Ethics Conference (2020), Contemporary Challenges for Just War Theory Conference (2021), International Criminology Conference (2022), Midwest Political Science Association Conference (2024), University of North Carolina Philosophy, Politics, and Economics Speaker Series (2025), and Philosophy, Politics, and Economics Society Annual Meeting (2025). I thank these audiences for their feedback, and in particular Melissa Schwartzberg, Jake Monaghan, Alex Tuckness, Eleanor Brown, Jud Mathews, Lee-Ann Chae, Andrew Johnson, Kirun Sankaran, Adam Hosein, Lauren Lyons, and Renée Jørgensen.

Earlier versions of portions of the book—Chapter 4, Chapter 6, and part of Chapter 7—appeared as the following journal articles:

- Jones, Ben. "Police-Generated Killings: The Gap Between Ethics and Law." *Political Research Quarterly* 75 (2): 366–78. © 2021 University of Utah. Available online: https://doi.org/10.1177/10659129211009596
- Jones, Ben. "Applying the Imminence Requirement to Police." *Criminal Justice Ethics* 42 (1): 52–63. © 2023 John Jay College of Criminal Justice of the City University of New York. Available online: https://doi.org/10.1080/0731129X.2023.2187188
- Jones, Ben. "Police Obligations to Aggressors with Mental Illness." *Journal of Politics* 86 (3): 864–76. © 2024 Southern Political Science Association. Available online: https://doi.org/10.1086/726972

Comments from anonymous reviewers and these journals' editors provided welcome feedback during the long odyssey of chipping away at a book manuscript. Their close engagement with my work gave me a better sense of where I was on track and blind spots that I needed to address.

Lucy Randall at Oxford University Press has been everything one could hope for in an editor: professional, responsive, encouraging, and a master at coordinating everything to move the project forward. She has been an amazing champion of this project and a pleasure to work with. Three anonymous reviewers provided exceptional feedback on the book manuscript, pressing me to confront difficult tradeoffs and counterarguments. Their incisive comments made for a better book. E. J. Graff made many helpful suggestions that improved style and readability. I am grateful to Victoria Akwamaa Yeboah for her meticulous work compiling the index.

Most importantly, my family was there throughout the long journey of writing this book. My wife Mackenzie, whose judgment I value more than anyone else's, was someone I could go to for sage advice on issues large and small related to the book. Whether it was a productive or slow day of writing, spending time with her afterward guaranteed it would be good day. Our two dogs, Sloopy and Lana, logged many hours at my side as the manuscript took form. Lana did eat one library book I had checked out for the project. But on the whole, their company was far more of a help than a hindrance. It's hard to imagine two more eager and faithful writing companions.

References

Addo, Fenaba, William Darity Jr., and Samuel Myers Jr. 2024. "Setting the Record Straight on Racial Wealth Inequality." *AEA Papers and Proceedings* 114: 169–73.

Alexander, Larry. 1987. "Justification and Innocent Aggressors." *Wayne Law Review* 33 (4): 1177–89.

Alexander, Larry. 2005. "Lesser Evils: A Closer Look at the Paradigmatic Justification." *Law and Philosophy* 24 (6): 611–43.

Alexander, Larry. 2013. "Can Self-Defense Justify Punishment?" *Law and Philosophy* 32 (2/3): 159–75.

Allhoff, Fritz. 2019. "Self-Defense without Imminence." *American Criminal Law Review* 56 (4): 1527–52.

Alpert, Geoffrey, and Cynthia Lum. 2014. *Police Pursuit Driving: Policy and Research*. New York: Springer.

Alpert, Geoffrey, and William Smith. 1994. "How Reasonable Is the Reasonable Man?: Police and Excessive Force." *Journal of Criminal Law and Criminology* 85 (2): 481–501.

Ang, Desmond. 2021. "The Effects of Police Violence on Inner-City Students." *Quarterly Journal of Economics* 136 (1): 115–68.

Ang, Desmond, and Jonathan Tebes. 2024. "Civic Responses to Police Violence." *American Political Science Review* 118 (2): 972–87.

Aristotle. 2000. *Nicomachean Ethics*. Translated and edited by Roger Crisp. New York: Cambridge University Press.

Arizona State Legislature. 2025. Arizona Revised Statutes § 13-404. https://www.azleg.gov/viewdocument/?docName=https://www.azleg.gov/ars/13/00404.htm

Armacost, Barbara. 2019. "Police Shooting: Is Accountability the Enemy of Prevention?" *Ohio State Law Journal* 80 (5): 907–86.

Arnold, David, Will Dobbie, and Crystal Yang. 2018. "Racial Bias in Bail Decisions." *Quarterly Journal of Economics* 133 (4): 1885–932.

Associated Press. 2018a. "Officer in Tamir Rice Shooting Has Suspension Cut in Half." July 24, 2018. https://apnews.com/article/2f6dbe4159114ac285768680a183996a

Associated Press. 2018b. "Officer who Fatally Shot Tamir Rice Gets New Police Job." October 5, 2018. https://apnews.com/article/8fab88f1023442749163a5e3dbeeb492

Association of State Criminal Investigative Agencies, Commission on Accreditation for Law Enforcement Agencies, Fraternal Order of Police, Federal Law Enforcement Officers Association, International Association of Chiefs of Police, Hispanic American Police Command Officers Association, International Association of Directors of Law Enforcement, National Association of Police Organizations, National Association of Women Law Enforcement Executives, National Organization of Black Law Enforcement Executives, and National Tactical Officers Association. 2020. "National Consensus Policy and Discussion Paper on Use of Force." https://www.theiacp.org/sites/default/files/2020-07/National_Consensus_Policy_On_Use_Of_Force%2007102020%20v3.pdf

Atlanta Police Department. 2022. "Standard Operating Procedure 3010: Use of Force." March 28. https://public.powerdms.com/APD13/list/documents/488591

Ba, Bocar, Dean Knox, Jonathan Mummolo, and Roman Rivera. 2021. "The Role of Officer Race and Gender in Police–Civilian Interactions in Chicago." *Science* 371: 696–702.

Barber, Elizabeth. 2014. "Kelly Thomas Case: Why Police Were Acquitted in Killing of Homeless Man." *Christian Science Monitor*, January 14. https://www.csmonitor.com/USA/USA-Update/2014/0114/Kelly-Thomas-case-why-police-were-acquitted-in-killing-of-homeless-man

Barnes v. Felix. 2025. 605 US.

Baron, Marcia. 2011. "Self-Defense: The Imminence Requirement." *Oxford Studies in Philosophy of Law* 1: 228–66.

Barry, Brian. 1973. "John Rawls and the Priority of Liberty." *Philosophy and Public Affairs* 2 (3): 274–90.

Baude, William. 2018. "Is Qualified Immunity Unlawful?" *California Law Review* 106: 45–90.

Baumgartner, Frank, Derek Epp, and Kelsey Shoub. 2018. *Suspect Citizens: What 20 Million Traffic Stops Tell Us about Policing and Race.* New York: Cambridge University Press.

BBC. 2002. "CIA 'Killed al-Qaeda Suspects' in Yemen." November 5. http://news.bbc.co.uk/2/hi/2402479.stm

Beck, Brendan, Joseph Antonelli, and Angela LaScala-Gruenewald. 2024. "Neck-Restraint Bans, Law Enforcement Officer Unions, and Police Killings." *Criminology and Public Policy* 23 (3): 663–88.

Bedau, Hugo. 1968. "The Right to Life." *Monist* 52 (4): 550–72.

Bennett, Brian. 2026. "On Thin ICE in Minneapolis: How Trump's Immigration Crackdown Sparked a Crisis of Trust." *Time*, January 26. https://time.com/7358027/ice-agents-minnesota-alex-pretti-abolish-ice/

Berman, Mark. 2017. "Trump Tells Police Not to Worry about Injuring Suspects during Arrests." *Washington Post*, July 28. https://www.washingtonpost.com/news/post-nation/wp/2017/07/28/trump-tells-police-not-to-worry-about-injuring-suspects-during-arrests/

Biden, Joseph. 2022. Executive Order on Advancing Effective, Accountable Policing and Criminal Justice Practices to Enhance Public Trust and Public Safety. Archived Biden White House Website, May 25. https://bidenwhitehouse.archives.gov/briefing-room/presidential-actions/2022/05/25/executive-order-on-advancing-effective-accountable-policing-and-criminal-justice-practices-to-enhance-public-trust-and-public-safety/

Bishop, Sydney. 2026. "Officials Say Alex Pretti 'Brandished' a Weapon, but Have Offered No Evidence. Why That Term Matters." *CNN*, January 25. https://www.cnn.com/2026/01/25/us/shooting-alex-pretti-gun-minneapolis

Bittner, Egon. 1970. *The Functions of the Police in Modern Society.* Chevy Chase, MD: National Institute of Mental Health.

Bolinger, Renée Jorgensen. 2017. "Reasonable Mistakes and Regulative Norms: Racial Bias in Defensive Harm." *Journal of Political Philosophy* 25 (2): 196–217.

Bolinger, Renée Jorgensen. 2021. "The Moral Grounds of Reasonably Mistaken Self-Defense." *Philosophy and Phenomenological Research* 103 (1): 140–56.

Bondurant, Samuel, Jason Lindo, and Isaac Swensen. 2018. "Substance Abuse Treatment Centers and Local Crime." *Journal of Urban Economics* 104: 124–33.

Bonilla-Silva, Eduardo. 1997. "Rethinking Racism: Toward a Structural Interpretation." *American Sociological Review* 62 (3): 465–80.

Bonilla-Silva, Eduardo. 2021. "What Makes Systemic Racism *Systemic*?" *Sociological Inquiry* 91 (3): 513–33.

Bouzat, Pierre. 1963. *Traité de droit pénal et de criminologie*, vol. 1. Paris: Librairie Dalloz.

Bradbury, Shelly. 2019. "Pa. Dems Discuss Proposal to Change Deadly Force Rules for Police." *Pittsburgh Post-Gazette*, August 27. https://www.post-gazette.com/news/crime-courts/2019/08/27/pennsylvania-deadly-force-law-change-antwon-rose-police-shooting-use-of-force/stories/201908270152

Brooks, Rosa. 2021. *Tangled Up in Blue: Policing the American City.* New York: Penguin Books.

Brown, Eleanor, and Ben Jones. 2020. "Why, Even in a Small Pa. College Town, Black People Distrust Police." *Philadelphia Inquirer*, June 30. https://www.inquirer.com/opinion/commentary/george-floyd-protests-police-reform-state-college-20200630.html

Brownlee, Kimberley, and Zofia Stemplowska. 2017. "Thought Experiments." *Methods in Analytical Political Theory*, edited by Adrian Blau. New York: Cambridge University Press, 21–45.

Bruner, Justin. 2018. "Decisions behind the Veil: An Experimental Approach." In *Oxford Studies in Experimental Philosophy*, vol. 2, edited by Tania Lombrozo, Joshua Knobe, and Shaun Nichols. New York: Oxford University Press, 167–80.

Bubola, Emma, and Aurelien Breeden. 2023. "What's behind the Unrest in France?" *New York Times*, June 29. https://www.nytimes.com/2023/06/29/world/europe/france-riots-nahel-shooting.html

Buchanan, Larry, Quoctrung Bui, and Jugal Patel. 2020. "Black Lives Matter May Be the Largest Movement in U.S. History." *New York Times*, July 3. https://www.nytimes.com/interactive/2020/07/03/us/george-floyd-protests-crowd-size.html

Bui, Anthony, Matthew Coates, and Ellicott Matthay. 2018. "Years of Life Lost due to Encounters with Law Enforcement in the USA, 2015–2016." *Journal of Epidemiology and Community Health* 72 (8): 715–18.

Burnham, Margaret. 2022. *By Hands Now Known: Jim Crow's Legal Executioners*. New York: W. W. Norton and Company.

Burri, Susanne. 2020a. "Morally Permissible Risk Imposition and Liability to Defensive Harm." *Law and Philosophy* 39 (4): 381–408.

Burri, Susanne. 2020b. "Why Moral Theorizing Needs Real Cases: The Redirection of V-Weapons during the Second World War." *Journal of Political Philosophy* 28 (2): 247–69.

Burri, Susanne. 2022. "Defensive Liability: A Matter of Rights Enforcement, Not Distributive Justice." *Criminal Law and Philosophy* 16 (3): 539–53.

Burri, Susanne, Daniela Lup, and Alexander Pepper. 2021. "What Do Business Executives Think about Distributive Justice?" *Journal of Business Ethics* 174 (1): 15–33.

Butler, Paul. 2016. "The System Is Working the Way It Is Supposed to: The Limits of Criminal Justice Reform." *Georgetown Law Journal* 104 (6): 1419–78.

Butler, Paul. 2017. *Chokehold: Policing Black Men*. New York: New Press.

Calamur, Krishnadev. 2017. "Officer in Tamir Rice Shooting is Fired." *Atlantic*, May 30. https://www.theatlantic.com/news/archive/2017/05/tamir-rice-officer-fired/528522/

California Legislative Information. 2024. Penal Code of California. https://leginfo.legislature.ca.gov/faces/codesTOCSelected.xhtml?tocCode=PEN&tocTitle=+Penal+Code+-+PEN

Campaign Zero. 2026. "Mapping Police Violence." https://mappingpoliceviolence.org

Carmichael, Stokely, and Charles Hamilton. 1967. *Black Power: The Politics of Liberation in America*. New York: Vintage Books.

Carter, Matilda. 2023. "Minority Minds: Mental Disability and the Presumption of Value Neutrality." *Journal of Applied Philosophy* 40 (2): 358–75.

Caruso, Stephen. 2019. "A Year after the Police Shooting of Antwon Rose, This State Rep. Wants to Change Pa.'s Deadly Force Rule." *Pennsylvania Capital-Star*, June 20. https://www.penncapital-star.com/government-politics/a-year-after-the-police-shooting-of-antwon-rose-this-state-rep-wants-to-change-pa-s-deadly-force-rule/

CBC. 2016. "UK Cops Disarm Man Wielding a Machete." YouTube. https://www.youtube.com/watch?v=9mzPj_IaMzY

CBS News. 2019. "We Asked 155 Police Departments About Their Racial Bias Training. Here's What They Told Us." August 7. https://www.cbsnews.com/news/racial-bias-training-de-escalation-training-policing-in-america/

CBS News. 2020. "Baltimore Police Release Body-Worn Camera Footage from July 1 Officer-Involved Shooting during 'Behavioral Crisis' Call." July 9. https://www.cbsnews.com/baltimore/news/baltimore-police-release-body-camera-footage-july-1-officer-involved-shooting-behavioral-crisic-call/

Cesario, Joseph. 2022. "What Can Experimental Studies of Bias Tell Us about Real-World Group Disparities?" *Behavioral and Brain Sciences* 45: 1–20.

Cesario, Joseph, and Alejandro Carrillo. 2024. "Racial Bias in Police Officer Deadly Force Decisions: What Has Social Cognition Learned?" In *The Oxford Handbook of Social Cognition*, 2nd ed., edited by Donal Carlston, Kurt Hugenberg, and Kerri Johnson. New York: Oxford University Press, 525–59.

Cesario, Joseph, David Johnson, and William Terrill. 2019. "Is There Evidence of Racial Disparity in Police Use of Deadly Force? Analyses of Officer-Involved Fatal Shootings in 2015–2016." *Social Psychological and Personality Science* 10 (5): 586–95.

Chicago Police Department. 2023. "General Order G03-02: De-escalation, Response to Resistance, and Use of Force." June 28. https://directives.chicagopolice.org/#directive/public/6214

Choe, Jeanne, Linda Teplin, and Karen Abram. 2008. "Perpetration of Violence, Violent Victimization, and Severe Mental Illness: Balancing Public Health Concerns." *Psychiatric Services* 59 (2): 153–64.

City and County of San Francisco v. Sheehan. 2015. 575 US 600.

City of Los Angeles v. Lyons. 1983. 461 US 95.

Clark, David. 2023. "The Demands of Necessity." *Ethics* 133 (4): 473–96.

CNN. 2009. "UK Police Settle over de Menezes Shooting." November 23. http://www.cnn.com/2009/WORLD/europe/11/23/uk.menezes.police/index.html

Coady, Tony, Steve James, Seumas Miller, and Michael O'Keefe. 2000. *Violence and Police Culture.* Melbourne: Melbourne University Press.

Cochrane, Emily, and Ben Stanley. 2025. "What to Know about the State Trial over Tyre Nichols's Death." *New York Times*, April 29. https://www.nytimes.com/article/tyre-nichols-death-memphis-police-trials.html

Cohen, G. A. 1997. "Where the Action Is: On the Site of Distributive Justice." *Philosophy and Public Affairs* 26 (1): 3–30.

Cohen, Howard. 1985. "Authority: The Limits of Discretion." In *Moral Issues in Police Work*, edited by Frederick Elliston and Michael Feldberg. Totowa, NJ: Rowman and Allanheld, 27–41.

Colorado General Assembly. 2020. "Senate Bill 20-217: Enhance Law Enforcement Integrity." https://leg.colorado.gov/bills/sb20-217

Commission on Accreditation for Law Enforcement Agencies. 2021. *Standards for Law Enforcement Agencies*, 6th ed. Washington, DC.

Commission on Accreditation for Law Enforcement Agencies. 2025. "CALEA Client Database." https://www.calea.org/calea-client-database

Coons, Christian, and Michael Weber, eds. 2016. *The Ethics of Self-Defense.* New York: Oxford University Press.

Correll, Joshua, Sean Hudson, Steffanie Guillermo, and Debbie Ma. 2014. "The Police Officer's Dilemma: A Decade of Research on Racial Bias in the Decision to Shoot." *Social and Personality Compass* 8 (5): 201–13.

Correll, Joshua, Bernadette Park, Charles Judd, and Bernd Wittenbrink. 2002. "The Police Officer's Dilemma: Using Ethnicity to Disambiguate Potentially Threatening Individuals." *Journal of Personality and Social Psychology* 83 (6): 1314–29.

Correll, Joshua, Bernadette Park, Charles Judd, Bernd Wittenbrink, Melody Sadler, and Tracie Keesee. 2007. "Across the Thin Blue Line: Police Officers and Racial Bias in the Decision to Shoot." *Journal of Personality and Social Psychology* 92 (6): 1006–23.

County of Los Angeles v. Mendez. 2017. 581 US ___.

Cournoyer, Caroline. 2016. "How Police Chiefs Plan to Avoid 'Lawful but Awful' Shootings." Governing, February 2. https://www.governing.com/topics/public-justice-safety/gov-police-chiefs-shootings.html

Crawford, Kimberly. 2015. "Review of Deadly Force Incident: Tamir Rice." https://www.documentcloud.org/documents/2455846-crawford-review-of-deadly-force-tamir-rice/

Cunningham, Mark, Jon Sorensen, and Thomas Reidy. 2009. "Capital Jury Decision-Making: Limitations of Predictions of Future Violence." *Psychology, Public Policy, and Law* 15 (4): 223–56.

Cunningham, Mark, Jon Sorensen, Mark Vigen, and S. O. Woods. 2011. "Life and Death in the Lone Star State: Three Decades of Violence Predictions by Capital Juries." *Behavioral Sciences and the Law* 29 (1): 1–22.

Curtis, David, Tessa Washburn, Hedwig Lee, Ken Smith, Jaewhan Kim, Connor Martz, Michael Kramer, and David Chae. 2021. "Highly Public Anti-Black Violence Is Associated with Poor Mental Health Days for Black Americans." *Proceedings of the National Academy of Sciences* 118 (17): e2019624118.

Dale, Maryclaire. 2020. "Philadelphia Pledges Better Response after Black Man's Death." Associated Press, October 29. https://apnews.com/article/body-cam-911-tapes-walter-wall ace-94132e6531132c5f498996abaf374361

Dallas Police Department. 2024. "General Order 906.00: Use of Deadly Force." November 4. https://dallaspolice.net/resources/Pages/General_Orders_900_Combined.aspx

Daly, Kathleen. 2025. "Justice: Word, Idea, Practice." *Criminology* 63 (4): 707–43.

Danahy, Anne. 2019. "Centre County DA Says No Charges for Police in Shooting of Black Man with Mental Health Issues." WPSU, May 8. https://radio.wpsu.org/crime-and-law-enforcem ent/2019-05-08/centre-county-da-says-no-charges-for-police-in-shooting-of-black-man-with-mental-health-issues

Dean, Kimberlie, Thomas Laursen, Carsten Pedersen, Roger Webb, Preben Mortensen, and Esben Agerbo. 2018. "Risk of Being Subjected to Crime, Including Violent Crime, after Onset of Mental Illness: A Danish National Registry Study Using Police Data." *JAMA Psychiatry* 75 (7): 689–96.

DeAngelis, Reed. 2024. "Systemic Racism in Police Killings: New Evidence from the Mapping Police Violence Database, 2013–2021." *Race and Justice* 14 (3): 413–22.

Dee, Thomas, and Jaymes Pyne. 2022. "A Community Response Approach to Mental Health and Substance Abuse Crises Reduced Crime." *Science Advances* 8 (23): eabm2106.

del Pozo, Brandon. 2019. "I'm a Police Chief. We Need to Change How Officers View Their Guns." *New York Times*, November 13. https://www.nytimes.com/2019/11/13/opinion/pol ice-shootings-guns.html

del Pozo, Brandon. 2023. *The Police and the State: Security, Social Cooperation, and the Public Good*. New York: Cambridge University Press.

del Pozo, Brandon, and Barry Friedman. 2023. "Policing in the Age of the Gun." *New York University Law Review* 98 (6): 1831–80.

Delmas, Candice. 2018. *A Duty to Resist: When Disobedience Should Be Uncivil*. New York: Oxford University Press.

Dennis, Brady, Mark Berman, and Elahe Izadi. 2016. "Dallas Police Chief Says 'We're Asking Cops to Do too much in This Country.'" *Washington Post*, July 11. https://www.washing tonpost.com/news/post-nation/wp/2016/07/11/grief-and-anger-continue-after-dallas-attacks-and-police-shootings-as-debate-rages-over-policing/

de Vries, Bertine, Jooske van Busschbach, Elisabeth van der Stouwe, André Aleman, Jan van Dijk, Paul Lysaker, Johan Arends, Saskia Nijman, and Gerdina Pijnenborg. 2019. "Prevalence Rate and Risk Factors of Victimization in Adult Patients with a Psychotic Disorder: A Systematic Review and Meta-Analysis." *Schizophrenia Bulletin* 45 (1): 114–26.

Dewan, Shaila. 2026. "'It's All Just Going Down the Toilet': Police Chiefs Fume at ICE Tactics." *New York Times*, January 30. https://www.nytimes.com/2026/01/30/us/its-all-just-going-down-the-toilet-police-chiefs-fume-at-ice-tactics.html

Dewan, Shaila, and Richard Oppel Jr. 2015. "In Tamir Rice Case, Many Errors by Cleveland Police, Then a Fatal One." *New York Times*, January 22. https://www.nytimes.com/2015/01/23/us/in-tamir-rice-shooting-in-cleveland-many-errors-by-police-then-a-fatal-one.html

Deza, Monica, Johanna Catherine Maclean, and Keisha Solomon. 2022. "Local Access to Mental Healthcare and Crime." *Journal of Urban Economics* 129: 103410.

DiPasquale, Denise, and Edward Glaeser. 1998. "The Los Angeles Riot and the Economics of Urban Unrest." *Journal of Urban Economics* 43 (1): 52–78.

Dobbin, Frank, and Alexandra Kalev. 2018. "Why Doesn't Diversity Training Work? The Challenge for Industry and Academia." *Anthropology Now* 10 (2): 48–55.

Dolan, Brian. 2019. "To Knock or Not to Knock? No-Knock Warrants and Confrontational Policing." *St. John's Law Review* 93 (1): 201–31.

Donelson, Raff. 2017. "Blacks, Cops, and the State of Nature." *Ohio State Journal of Criminal Law* 15 (1): 183–92.

Downes, Chris. 2004. "'Targeted Killings' in an Age of Terror: The Legality of the Yemen Strike." *Journal of Conflict and Security Law* 9 (2): 277–94.

Draper, George. 1993. "Fairness and Self-Defense." *Social Theory and Practice* 19 (1): 73–92.

Dubber, Markus. 2015. *An Introduction to the Model Penal Code.* 2nd ed. New York: Oxford University Press.

Dube, Oeindrila, Sandy Jo MacArthur, and Anuj Shah. 2025. "A Cognitive View of Policing." *Quarterly Journal of Economics* 140 (1): 745–91.

Du Bois, W. E. B. 2007. *Black Reconstruction in America.* New York: Oxford University Press.

Dwyer, Jim, and Kevin Flynn. 2002. "Fatal Confusion: A Troubled Emergency Response; 9/11 Exposed Deadly Flaws in Rescue Plan." *New York Times*, July 7. https://www.nytimes.com/2002/07/07/nyregion/fatal-confusion-troubled-emergency-response-9-11-exposed-deadly-flaws-rescue.html

Eberhardt, Jennifer, Paul Davies, Valerie Purdie-Vaughns, and Sheri Lynn Johnson. 2006. "Looking Deathworthy: Perceived Stereotypicality of Black Defendants Predicts Capital-Sentencing Outcomes." *Psychological Science* 17 (5): 383–86.

Edens, John, Jacqueline Buffington-Vollum, Andrea Keilen, Phillip Roskamp, and Christine Anthony. 2005. "Predictions of Future Dangerousness in Capital Murder Trials: Is It Time to 'Disinvent the Wheel?'" *Law and Human Behavior* 29 (1): 55–86.

Edmondson, Carla. 2016. "Nothing Is Certain but Death: Why Future Dangerousness Mandates Abolition of the Death Penalty." *Lewis and Clark Law Review* 20 (3): 857–917.

Edwards, Frank, Michael Esposito, and Hedwig Lee. 2018. "Risk of Police-Involved Death by Race/Ethnicity and Place, United States, 2012–2018." *American Journal of Public Health* 108 (9): 1241–48.

Edwards, Frank, Hedwig Lee, and Michael Esposito. 2019. "Risk of Being Killed by Police Use of Force in the United States by Age, Race–Ethnicity, and Sex." *Proceedings of the National Academy of Sciences* 116 (34): 16793–98.

Eichstaedt, Johannes, Garrick Sherman, Salvatore Giorgi, Steven Roberts, Megan Reynolds, Lyle Ungar, and Sharath Chandra Guntuku. 2021. "The Emotional and Mental Health Impact of the Murder of George Floyd on the US Population." *Proceedings of the National Academy of Sciences* 118 (39): e2109139118.

Engel, Robin, Nicholas Corsaro, Gabrielle Isaza, and Hannah McManus. 2022. "Assessing the Impact of De-escalation Training on Police Behavior: Reducing Police Use of Force in the Louisville, KY Metro Police Department." *Criminology and Public Policy* 21 (2): 199–233.

Epp, Charles, Steven Maynard-Moody, and Donald Haider-Markel. 2014. *Pulled Over: How Police Stops Define Race and Citizenship.* Chicago: Chicago University Press.

Fabre, Cécile. 2007. "Mandatory Rescue Killings." *Journal of Political Philosophy* 15 (4): 363–84.

Fabre, Cécile. 2012. *Cosmopolitan War.* New York: Oxford University Press.

Fabre, Cécile. 2018. "Children and War." In *The Routledge Handbook of the Philosophy of Childhood and Children*, edited by Anca Gheaus, Gideon Calder, and Jurgen De Wispelaere. New York: Routledge, 406–15.

Fagan, Jeffrey, and Alexis Campbell. 2020. "Race and Reasonableness in Police Killings." *Boston University Law Review* 100 (3): 951–1015.

Fazel, Seena, Gautam Gulati, Louise Linsell, John Geddes, and Martin Grann. 2009. "Schizophrenia and Violence: Systematic Review and Meta-Analysis." *PLOS Medicine* 6 (8): e1000120.

Fazel, Seena, and Katharina Seewald. 2012. "Severe Mental Illness in 33 588 Prisoners Worldwide: Systematic Review and Meta-Regression Analysis." *British Journal of Psychiatry* 200 (5): 364–73.

Federal Bureau of Investigation. 2024. "Table 28. Law Enforcement Officers Feloniously Killed: Type of Weapon, 2014–2023." Law Enforcement Officers Killed and Assaulted Annual Reports. https://cde.ucr.cjis.gov/LATEST/webapp/#

Ferré-Sadurní, Luis, and Jesse McKinley. 2020. "N.Y. Bans Chokeholds and Approves Other Measures to Restrict Police." *New York Times*, June 12. https://www.nytimes.com/2020/06/12/nyregion/50a-repeal-police-floyd.html

Ferzan, Kimberly Kessler. 2004. "Defending Imminence: From Battered Women to Iraq." *Arizona Law Review* 46 (2): 213–62.

Ferzan, Kimberly Kessler. 2005. "Justifying Self-Defense." *Law and Philosophy* 24 (6): 711–49.

Ferzan, Kimberly Kessler. 2012. "Culpable Aggression: The Basis for Moral Liability to Defensive Killing." *Ohio State Journal of Criminal Law* 9 (2): 669–97.

Ferzan, Kimberly Kessler, and Rachel Harmon. 2023. "Flight and Force." *Criminal Law and Philosophy* 17 (3): 597–613.

Fineman, Martha Albertson. 2008. "The Vulnerable Subject: Anchoring Equality in the Human Condition." *Yale Journal of Law and Feminism* 20 (1): 1–24.

Fletcher, George. 1973. "Proportionality and the Psychotic Aggressor: A Vignette in Comparative Criminal Theory." *Israel Law Review* 8 (3): 367–90.

Fliss, Mike, Frank Baumgartner, Paul Delamater, Steve Marshall, Charles Poole, and Whitney Robinson. 2020. "Re-Prioritizing Traffic Stops to Reduce Motor Vehicle Crash Outcomes and Racial Disparities." *Injury Epidemiology* 7 (1): 3.

Flores-Macías, Gustavo, and Jessica Zarkin. 2021. "The Militarization of Law Enforcement: Evidence from Latin America." *Perspectives on Politics* 19 (2): 519–38.

Ford, Shannon Brandt. 2022. "Restraining Police Use of Lethal Force and the Moral Problem of Militarization." *Criminal Justice Ethics* 41 (1): 1–20.

Forman Jr., James. 2017. *Locking Up Our Own: Crime and Punishment in Black America*. New York: Farrar, Straus, and Giroux.

Forscher, Patrick, Calvin Lai, Jordan Axt, Charles Ebersole, Michelle Herman, Patricia Devine, and Brian Nosek. 2019. "A Meta-Analysis of Procedures to Change Implicit Measures." *Journal of Personality and Social Psychology* 117 (3): 522–59.

Foy, Nicole, and McKenzie Funk. 2026. "We Found More Than 40 Cases of Immigration Agents Using Banned Chokeholds and Other Moves That Can Cut Off Breathing." *ProPublica*, January 13. https://www.propublica.org/article/videos-ice-dhs-immigration-agents-using-chokeholds-citizens

Fraternal Order of Police and International Association of Chiefs of Police. 2016. "Statement of the Fraternal Order of Police and International Association of Chiefs of Police on Use of Force Standards." Fraternal Order of Police. https://fop.net/wp-content/uploads/2021/04/fop-iacp-use-of-force-statement.pdf

Friedman, Barry. 2017. *Unwarranted: Policing without Permission*. New York: Farrar, Strauss and Giroux.

Friedman, Barry. 2021. "Disaggregating the Policing Function." *University of Pennsylvania Law Review* 169 (4): 925–99.

Friedman, Willa. 2016. "The Economics of Genocide in Rwanda." In *Economic Aspects of Genocides, Other Mass Atrocities, and Their Preventions*, edited by Charles Anderton and Jurgen Brauer. New York: Oxford University Press, 339–55.

Frowe, Helen. 2014. *Defensive Killing*. New York: Oxford University Press.

Frowe, Helen. 2018. "Lesser-Evil Justifications for Harming: Why We're Required to Turn the Trolley." *Philosophical Quarterly* 68 (272): 460–80.

Fryer Jr., Roland. 2019. "An Empirical Analysis of Racial Differences in Police Use of Force." *Journal of Political Economy* 127 (3): 1210–61.

Fyfe, James. 1979. "Administrative Interventions on Police Shooting Discretion: An Empirical Examination." *Journal of Criminal Justice* 7 (4): 309–23.

Fyfe, James. 1988. "Police Use of Deadly Force: Research and Reform." *Justice Quarterly* 5 (2): 165–205.

Gaebler, Johann, and Sharad Goel. 2025. "A Simple, Statistically Robust Test of Discrimination." *Proceedings of the National Academy of Sciences* 122 (10): e2416348122.

Gardner, Andrea, and Kevin Scott. 2022. "Census of State and Local Law Enforcement Agencies, 2018—Statistical Tables." Bureau of Justice Statistics. https://bjs.ojp.gov/library/publications/census-state-and-local-law-enforcement-agencies-2018-statistical-tables

Gardner, John. 2013. "Criminals in Uniform." In *The Constitution of the Criminal Law*, edited by R. A. Duff, Lindsay Farmer, S. E. Marshall, Massimo Renzo, and Victor Tadros. New York: Oxford University Press, 97–118.

Gardner, Trevor George, and Esam Al-Shareffi. 2022. "Regulating Police Chokeholds." *Journal of Criminal Law and Criminology Online* 112: 111–33.

Garrett, Brandon, and Seth Stoughton. 2017. "A Tactical Fourth Amendment." *Virginia Law Review* 103 (2): 211–307.

GBD 2019 Police Violence US Subnational Collaborators. 2021. "Fatal Police Violence by Race and State in the USA, 1980–2019: A Network Meta-Regression." *Lancet* 398 (10307): 1239–55.

Gelman, Andrew, Jeffrey Fagan, and Alex Kiss. 2007. "An Analysis of the New York City Police Department's 'Stop-and-Frisk' Policy in the Context of Claims of Racial Bias." *Journal of the American Statistical Association* 102 (479): 813–23.

General Court of the Commonwealth of Massachusetts. 2020. "Bill S.2963 191st (2019–2020)." https://malegislature.gov/Bills/191/S2963/BillHistory?pageNumber=2

Gershenson, Seth, and Michael Hayes. 2018. "Police Shootings, Civic Unrest, and Student Achievement: Evidence from Ferguson." *Journal of Economic Geography* 18 (3): 663–85.

Gilbert, Curtis. 2017. "Not Trained to Not Kill." APM Reports, May 5. https://www.apmreports.org/story/2017/05/05/police-de-escalation-training

Glaser, Jack. 2014. *Suspect Race: Causes and Consequences of Racial Profiling*. New York: Oxford University Press.

Goh, Li Sian. 2021. "Did De-escalation Successfully Reduce Serious Use of Force in Camden County, New Jersey? A Synthetic Control Analysis of Force Outcomes." *Criminology and Public Policy* 20 (2): 207–41.

Goldman, Roger. 2003. "State Revocation of Law Enforcement Officers' Licenses and Federal Criminal Prosecution: An Opportunity for Cooperative Federalism." *Saint Louis University Public Law Review* 22 (1): 121–51.

Goldman, Roger. 2012. "A Model Decertification Law." *Saint Louis University Public Law Review* 32 (1): 147–56.

Goldman, Roger. 2016. "Importance of State Law in Police Reform." *Saint Louis University Law Journal* 60 (3): 363–90.

Goldstein, Joseph, and Marc Santora. 2014. "Staten Island Man Died from Chokehold during Arrest, Autopsy Finds." *New York Times*, August 1. https://www.nytimes.com/2014/08/02/nyregion/staten-island-man-died-from-officers-chokehold-autopsy-finds.html

Gollan, Jennifer, and Susie Neilson. 2024. "Police Chases Are Killing More and More Americans. With Lax Rules, It's No Accident." *San Francisco Chronicle*, February 28. https://www.sfchronicle.com/projects/2024/police-chases/

González, Yanilda María. 2021. *Authoritarian Police in Democracy: Contested Security in Latin America*. New York: Cambridge University Press.

Goodin, Robert. 1985. *Protecting the Vulnerable: A Reanalysis of Our Social Responsibilities*. Chicago: University of Chicago Press.

Gordon-Solmon, Kerah. 2018. "What Makes a Person Liable to Defensive Harm?" *Philosophy and Phenomenological Research* 97 (3): 543–67.

Gordon-Solmon, Kerah. 2023. "How (and How Not) to Defend Lesser-Evil Options." *Journal of Moral Philosophy* 20 (3–4): 211–32.

Gorman, Steve, and Brendan O'Brien. 2021. "Parents of Girl Shot Dead in Dressing Room by Los Angeles Police Call for Justice." *Reuters*, December 29. https://www.reuters.com/world/us/parents-girl-shot-dead-dressing-room-by-los-angeles-police-call-justice-2021-12-28/

Graham v. Connor. 1989. 490 US 386.

Grant-Thomas, Andrew, and john a. powell. 2006. "Toward a Structural Racism Framework." *Poverty and Race Journal* 15 (6): 3–6.

Grunwald, Ben, and John Rappaport. 2020. "The Wandering Officer." *Yale Law Journal* 129 (6): 1676–782.

Guardian. 2014. "'I Can't Breathe.' Eric Garner Put in Chokehold by NYPD Officer." December 4. https://www.theguardian.com/us-news/video/2014/dec/04/i-cant-breathe-eric-garner-chokehold-death-video

Guardian. 2016. "The Counted: People Killed by Police in the US." https://www.theguardian.com/us-news/ng-interactive/2015/jun/01/the-counted-police-killings-us-database

Haberman, Maggie, Nicholas Nehamas, and Alyce McFadden. 2023. "Trump Said Shoplifters Should Be Shot, Part of a String of Violent Remarks." *New York Times*, October 3. https://www.nytimes.com/2023/10/03/us/politics/trump-indictments-shoplifters-violence.html

Hamilton, Darrick, and William Darity Jr. 2017. "The Political Economy of Education, Financial Literacy, and the Racial Wealth Gap." *Federal Reserve Bank of St. Louis Review* 99 (1): 59–76.

Harmon, Rachel. 2008. "When Is Police Violence Justified?" *Northwestern University Law Review* 102 (3): 1119–87.

Haslanger, Sally. 2012. "Oppressions: Racial and Other." In *Resisting Reality: Social Construction and Social Critique.* New York: Oxford University Press, 311–38.

Heath, Joseph. 2024. "The Challenge of Policing Minorities in a Liberal Society." *Journal of Political Philosophy* 32 (1–4): 28–55.

Heckman, James, Seong Hyeok Moon, Rodrigo Pinto, Peter Savelyev, and Adam Yavitz. 2010. "The Rate of Return to the HighScope Perry Preschool Program." *Journal of Public Economics* 94 (1–2): 114–28.

Hehman, Eric, Jessica Flake, and Jimmy Calanchini. 2018. "Disproportionate Use of Lethal Force in Policing Is Associated with Regional Racial Biases of Residents." *Social Psychological and Personality Science* 9 (4): 393–401.

Heller, Sara. 2022. "When Scale and Replication Work: Learning from Summer Youth Employment Experiments." *Journal of Public Economics* 209: 104617.

Hendrix, Burke. 2019. *Strategies of Justice: Aboriginal Peoples, Persistent Injustice, and the Ethics of Political Action.* New York: Oxford University Press.

Henning, Allyson. 2020. "Sarasota Family Pushing for Mental Health Resources for Families and Law Enforcement following Personal Tragedy." WFLA News Channel 8, August 12. https://www.wfla.com/news/sarasota-county/sarasota-family-pushing-for-mental-health-resources-for-families-and-law-enforcement-following-personal-tragedy/

Hinton, Elizabeth. 2021. *America on Fire: The Untold History of Police Violence and Black Rebellion since the 1960s.* New York: Liveright Publishing Corporation.

Hirschfield, Paul. 2023. "Exceptionally Lethal: American Police Killings in a Comparative Perspective." *Annual Review of Criminology* 6: 471–98.

Hoekstra, Mark, and CarlyWill Sloan. 2022. "Does Race Matter for Police Use of Force? Evidence from 911 Calls." *American Economic Review* 112 (3): 827–60.

Holloway, Philip. 2015. "Tamir Rice's Death: A Lawful Tragedy." CNN, December 28. https://www.cnn.com/2015/12/28/opinions/holloway-tamir-rice-case/index.html

Hosein, Adam Omar. 2014. "Doing, Allowing, and the State." *Law and Philosophy* 33 (2): 235–64.

Houston Police Department. 2022. "General Order 600-17: Use of Force." March 4. https://www.houstontx.gov/police/general_orders/600/600-17%20Use%20of%20Force.pdf

Hughes, Karen, Mark Bellis, Lisa Jones, Sara Wood, Geoff Bates, Lindsey Eckley, Ellie McCoy, Christopher Mikton, Tom Shakespeare, and Alana Officer. 2012. "Prevalence and Risk of Violence against Adults with Disabilities: A Systematic Review and Meta-Analysis of Observational Studies." *Lancet* 379 (9826): 1621–29.

Hunt, Luke William. 2019. *The Retrieval of Liberalism in Policing.* New York: Oxford University Press.

Hunt, Luke William. 2021. *The Police Identity Crisis: Hero, Warrior, Guardian, Algorithm.* New York: Routledge.

Illinois General Assembly. 2024. Illinois Compiled Statutes. https://www.ilga.gov/legislation/ilcs/ilcs.asp

Independent Police Complaints Commission. 2007. *Stockwell One: Investigation into the Shooting of Jean Charles de Menezes at Stockwell Underground Station on 22 July 2005.* http://policeauthority.org/metropolitan/scrutinies/stockwell/index.html

Iowa Legislature. 2024. Iowa Code §704.6. https://www.legis.iowa.gov/docs/code/2024/704.6.pdf

Jackman, Tom. 2016. "Protocol for Reducing Police Shootings Draws Backlash from Unions, Chiefs Groups." *Washington Post*, March 31. https://www.washingtonpost.com/local/public-safety/move-to-reduce-police-shootings-draws-sharp-backlash-from-unions-chiefs-group/2016/03/30/03c81e6a-ec55-11e5-bc08-3e03a5b41910_story.html

Jacobs, Jonathan. 2020. "How Is Criminal Justice Related to the Rest of Justice?" *Criminal Justice Ethics* 39 (2): 111–36.

Jacoby, Sara, Beidi Dong, Jessica Beard, Douglas Wiebe, and Christopher Morrison. 2018. "The Enduring Impact of Historical and Structural Racism on Urban Violence in Philadelphia." *Social Science and Medicine* 199: 87–95.

James, Lois, Stephen James, and Renée Jean Mitchell. 2023. "Results from an Effectiveness Evaluation of Anti-Bias Training on Police Behavior and Public Perceptions of Discrimination." *Policing: An International Journal* 46 (5–6): 831–45.

Joffe, Lawrence. 2003. "Obituary: Shlomo Argov." *Guardian*, February 24. https://www.theguardian.com/world/2003/feb/25/israelandthepalestinians.lebanon

Johnson, Richard. 2016. "Dispelling the Myths Surrounding Police Use of Lethal Force." Dolan Consulting Group. https://www.dolanconsultinggroup.com/wp-content/uploads/2019/02/Dispelling-the-Myths-Surrounding-Police-Use-of-Lethal-Force.pdf

Johnson, Vida. 2022. "White Supremacy's Police Siege on the United States Capitol." *Brooklyn Law Review* 87 (2): 557–607.

Jones, Ben. 2021. "Eating Meat and Not Vaccinating: In Defense of the Analogy." *Bioethics* 35 (2): 135–42.

Jones, Ben. 2022. "Police-Generated Killings: The Gap between Ethics and Law." *Political Research Quarterly* 75 (2): 366–78.

Jones, Ben. 2023a. "Applying the Imminence Requirement to Police." *Criminal Justice Ethics* 42 (1): 52–63.

Jones, Ben. 2023b. "Death Penalty Abolition, the Right to Life, and Necessity." *Human Rights Review* 24 (1): 77–95.

Jones, Ben. 2024. "Police Obligations to Aggressors with Mental Illness." *Journal of Politics* 86 (3): 864–76.

Jones, Ben. 2026. "ICE Killing of Driver in Minneapolis Involved Tactics Many Police Departments Warn Against—But Not ICE Itself." *Conversation*, January 8. https://doi.org/10.64628/AAI.cx3d5q5wk

Jones, Ben. Forthcoming. "Narrow and Wide Necessity." *Analysis.* https://doi.org/10.1093/analys/anaf096

Jones, Ben, and Désirée Lim. Forthcoming. "The Ethics of Defunding the Policing." *Perspectives on Politics.* https://doi.org/10.1017/S1537592725101850

Jones, Ben, and Karin Martin. Forthcoming. *Antiracist Policing.* New York: Oxford University Press.

Jones, Ben, and Eduardo Mendieta. 2021. "Introduction: Police Ethics after Ferguson." In *The Ethics of Policing: New Perspectives on Law Enforcement*, edited by Ben Jones and Eduardo Mendieta. New York: New York University Press, 1–22.

Jones, Ben, and John Parrish. 2016. "Drones and Dirty Hands." In *Preventive Force: Drones, Targeted Killing, and the Transformation of Contemporary Warfare*, edited by Kerstin Fisk and Jennifer Ramos. New York: New York University Press, 283–312.

Jones, Ben, and Manshu Tian. 2022. "Hobbes's Lesser Evil Argument for Political Authority." *Hobbes Studies* 35 (2): 115–34.

Jones, Ben, and Manshu Tian. 2025. "The Lesser Evil Argument for (and Against) Political Obligation." *Law and Philosophy* 44 (2): 207–34.

Jones, Jeffrey. 2020. "Black, White Adults' Confidence Diverges Most on Police." *Gallup*, August 12. https://news.gallup.com/poll/317114/black-white-adults-confidence- diverges-police. aspx

Jun, Hyun-Jin, Jordan DeVylder, and Lisa Fedina. 2020. "Police Violence among Adults Diagnosed with Mental Disorders." *Health and Social Work* 45 (2): 81–89.

Kant, Immanuel. 1996. *Groundwork of the Metaphysics of Morals*. In *Practical Philosophy*, translated and edited by Mary Gregor. New York: Cambridge University Press, 37–108.

Karnowski, Steve. 2022. "No Charges Filed in No-Knock Warrant Killing of Amir Locke." Associated Press, April 6. https://apnews.com/article/amir-locke-keith-ellison-minneapo lis-minnesota-shootings-8991aa0d4d817a591ea9200a8b17a70f

Kaufman, Whitley. 2008. "Torture and the 'Distributive Justice' Theory of Self-Defense: An Assessment." *Ethics and International Affairs* 22 (1): 93–115.

Kaufman, Whitley. 2010. "Self-Defense, Innocent Aggressors, and the Duty of Martyrdom." *Pacific Philosophical Quarterly* 91 (1): 78–96.

Kindy, Kimberly. 2016. "The Post Asked Experts to Examine 5 Viral Videos of Police Shootings. Here's Their Analysis." *Washington Post*, July 22. https://www.washingtonpost.com/natio nal/the-post-asked-experts-to-examine-5-viral-videos-of-police-shootings-heres-their- analysis/2016/07/22/47a0a446-4df2-11e6-a422-83ab49ed5e6a_story.html

King Jr., Martin Luther. 2015. "The Other America." In *The Radical King*, edited by Cornel West. Boston, MA: Beacon Press, 235–44.

Kivisto, Aaron, Bradley Ray, and Peter Phalen. 2017. "Firearm Legislation and Fatal Police Shootings in the United States." *American Journal of Public Health* 107 (7): 1068–75.

Kleinig, John. 1991. *Valuing Life*. Princeton, NJ: Princeton University Press.

Kleinig, John. 1996. *The Ethics of Policing*. New York: Cambridge University Press.

Klinger, David. 2021. "Prioritization of Life as a Guiding Principle for Police Use of Deadly Force." In *The Ethics of Policing: New Perspectives on Law Enforcement*, edited by Ben Jones and Eduardo Mendieta. New York: New York University Press, 120–45.

Knox, Dean, Will Lowe, and Jonathan Mummolo. 2020. "Administrative Records Mask Racially Biased Policing." *American Political Science Review* 114 (3): 619–37.

Kochel, Tammy. 2022. "Effectiveness of Online Implicit Bias Training: Evaluating Officer Outcomes from a Cultural Diversity Training versus a Skills-Based Course on Communication." In *Exploring Contemporary Police Challenges*, edited by Sanja Kutnjak Ivković, Jon Maskály, Christopher Donner, Irena Cajner Mraović, and Dilip Das New York: Routledge, 251–65.

Kochel, Tammy, and Seyvan Nouri. 2024. "Impact of In-Service Implicit Bias Training: A Study of Attitudinal Changes and Intention to Apply Anti-Bias Techniques." *Police Quarterly* 27 (4): 561–81.

Kramer, Rory, and Brianna Remster. 2018. "Stop, Frisk, and Assault? Racial Disparities in Police Use of Force during Investigatory Stops." *Law and Society Review* 52 (4): 960–93.

Kraska, Peter. 2007. "Militarization and Policing—Its Relevance to 21st Century Police." *Policing: A Journal of Policy and Practice* 1 (4): 501–13.

LaFraniere, Sharon, and Mitch Smith. 2016. "Philando Castile Was Pulled over 49 Times in 13 Years, often for Minor Infractions." *New York Times*, July 16. https://www.nytimes.com/2016/07/17/us/before-philando-castiles-fatal-encounter-a-costly-trail-of-minor-traffic-stops.html

Lai, Calvin, and Jaclyn Lisnek. 2023. "The Impact of Implicit-Bias-Oriented Diversity Training on Police Officers' Beliefs, Motivations, and Actions." *Psychological Science* 34 (4): 424–34.

Latalova, Klara, Dana Kamaradova, and Jan Prasko. 2014. "Violent Victimization of Adult Patients with Severe Mental Illness: A Systematic Review." *Neuropsychiatric Disease and Treatment* 10: 1925–39.

La Tour, Jesse. 2020. "The Kelly Thomas Files Part 1: Notices to the Officers Who Were Fired and Disciplined." *Fullerton Observer*, July 18. https://fullertonobserver.com/2020/07/18/the-kelly-thomas-files-part-1-notices-to-the-officers-who-were-fired-and-disciplined/

Lazar, Seth. 2009. "Responsibility, Risk, and Killing in War." *Ethics* 119 (4): 699–728.

Lazar, Seth. 2012. "Necessity in Self-Defense and War." *Philosophy and Public Affairs* 40 (1): 3–44.

Lazar, Seth. 2015. *Sparing Civilians*. New York: Oxford University Press.

Lazar, Seth. 2017. "Just War Theory: Revisionists versus Traditionalists." *Annual Review of Political Science* 20: 37–54.

Lazar, Seth. 2018. "In Dubious Battle: Uncertainty and the Ethics of Killing." *Philosophical Studies* 175 (4): 859–83.

Lee, Cynthia. 2018. "Reforming the Law on Police Use of Deadly Force: De-escalation, Preseizure Conduct, and Imperfect Self-Defense." *University of Illinois Law Review* 2018 (2): 629–91.

Lee, Cynthia. 2021. "Officer-Created Jeopardy: Broadening the Time Frame for Assessing a Police Officer's Use of Deadly Force." *George Washington Law Review* 89 (6): 1362–451.

Lee, Summer, and Ed Gainey. 2019. "Co-Sponsorship Memo: Law Enforcement Deadly Use of Force." Pennsylvania General Assembly. https://www.legis.state.pa.us//cfdocs/Legis/CSM/showMemoPublic.cfm?chamber=H&SPick=20190&cosponId=29033

Leider, Robert. 2018. "Taming Self-Defense: Using Deadly Force to Prevent Escapes." *Florida Law Review* 70 (5): 971–1017.

Levenson, Michael. 2023. "Video Released of Officer Fatally Shooting Pregnant Black Woman." *New York Times*, September 1. https://www.nytimes.com/2023/09/01/us/takiya-young-ohio-police-shooting.html

Leverick, Fiona. 2006. *Killing in Self-Defence*. New York: Oxford University Press.

LexisNexis. 2025. Official Code of Georgia Annotated. http://www.lexisnexis.com/hottopics/gacode

Light, Michael, and Jeffrey Ulmer. 2016. "Explaining the Gaps in White, Black, and Hispanic Violence since 1990: Accounting for Immigration, Incarceration, and Inequality." *American Sociological Review* 81 (2): 290–315.

Lum, Devon, Haley Willis, Alexander Cardia, Dmitriy Khavin, and Ainara Tiefenthäler. 2026. "New Video Analysis Reveals Flawed and Fatal Decisions in Shooting of Pretti." *New York Times*, January 26. https://www.nytimes.com/video/us/100000010668660/new-video-analysis-reveals-flawed-and-fatal-decisions-in-shooting-of-pretti.html

Mac Donald, Heather. 2016. *The War on Cops: How the New Attack on Law and Order Makes Everyone Less Safe*. New York: Encounter Books.

Mac Donald, Heather. 2020. "The Myth of Systemic Police Racism." *Wall Street Journal*, June 2. https://www.wsj.com/articles/the-myth-of-systemic-police-racism-11591119883

MacDonald, John, and Anthony Braga. 2019. "Did Post-*Floyd et al.* Reforms Reduce Racial Disparities in NYPD Stop, Question, and Frisk Practices? An Exploratory Analysis Using External and Internal Benchmarks." *Justice Quarterly* 36 (5): 954–83.

Mackenzie, Catriona, Wendy Rogers, and Susan Dodds, eds. 2013. *Vulnerability: New Essays in Ethics and Feminist Philosophy*. New York: Oxford University Press.

Maniglio, R. 2009. "Severe Mental Illness and Criminal Victimization: A Systematic Review." *Acta Psychiatrica Scandinavica* 119 (3): 180–91.

Mann, Olivia, Kathryn Edin, and H. Luke Shaefer. 2024. "Understanding the Relationship between Intergenerational Mobility and Community Violence." *Proceedings of the National Academy of Sciences* 121 (33): e2309066121.

Marcus, Nancy. 2016. "From Edward to Eric Garner and Beyond: The Importance of Constitutional Limitations on Lethal Use of Force in Police Reform." *Duke Journal of Constitutional Law and Public Policy* 12 (1): 53–106.

Marcus, Natania, and Vicky Stergiopoulos. 2022. "Examining Mental Health Crisis Intervention: A Rapid Review Comparing Outcomes across Police, Co-Responder, and Non-Police Models." *Health and Social Care in the Community* 30 (5): 1665–79.

Marquart, James, Sheldon Ekland-Olson, and Jonathan Sorensen. 1989. "Gazing into the Crystal Ball: Can Jurors Accurately Predict Dangerousness in Capital Case?" *Law and Society Review* 23 (3): 449–68.

Marshall, Gordon, Adam Swift, David Routh, and Carole Burgoyne. 1999. "What Is and What Ought to Be: Popular Beliefs about Distributive Justice in Thirteen Countries." *European Sociological Review* 15 (4): 349–67.

Maruschak, Laura, Jennifer Bronson, and Mariel Alper. 2021. "Indicators of Mental Health Problems Reported by Prisoners: Survey of Prison Inmates, 2016." Bureau of Justice Statistics, June. https://bjs.ojp.gov/library/publications/indicators-mental-health-probl ems-reported-prisoners-survey-prison-inmates

Matteis, Laura Rose. 2015. "Stay Away from the Neck: Why Police Chokeholds and Other Neck Restraints Violate International Human Rights." *Thomas Jefferson Law Review* 38 (1): 101–41.

McGrady, Clyde. 2023. "Tyre Nichols Beating Opens a Complex Conversation on Race and Policing." *New York Times*, January 28. https://www.nytimes.com/2023/01/28/us/police-tyre-nichols-beating-race.html

McLeod, Allegra. 2019. "Envisioning Abolition Democracy." *Harvard Law Review* 132 (6): 1613–49.

McMahan, Jeff. 1994. "Self-Defense and the Problem of the Innocent Attacker." *Ethics* 104 (2): 252–90.

McMahan, Jeff. 2002. *The Ethics of Killing: Problems at the Margins of Life*. New York: Oxford University Press.

McMahan, Jeff. 2005a. "The Basis of Moral Liability to Defensive Killing." *Philosophical Issues* 15: 386–405.

McMahan, Jeff. 2005b. "Self-Defense and Culpability." *Law and Philosophy* 24 (6): 751–74.

McMahan, Jeff. 2009. *Killing in War*. New York: Oxford University Press.

McMahan, Jeff. 2010. "An Ethical Perspective on Child Soldiers." In *Child Soldiers in the Age of Fractured States*, edited by Scott Gates and Simon Reich. Pittsburgh, PA: University of Pittsburgh Press, 27–36.

McMahan, Jeff. 2011. "Who Is Morally Liable to Be Killed in War." *Analysis* 71 (3): 544–59.

McMahan, Jeff. 2014. "Proportionate Defense." *Journal of Transnational Law and Policy* 23: 1–36.

McMahan, Jeff. 2016. "The Limits of Self-Defense." In *The Ethics of Self-Defense*, edited by Christian Coons and Michael Weber. New York: Oxford University Press, 185–210.

McMahan, Jeff. 2021. "Necessity and Proportionality in Morality and Law." In *Necessity and Proportionality in International Peace and Security Law*, edited by Claus Kreß and Robert Lawless. New York: Oxford University Press, 3–38.

McMillen, Daniel, Ignacio Sarmiento-Barbieri, and Ruchi Singh. 2019. "Do More Eyes on the Street Reduce Crime? Evidence from Chicago's Safe Passage Program." *Journal of Urban Economics* 110: 1–25.

McNamara, Robert, Charles Crawford, and Ronald Burns. 2013. "Policing the Homeless: Policy, Practice, and Perceptions." *Policing: An International Journal* 36 (2): 357–74.

Mekawi, Yara, and Konrad Bresin. 2015. "Is the Evidence from Racial Bias Shooting Task Studies a Smoking Gun? Results from a Meta-Analysis." *Journal of Experimental Social Psychology* 61: 120–30.

Melzer, Nils. 2008. *Targeted Killing in International Law*. New York: Oxford University Press.

Menifield, Charles, Geiguen Shin, and Logan Strother. 2019. "Do White Law Enforcement Officers Target Minority Suspects?" *Public Administration Review* 79 (1): 56–68.

Mentch, Lucas. 2020. "On Racial Disparities in Recent Fatal Police Shootings." *Statistics and Public Policy* 7 (1): 9–18.

Metropolitan Police Department of the District of Columbia. 2023. "General Order 301.03: Vehicle Pursuits." July 20. https://go.mpdconline.com/GO/GO_301_03.pdf

Metropolitan Police Department of the District of Columbia. 2024. "General Order 901.07: Use of Force." March 28. https://go.mpdconline.com/GO/GO_901_07.pdf

Metzl, Jonathan, and Kenneth MacLeish. 2015. "Mental Illness, Mass Shootings, and the Politics of American Firearms." *American Journal of Public Health* 105 (2): 240–49.

Michelbach, Philip, John Scott, Richard Matland, and Brian Bornstein. 2003. "Doing Rawls Justice: An Experimental Study of Income Distribution Norms." *American Journal of Political Science* 47 (3): 523–39.

Midgette, Greg, and Peter Reuter. 2024. "Diverting 911 Calls: Lessons from Early Adopting Urban Jurisdictions." *Criminology and Public Policy* 23 (3): 777–99.

Miller, Dinah, and Annette Hanson. 2016. *Committed: The Battle over Involuntary Psychiatric Care*. Baltimore: Johns Hopkins University Press.

Miller, Joel, Paul Quinton, Banos Alexandrou, and Daniel Packham. 2020. "Can Police Training Reduce Ethnic/Racial Disparities in Stop and Search? Evidence from a Multisite UK Trial." *Criminology and Public Policy* 19 (4): 1259–87.

Miller, Seumas. 2016. *Shooting to Kill: The Ethics of Police and Military Use of Lethal Force*. New York: Oxford University Press.

Miller, Seumas, and John Blackler. 2005. *Ethical Issues in Policing*. Burlington, VT: Ashgate Publishing Company.

Mitchell, Ojmarrh, and Michael Caudy. 2015. "Examining Racial Disparities in Drug Arrests." *Justice Quarterly* 32 (2): 288–313.

Monaghan, Jake. 2017. "The Special Moral Obligations of Law Enforcement." *Journal of Political Philosophy* 25 (2): 218–37.

Monaghan, Jake. 2021a. "Boundary Policing." *Philosophy and Public Affairs* 49 (1): 26–50.

Monaghan, Jake. 2021b. "Legitimate Policing and Professional Norms." In *The Ethics of Policing: New Perspectives on Law Enforcement*, edited by Ben Jones and Eduardo Mendieta. New York: New York University Press, 39–65.

Monaghan, Jake. 2022. "Idealizations and Ideal Policing." *Philosophers' Imprint* 22 (9). https://doi.org/10.3998/phimp.882

Monaghan, Jake. 2023. *Just Policing*. New York: Oxford University Press.

Montague, Phillip. 1981. "Self-Defense and Choosing between Lives." *Philosophical Studies* 40 (2): 207–19.

Montague, Phillip. 2010. "Self-Defense, Culpability, and Distributive Justice." *Law and Philosophy* 29 (1): 75–91.

Morabito, Melissa Schaefer. 2014. "Policing Vulnerable Populations." In *The Oxford Handbook of Police and Policing*, edited by Michael Reisig and Robert Kane. New York: Oxford University Press, 197–213.

Moreland, Roy. 1952. *The Law of Homicide*. Indianapolis: Bobbs-Merrill.

Morris, Kevin, and Kelsey Shoub. 2024. "Contested Killings: The Mobilizing Effects of Community Contact with Police Violence." *American Political Science Review* 118 (1): 458–74.

Mosby, Marilyn. 2020. "Report by the Office of the Baltimore City State's Attorney on the Non-Fatal Police-Involved Shooting in the 5800 Block of Falkirk Rd." https://www.stattorney.org/images/police_involved_shooting/Declination%20Report%20-%205800%20BLOCK%20FALKIRK%20ROAD.pdf

Mullenix v. Luna. 2015. 577 US 7.

Mummolo, Jonathan. 2018a. "Militarization Fails to Enhance Police Safety or Reduce Crime but May Harm Police Reputation." *Proceedings of the National Academy of Sciences* 115 (37): 9181–86.

Mummolo, Jonathan. 2018b. "Modern Police Tactics, Police-Citizen Interactions, and the Prospects for Reform." *Journal of Politics* 80 (1): 1–15.

Munoz, Carlos. 2020. "After Sarasota Deputy Kills Woman, Sheriff Talks of Alternatives." *Herald-Tribune*, August 3. https://www.heraldtribune.com/story/news/local/sarasota/2020/08/03/after-sarasota-deputy-kills-woman-sheriff-talks-of-alternatives/42183447/

NAACP Legal Defense Fund. 2020. "Civil Rights Groups Demand Action Following Baltimore Police Shooting of Ricky Walker, Jr." July 22. https://www.naacpldf.org/press-release/civil-rights-groups-demand-action-following-baltimore-police-killing-of-ricky-walker-jr/

National Institute on Drug Abuse. 2020. "Common Comorbidities with Substance Use Disorders Research Report." April. https://www.ncbi.nlm.nih.gov/books/NBK571451/

New York City Civilian Complaint Review Board. 2014. *A Mutated Rule: Lack of Enforcement in the Face of Persistent Chokehold Complaints in New York City.* http://www.nyc.gov/html/ccrb/downloads/pdf/Chokehold%20Study_20141007.pdf

New York Times. 2015. "Video Shows Fatal Police Shooting." April 7. https://www.nytimes.com/video/us/100000003615939/video-shows-fatal-police-shooting.html

Nix, Justin, Bradley Campbell, Edward Byers, and Geoffrey Alpert. 2017. "A Bird's Eye View of Civilians Killed by Police in 2015: Further Evidence of Implicit Bias." *Criminology and Public Policy* 16 (1): 309–40.

Nix, Justin, and John Shjarback. 2021. "Factors Associated with Police Shooting Mortality: A Focus on Race and a Plea for More Comprehensive Data." *PLOS One* 16 (11): e0259024.

Noble, Jeffrey, and Geoffrey Alpert. 2010. "State-Created Danger: Should Police Officers Be Accountable for Reckless Tactical Decision Making?" In *Critical Issues in Policing: Contemporary Readings*, 6th ed., edited by Roger Dunham and Geoffrey Alpert. Long Grove, IL: Waveland Press, 481–95.

Nosek, Brian, Frederick Smyth, N. Sriram, Nicole Lindner, Thierry Devos, Alfonso Ayala, Yoav Bar-Anan, Robin Bergh, Huajian Cai, Karen Gonsalkorale, Selin Kesebir, Norbert Maliszewski, Félix Neto, Eero Olli, Jaihyun Park, Konrad Schnabel, Kimihiro Shiomura, Bogdan Tudor Tulbure, Reinout Wiers, Mónika Somogyi, Nazar Akrami, Bo Ekehammar, Michelangelo Vianello, Mahzarin Banaji, and Anthony Greenwald. 2009. "National Differences in Gender–Science Stereotypes Predict National Sex Differences in Science and Math Achievement." *Proceedings of the National Academy of Science* 106 (26): 10593–97.

Nowacki, Jeffrey. 2015. "Organizational-Level Police Discretion: An Application for Police Use of Lethal Force." *Crime and Delinquency* 61 (5): 643–68.

Obama, Barack. 2016. *Report on the Legal and Policy Frameworks Guiding the United States' Use of Military Force and Related National Security Operations.* https://obamawhitehouse.archives.gov/sites/whitehouse.gov/files/documents/Legal_Policy_Report.pdf

Obasogie, Osagie, and Zachary Newman. 2017. "Police Violence, Use of Force Policies, and Public Health." *American Journal of Law and Medicine* 43 (2–3): 279–95.

Obasogie, Osagie, and Zachary Newman. 2018. "The Futile Fourth Amendment: Understanding Police Excessive Force Doctrine through an Empirical Assessment of *Graham v. Connor.*" *Northwestern University Law Review* 112 (6): 1465–500.

O'Hara, Brian. 2026. "Minneapolis Police Chief O'Hara: We Rebuilt Trust. ICE Is Destroying It." *USA Today*, January 27. https://www.usatoday.com/story/opinion/voices/2026/01/27/minneapolis-police-chief-ice-shootings-public-trust/88338271007/

Olsaretti, Serena. 2018. "Introduction: The Idea of Distributive Justice." In *The Oxford Handbook of Distributive Justice*, edited by Serena Olsaretti. New York: Oxford University Press, 1–10.

Onyeador, Ivuoma, Sa-kiera Hudson, and Neil Lewis Jr. 2021. "Moving beyond Implicit Bias Training: Policy Insights for Increasing Organizational Diversity." *Policy Insights from the Behavioral and Brain Sciences* 8 (1): 19–26.

Oramas Mora, Daniela, William Terrill, and Jacob Foster. 2023. "A Decade of Police Use of Deadly Force Research (2011–2020)." *Homicide Studies* 27 (1): 6–33.

Oswald, Frederick, Gregory Mitchell, Hart Blanton, James Jaccard, and Philip Tetlock. 2013. "Predicting Ethnic and Racial Discrimination: A Meta-Analysis of IAT Criterion Studies." *Journal of Personality and Social Psychology* 105 (2): 171–92.

Otsuka, Michael. 1994. "Killing the Innocent in Self-Defense." *Philosophy and Public Affairs* 23 (1): 74–94.

Otsuka, Michael. 2016. "The Moral-Responsibility Account of Liability to Defensive Killing." In *The Ethics of Self-Defense*, edited by Christian Coons and Michael Weber. New York: Oxford University Press, 51–68.

Ousey, Graham. 1999. "Homicide, Structural Factors, and the Racial Invariance Assumption." *Criminology* 37 (2): 405–26.

Page, Jennifer. 2019. "Reparations for Police Killings." *Perspectives on Politics* 17 (4): 958–72.

Page, Jennifer. 2023. "Defensive Killing by Police: Analyzing Uncertain Threat Scenarios." *Journal of Ethics and Social Philosophy* 24 (3): 315–51.

Pallotto, Bret. 2021. "State College Responds to Osagie Lawsuit, Citing Officers' Experience and Training." *Centre Daily Times*, January 5. https://www.centredaily.com/article248266965.html

Palmer, Chris. 2019. "It Should Be Unconstitutional When Police Officers Kill Fleeing Felony Suspects, Philly DA's Office Says." *Philadelphia Inquirer*, December 5. https:// www.inquirer.com/news/ryan-pownall-police-shooting- david-jones-larry-krasner-20191205.html

Paluck, Elizabeth, Roni Porat, Chelsey Clark, and Donald Green. 2021. "Prejudice Reduction: Progress and Challenges." *Annual Review of Psychology* 72: 533–60.

Parfit, Derek. 2002. "Equality or Priority?" In *The Ideal of Equality*, edited by Matthew Clayton and Andrew Williams. New York: Palgrave Macmillan, 81–125.

Park, Haeyoun, and Robin Lindsay. 2015. "A Timeline of the Tamir Rice Shooting." *New York Times*, January 22. https://www.nytimes.com/video/us/100000003464054/a-timeline-of-the-tamir-rice-shooting.html

Patil, Shefali. 2018. "Public Support for the Punishment of Police Use of Force Errors: Evidence of Ideological Divergence and Convergence." *Police Quarterly* 21 (3): 358–86.

Payne, B. Keith, and Jason Hannay. 2021. "Implicit Bias Reflects Systemic Racism." *Trends in Cognitive Sciences* 25 (11): 927–36.

Pearson v. Callahan. 2009. 555 US 223.

Pennsylvania General Assembly. 2019. "House Bill 1664." https://www.legis.state.pa.us/cfdocs/billInfo/billInfo.cfm?sYear=2019&sInd=0&body=h&type=b&bn=1664

Pennsylvania General Assembly. 2025. Pennsylvania Consolidated Statutes. https://www.palegis.us/statutes/consolidated

Peralta, Eyder, and Cheryl Corley. 2016. "The Driving Life and Death of Philando Castile." NPR, July 15. https://www.npr.org/sections/thetwo-way/2016/07/15/485835272/the-driving-life-and-death-of-philando-castile

Perez, Nicholas, and Emilie Whitehouse. 2024. "Incident Characteristics of Forcible Entry Warrant Raids in the USA (2010–6)." *Policing: A Journal of Policy and Practice* 18: paae129.

Peterson, Ruth, and Lauren Krivo. 2005. "Macrostructural Analyses of Race, Ethnicity, and Violent Crime: Recent Lessons and New Directions for Future Research." *Annual Review of Sociology* 31: 331–56.

Philadelphia Police Department. 2024. "Directive 10.1: Use of Force—Involving the Discharge of Firearms." July 23. https://www.phillypolice.com/wp-content/uploads/2021/05/D10.1-REV-7-23-24-REDACTED-1.pdf

Phillips, Julie. 2002. "White, Black, and Latino Homicide Rates: Why the Difference?" *Social Problems* 49 (3): 349–73.

Pickard, Hanna. 2015. "Psychopathology and the Ability to Do Otherwise." *Philosophy and Phenomenological Research* 90 (1): 135–63.

Pickering, Jordan, and David Klinger. 2016. "Enhancing Police Legitimacy by Promoting Safety Culture." In *The Politics of Policing: Between Force and Legitimacy*, edited by Mathieu Deflem. Bingley, UK: Emerald, 21–39.

Pierson, Emma, Camelia Simoiu, Jan Overgoor, Sam Corbett-Davies, Daniel Jenson, Amy Shoemaker, Vignesh Ramachandran, Phoebe Barghouty, Cheryl Phillips, Ravi Shroff, and Sharad Goel. 2020. "A Large-Scale Analysis of Racial Disparities in Police Stops across the United States." *Nature Human Behaviour* 4 (7): 736–45.

Police Executive Research Forum. 2016. *Guiding Principles on Police Force*. https://www.poli ceforum.org/assets/guidingprinciples1.pdf

Policing Project. 2025. "Policing Project Commends the Supreme Court's Unanimous Decision in *Barnes v. Felix*, Citation to Our Amicus Brief." May 15. https://www.policing project.org/news-main/2025/4/10/nqnd1nid2h7uegopn9rrm3sl8q7xlh-pc99n-g9twx

Powell, Zachary, and Sishi Wu. 2025. "Supreme Court Decisions and Fatal Officer-Involved Shootings." *Policing: A Journal of Policy and Practice* 19: paaf003.

Pratt, Travis, and Francis Cullen. 2005. "Assessing Macro-Level Predictors and Theories of Crime: A Meta-Analysis." *Crime and Justice* 32: 373–450.

Project Implicit. 2024. "Take a Test." https://implicit.harvard.edu/implicit/selectatest.html

Quinn, Warren. 1989. "Actions, Intentions, and Consequences: The Doctrine of Doing and Allowing." *Philosophical Review* 98 (3): 287–312.

Quong, Jonathan. 2009. "Killing in Self-Defense." *Ethics* 119 (3): 507–37.

Quong, Jonathan. 2012. "Liability to Defensive Harm." *Philosophy and Public Affairs* 40 (1): 45–77.

Quong, Jonathan. 2020. *The Morality of Defensive Force*. New York: Oxford University Press.

Quong, Jonathan. 2023. "Legitimate Injustice: A Response to Wellman." *Journal of Political Philosophy* 31 (2): 222–32.

Raim, Sam. 2024. "Police Are Stopping Fewer Drivers—and It's Increasing Safety." Vera Institute, January 11. https://www.vera.org/news/police-are-stopping-fewer-drivers-and-its-increasing-safety

Ratner, Steven. 2007. "Predator and Prey: Seizing and Killing Suspected Terrorists Abroad." *Journal of Political Philosophy* 15 (3): 251–75.

Rawls, John. 1999. *A Theory of Justice*, rev. ed. Cambridge, MA: Harvard University Press.

Reidy, Thomas, Jon Sorensen, and Mark Cunningham. 2013. "Probability of Criminal Acts of Violence: A Test of Jury Predictive Accuracy." *Behavioral Sciences and the Law* 31 (2): 286–305.

Reiman, Jeffrey. 1985. "The Social Contract and the Police Use of Deadly Force." In *Moral Issues in Police Work*, edited by Frederick Elliston and Michael Feldberg. Totowa, NJ: Rowman and Allanheld, 237–49.

Richards v. Wisconsin. 1997. 520 US 385.

Risi, Joseph, and Corina Graif. 2024. "Community Representation and Policing: Effects on Black Civilians." *Criminology* 62 (3): 454–502.

Robeyns, Ingrid. 2005. "The Capability Approach: A Theoretical Survey." *Journal of Human Development* 6 (1): 93–114.

Robinson, Paul. 1982. "Criminal Law Defenses: A Systematic Analysis." *Columbia Law Review* 82 (2): 199–291.

Robinson, Paul. 1985. "Causing the Conditions of One's Own Defense: A Study in the Limits of Theory in Criminal Law Doctrine." *Virginia Law Review* 71 (1): 1–63.

Rodin, David. 2002. *War and Self-Defense*. New York: Oxford University Press.

Rodin, David. 2011. "Justifying Harm." *Ethics* 122 (1): 74–110.

Rogers, Katie, and Hamed Aleaziz. 2026. "Trump and Federal Officials Try to Blame Minnesota Authorities and Slain Man." *New York Times*, January 24. https://www.nytimes.com/2026/01/24/us/trump-administration-minneapolis-shooting.html

Rogers, Michael, Dale McNiel, and Renée Binder. 2019. "Effectiveness of Police Crisis Intervention Training Programs." *Journal of the American Academy of Psychiatry and the Law* 47 (4): 414–21.

Rogna, Marco, and Bich Diep Nguyen. 2022. "Firearms Law and Fatal Police Shootings: A Panel Data Analysis." *Applied Economics* 54 (27): 3121–37.

Ross, Cody, Bruce Winterhalder, and Richard McElreath. 2021. "Racial Disparities in Police Use of Deadly Force against Unarmed Individuals Persist after Appropriately Benchmarking Shooting Data on Violent Crime Rates." *Social Psychological and Personality Sciences* 12 (3): 323–32.

Rothstein, Richard. 2017. *The Color of Law: A Forgotten History of How Our Government Segregated America.* New York: Liveright.

Rushin, Stephen. 2019. "Police Disciplinary Appeals." *University of Pennsylvania Law Review* 167 (3): 545–610.

Saleh, Amam, Paul Appelbaum, Xiaoyu Liu, T. Scott Stroup, and Melanie Wall. 2018. "Deaths of People with Mental Illness during Interactions with Law Enforcement." *International Journal of Law and Psychiatry* 58: 110–16.

Sampson, Robert, Jeffrey Morenoff, and Stephen Raudenbush. 2005. "Social Anatomy of Racial and Ethnic Disparities in Violence." *American Journal of Public Health* 95 (2): 224–32.

Sampson, Robert, William Wilson, and Hannah Katz. 2018. "Reassessing 'Toward a Theory of Race, Crime, and Urban Inequality.'" *Du Bois Review* 15 (1): 13–34.

Sandel, William, M. Hunter Martaindale, and J. Pete Blair. 2021. "A Scientific Examination of the 21-Foot Rule." *Police Practice and Research* 22 (3): 1314–29.

Sangero, Boaz. 2006. *Self-Defence in Criminal Law.* Portland: Hart Publishing.

Sarasota County Sheriff's Office. 2018. "News Release 18-034." February 20. https://web.arch ive.org/web/20190706115646/

Sariaslan, Amir, Louise Arseneault, Henrik Larsson, Paul Lichtenstein, and Seena Fazel. 2020. "Risk of Subjection to Violence and Perpetration of Violence in Persons with Psychiatric Disorders in Sweden." *JAMA Psychiatry* 77 (4): 359–67.

Savage, Charlie. 2026. "Killings in Minneapolis Invert Usual Dynamic over Policing the Police." *New York Times*, January 26. https://www.nytimes.com/2026/01/26/us/politics/minneapo lis-killings-federal-state-police.html

Schmidtz, David. 2006. *Elements of Justice.* New York: Cambridge University Press.

Schwartz, Joanna. 2014. "Police Indemnification." *New York University Law Review* 89 (3): 885–1005.

Schwartz, Joanna. 2017. "How Qualified Immunity Fails." *Yale Law Journal* 127 (2): 2–76.

Scott v. Harris. 2007. 550 US 372.

Scully, Jackie Leach. 2013. "Disability and Vulnerability: On Bodies, Dependence, and Power." In *Vulnerability: New Essays in Ethics and Feminist Philosophy*, edited by Catriona Mackenzie, Wendy Rogers, and Susan Dodds. New York: Oxford University Press, 204–21.

Shao, Elena, Arijeta Lajka, Helmuth Rosales, and Raj Saha. 2026. "Videos Showing Aggressive ICE Tactics in Minnesota Fuel a Backlash." *New York Times*, January 24. https://www.nyti mes.com/interactive/2026/01/24/us/minnesota-ice-violence-tactics-videos.html

Sharkey, Patrick. 2018. *Uneasy Peace: The Great Crime Decline, the Renewal of City Life, and the Next War on Violence.* New York: W. W. Norton and Company.

Shelby, Tommie. 2016. *Dark Ghettos: Injustice, Dissent, and Reform.* Cambridge, MA: Harvard University Press.

Sherman, Lawrence. 1980. "Execution without Trial: Police Homicide and the Constitution." *Vanderbilt Law Review* 33 (1): 71–100.

Sherman, Lawrence. 1983. "Reducing Police Gun Use: Critical Events, Administrative Policy, and Organizational Change." In *Control in the Police Organization*, edited by Maurice Punch. Cambridge, MA: MIT Press, 98–125.

Sherman, Lawrence. 2018. "Reducing Fatal Police Shootings as System Clashes: Research, Theory, and Practice." *Annual Review of Criminology* 1: 421–49.

Shjarback, John, and Julie Ward. 2025. "Moving Targets: An Examination of Departmental Deadly Force Policies and Police Shootings at Vehicles." *Policing: A Journal of Policy and Practice* 19: paaf004.

Shjarback, John, Michael White, and Stephen Bishopp. 2021. "Can Police Shootings Be Reduced by Requiring Officers to Document When They Point Firearms at Citizens?" *Injury Prevention* 27 (6): 508–13.

Sierra-Arévalo, Michael. 2024. *The Danger Imperative: Violence, Death, and the Soul of Policing.* New York: Columbia University Press.

Simes, Jessica, Bruce Western, and Angela Lee. 2022. "Mental Health Disparities in Solitary Confinement." *Criminology* 60 (3): 538–75.

Sims, S. Lamar. 2015. "Investigation into the Officer-Involved Shooting of Tamir Rice." https://www.google.com/url?sa=t&rct=j&q=&esrc=s&source=web&cd=10&ved=2ahUKEwjHxvKG-PXdAhUNpFkKHQbdC2MQFjAJegQIBRAC&url=https%3A%2F%2Fcdn3.vox-cdn.com%2Fuploads%2Fchorus_asset%2Ffile%2F4149926%2FColorado_prosecutor_Tamir_Rice.0.pdf&usg=AOvVaw01HEYIF-mcvT-F4x36VxCw

Singer, Peter. 1972. "Famine, Affluence, and Morality." *Philosophy and Public Affairs* 1 (3): 229–43.

Smith, Michael. 1997. "Police Use of Deadly Force: How Courts and Policy-Makers Have Misapplied *Tennessee v. Garner.*" *Kansas Journal of Law and Public Policy* 7 (2): 100–21.

Smith, Michael. 2022. "Reimagining the Use of Force by Police in a Post-Floyd Nation." *Police Quarterly* 25 (2): 228–51.

Smith, Mitch. 2016. "Philando Castile's Last Night: Tacos and Laughs, Then a Drive." *New York Times*, July 12. https://www.nytimes.com/2016/07/13/us/philando-castile-minnesota-police-shooting.html

Sonmez, Felicia, Paul Kane, and Rhonda Colvin. 2020. "House Passes Broad Police Reform Legislation in Wake of George Floyd's Killing." *Washington Post*, June 25. https://www.washingtonpost.com/powerpost/house-poised-to-pass-broad-police-reform-legislation-in-wake-of-george-floyds-killing/2020/06/25/445307f8-b5ed-11ea-a8da-693df3d7674a_story.html

Spencer, Katherine, Amanda Charbonneau, and Jack Glaser. 2016. "Implicit Bias and Policing." *Social and Personality Psychology Compass* 10 (1): 50–63.

State v. Bush. 1982. 307 NC 152.

State v. Moore. 1975. 112 AZ 271.

Steffensmeier, Darrell, Jeffrey Ulmer, Ben Feldmeyer, and Casey Harris. 2010. "Scope and Conceptual Issues in Testing the Race—Crime Invariance Thesis: Black, White, and Hispanic Comparisons." *Criminology* 48 (4): 1133–69.

Stein, Robin, Devon Lum, Dmitriy Khavin, Alexander Cardia, Aric Toler, and Jeff Bernier. 2026. "Video Analysis of ICE Shooting Sheds Light on Contested Final Moments." *New York Times*, January 15. https://www.nytimes.com/video/us/100000010648638/ice-shooting-renee-good-minneapolis-videos-analysis.html

Stevenson, Bryan. 2017. "A Presumption of Guilt: The Legacy of America's History of Racial Injustice." In *Policing the Black Man: Arrest, Prosecution, and Imprisonment*, edited by Angela J. Davis. New York: Pantheon Books, 3–30.

Stoughton, Seth. 2015. "Law Enforcement's 'Warrior' Problem." *Harvard Law Review Forum* 128 (6): 225–34.

Stoughton, Seth. 2016. "Principled Policing: Warrior Cops and Guardian Officers." *Wake Forest Law Review* 51: 611–76.

Stoughton, Seth. 2021. "How the Fourth Amendment Frustrates the Regulation of Police Violence." *Emory Law Journal* 70 (3): 521–85.

Stoughton, Seth, Jeffrey Noble, and Geoffrey Alpert. 2020. *Evaluating Police Uses of Force.* New York: New York University Press.

Subramanian, Ram, and Leily Arzy. 2021. "State Policing Reforms since George Floyd's Murder." Brennan Center for Justice, May 21. https://www.brennancenter.org/our-work/research-reports/state-policing-reforms-george-floyds-murder

Swanson, Jeffrey, and Mark Rosenberg. 2023. "American Gun Violence and Mental Illness: Reducing Risk, Restoring Health, Respecting Rights and Reviving Communities." *Daedalus* 152 (4): 45–74.

Tadros, Victor. 2009. "Poverty and Criminal Responsibility." *Journal of Value Inquiry* 43 (3): 391–413.

Tennenbaum, Abraham. 1994. "The Influence of the *Garner* Decision on Police Use of Deadly Force." *Journal of Criminal Law and Criminology* 85 (1): 241–60.

Tennessee v. Garner. 1985. 471 US 1.

Thacher, David. 2024. "Policing a Neurodiverse World: Lessons from the Social Model of Disability." *Policing: A Journal of Policy and Practice* 18: paae012.

Thomson, Judith Jarvis. 1991. "Self-Defense." *Philosophy and Public Affairs* 20 (4): 283–310.

Tregle, Brandon, Justin Nix, and Geoffrey Alpert. 2019. "Disparity Does Not Mean Bias: Making Sense of Observed Racial Disparities in Fatal Officer-Involved Shootings with Multiple Benchmarks." *Journal of Crime and Justice* 42 (1): 18–31.

United Nations. 1990. *Basic Principles on the Use of Force and Firearms by Law Enforcement Officials.* Office of the High Commissioner for Human Rights. https://www.ohchr.org/en/professionalinterest/pages/useofforceandfirearms.aspx

Unnever, James. 2018. "The Racial Invariance Thesis." In *Building a Black Criminology: Race, Theory, and Crime,* edited by James Unnever, Shaun Gabbidon, and Cecilia Chouhy. New York: Routledge, 77–100.

Unnever, James, J. C. Barnes, and Francis Cullen. 2016. "The Racial Invariance Thesis Revisited: Testing an African American Theory of Offending." *Journal of Contemporary Criminal Justice* 32 (1): 7–26.

Unnever, James, Akwasi Owusu-Bempah, and Rustu Deryol. 2019. "A Test of the Differential Involvement Hypothesis." *Race and Justice* 9 (2): 197–224.

US Department of Justice. 1995a. "Commentary Regarding the Use of Deadly Force in Non-Custodial Situations." October 17. https://www.justice.gov/archives/ag/attorney-general-october-17-1995-memorandum-resolution-14-attachment-1

US Department of Justice. 1995b. "Policy Statement: Use of Deadly Force." October 17. https://www.justice.gov/archives/ag/attorney-general-october-17-1995-memorandum-resolution-14-attachment-0

US Department of Justice. 2012. *Investigation of the Portland Police Bureau.* September 12. https://www.justice.gov/iso/opa/resources/9362012917111254750409.pdf

US Department of Justice. 2014. *Investigation of the Cleveland Division of Police.* December 4. https://www.justice.gov/sites/default/files/opa/press-releases/attachments/2014/12/04/cleveland_division_of_police_findings_letter.pdf

US Department of Justice. 2016. *Investigation of the Baltimore City Police Department.* August 10. https://www.justice.gov/crt/file/883296/download

US Department of Justice. 2022. "Department of Justice Policy on Use of Force." July. https://www.justice.gov/jm/1-16000-department-justice-policy-use-force

US Department of Justice. 2023. *Investigation of the City of Minneapolis and the Minneapolis Police Department.* June 16. https://www.justice.gov/opa/press-release/file/1587661/dl

Vallentyne, Peter. 2007. "Distributive Justice." In *A Companion to Contemporary Political Philosophy,* 2nd ed., edited by Robert Goodin, Philip Pettit, and Thomas Pogge. Malden, MA: Blackwell Publishers, 548–62.

Van Dorn, Richard, Jan Volavka, and Norman Johnson. 2012. "Mental Disorder and Violence: Is There a Relationship beyond Substance Abuse?" *Social Psychiatry and Psychiatric Epidemiology* 47 (3): 487–503.

Van Shoelandt, Chad, and Gerald Gaus. 2018. "Political and Distributive Justice." In *The Oxford Handbook of Distributive Justice*, edited by Serena Olsaretti. New York: Oxford University Press, 283–305.

Venice Gondolier. 2020. "'It's a Tragic Situation' Woman Shot, Killed by Officer." August 3. https://www.yoursun.com/venice/its-a-tragic-situation-woman-shot-killed-by-officer/article_99db8ee8-d5bf-11ea-b58b-6f34e52a8098.html

Virginia General Assembly. 2025. Code of Virginia. https://law.lis.virginia.gov/vacode/

Walzer, Michael. 1983. *Spheres of Justice: A Defense of Pluralism and Equality*. New York: Basic Books.

Walzer, Michael. 2021. "Soldiers and Police." In *The Ethics of Policing: New Perspectives on Law Enforcement*, edited by Ben Jones and Eduardo Mendieta. New York: New York University Press, 93–106.

Ward, Geoff. 2018. "Living Histories of White Supremacist Policing: Towards Transformative Justice." *Du Bois Review* 15 (1): 167–84.

Ward, Julie, Rebecca Fix, Javier Cepeda, Paul Nestadt, and Cassandra Crifasi. Forthcoming. "Mental and Behavioral Health Characteristics among Individuals Injuriously Shot by Police in the United States." *Journal of Mental Health*. https://doi.org/10.1080/09638237.2025.2585191

Ward, Paula Reed. 2019. "Teen Pleads Guilty to N. Braddock Drive-By that Preceded Antwon Rose Shooting." *Pittsburgh Post-Gazette*, March 15. https://www.post-gazette.com/news/crime-courts/2019/03/15/zaijuan-hester-antwon-rose-north-braddock-drive-by-shooting-police-rosfeld-east-pittsburgh/stories/201903150073

Washington Post. 2024. "Fatal Force." https://www.washingtonpost.com/graphics/investigations/police-shootings-database/

Watson, Amy, and Jennifer Wood. 2017. "Everyday Police Work during Mental Health Encounters: A Study of Call Resolutions in Chicago and Their Implications for Diversion." *Behavioral Sciences and the Law* 35 (5–6): 442–55.

Weaver, Vesla, Andrew Papachristos, and Michael Zanger-Tishler. 2019. "The Great Decoupling: The Disconnection between Criminal Offending and Experience of Arrest across Two Cohorts." *RSF: The Russell Sage Foundation Journal of the Social Sciences* 5 (1): 89–123.

Weisburd, David, and Malay Majmundar, eds. 2018. *Proactive Policing: Effects on Crime and Communities*. Washington, DC: National Academies Press. https://doi.org/10.17226/24928

Weitzer, Ronald. 2002. "Incidents of Police Misconduct and Public Opinion." *Journal of Criminal Justice* 30 (5): 397–408.

Wen, Hefei, Jason Hockenberry, and Janet Cummings. 2017. "The Effect of Medicaid Expansion on Crime Reduction: Evidence from HIFA-Waiver Expansions." *Journal of Public Economics* 154: 67–94.

Williams, Christian. 1984. "Abu Nidal Targets Backers of Mideast Compromise." *Washington Post*, February 5. https://www.washingtonpost.com/archive/politics/1984/02/05/abu-nidal-targets-backers-of-mideast-compromise/06d616a1-710f-4964-8db7-e06fc9917515/

Williams, Timothy, and Mitch Smith. 2015. "Cleveland Officer Will Not Face Charges in Tamir Rice Shooting Death." *New York Times*, December 28. https://www.nytimes.com/2015/12/29/us/tamir-rice-police-shootiing-cleveland.html

Williamson, Vanessa, Kris-Stella Trump, and Katherine Levine Einstein. 2018. "Black Lives Matter: Evidence that Police-Caused Deaths Predict Protest Activity." *Perspectives on Politics* 16 (2): 400–15.

Willis, Haley, Evan Hill, Robin Stein, Christiaan Triebert, Ben Laffin, and Drew Jordan. 2021. "New Footage Shows Delayed Medical Response to George Floyd." *New York Times*, January 6. https://www.nytimes.com/2020/08/11/us/george-floyd-body-cam-full-video.html

Wisconsin State Legislature. 2024. Wisconsin Statutes and Annotations. https://docs.legis.wisconsin.gov/statutes/prefaces/toc

Womack, Morgan, and Drew Johnson. 2026. "Cumberland County Sheriff: ICE Arrest of Corrections Officer Was 'Bush League.'" *Portland Press Herald*, January 22. https://www.pressherald.com/2026/01/22/cumberland-county-corrections-officers-ice-arrest-prompts-criticism-from-sheriff/

Wood, Jennifer, Amy Watson, and Christine Barber. 2021. "What Can We Expect of Police in the Face of Deficient Mental Health Systems? Qualitative Insights from Chicago Police Officers." *Journal of Psychiatric and Mental Health Nursing* 28 (1): 28–42.

Woods, Chris. 2015. "The Story of America's Very First Drone Strike." *Atlantic*, May 30. https://www.theatlantic.com/international/archive/2015/05/america-first-drone-strike-afghanistan/394463/

Woollard, Fiona. 2015. *Doing and Allowing Harm.* New York: Oxford University Press.

Worden, Robert, Cynthia Najdowski, Sarah McLean, Kenan Worden, Nicholas Corsaro, Hannah Cochran, and Robin Engel. 2024. "Implicit Bias Training for Police: Evaluating Impacts on Enforcement Disparities." *Law and Human Behavior* 48 (5–6): 338–55.

Young, Iris Marion. 2011. *Responsibility for Justice.* New York: Oxford University Press.

Yukhnenko, Denis, Nigel Blackwood, Paul Lichtenstein, and Seena Fazel. 2023. "Psychiatric Disorders and Reoffending Risk in Individuals with Community Sentences in Sweden: A National Cohort Study." *Lancet Public Health* 8 (2): e119–29.

Zalman, Marvin, and Robert Norris. 2021. "Measuring Innocence: How to Think about the Rate of Wrongful Conviction." *New Criminal Law Review* 24 (4): 601–54.

Zheng, Robin. 2018. "What Is My Role in Changing the System? A New Model of Responsibility for Structural Injustice." *Ethical Theory and Moral Practice* 21 (4): 869–85.

Zimring, Franklin. 2017. *When Police Kill.* Cambridge, MA: Harvard University Press.

Index

For the benefit of digital users, indexed terms that span two pages (e.g., 52–53) may, on occasion, appear on only one of those pages.

Tables and figures are indicated by an italic *t* and *f* following the page number.

14th Amendment, 172
21-foot rule, 104, 106, 140

Abu Ghraib, 180
account
   culpability, 85, 93–95, 98
   diminished protections, 85, 86, 90–91
   fusion, 86, 98–104, 105, 107–8, 110, 111
   traditional, 85, 86, 92–94, 95
   vulnerability, 86, 95–98, 99
accountability, 10, 99–100, 106, 107, 110, 134,
    143, 150–51, 184
Afghanistan, 21
aggressor, 15, 17, 23–36, 44–47, 56–59, 66–81,
    85–111, 134–35, 140, 144, 152, 158
   innocent, 85, 90–91, 92, 93–95
   vulnerable with diminished culpability, 85–
    87, 89–91, 92, 93–94, 95, 96–110
Alexander, Larry, 94
Ali Qaed Senyan al-Harthi, 110
Allhoff, Fritz, 177
Alpert, Geoffrey, 162
al Qaeda, 21
Americans with Disabilities Act, 110
Argov, Shlomo, 178
Aristotle, 72
Arizona, 144
Atlanta Police Department, 168, 168t
autism, 1, 105–6

Baltimore, MD, 89, 101, 102
   Police Department, 89
Barnes v. Felix, 149
bias, 112, 113, 115–18, 122–23, 127–31
Biden, Joe, 42–43
bipolar disorder. *See* mental illness
Bittner, Egon, 153
Black Americans, 3–4, 7, 53–54, 69–70, 75–76,
    78–79, 112–18, 119, 120–21, 123, 124,
    126–27, 134, 136–37, 185

Black Lives Matter, 2, 4, 5, 120, 131–32, 151, 166
Blue Lives Matter, 5
Brooks, Rosa, 41–42, 59, 60, 61
Brown, David, 7–8
Brown, Michael, 3
burglary, 41, 59, 161, 177
Burri, Susanne, 68
Butler, Paul, 120, 121
bystander, 6, 26, 32, 33–34, 35–37, 43, 101, 112,
    137–38, 140, 155

California, 33
Campaign Zero, 114
Castile, Philando, 63, 79
Central Intelligence Agency (CIA), 21
Cesario, Joseph, 121–22
Chicago, 129
   Police Department, 129, 167, 168t, 173–74
chokehold, 138–39, 142, 150, 151, 183, 184
City and County of San Francisco v. Sheehan,
    110, 150
City of Los Angeles v. Lyons, 150
civil damages, 146, 147, 149–50
civil rights movement, 131–32
civilian crisis response, 11, 86–87
Cleveland, OH, 89, 138
   Division of Police, 145, 162
Colorado, 167
Columbus, OH, 141
Commission on Accreditation for Law
    Enforcement Agencies (CALEA), 167,
    168, 169t
common law, 9, 22, 30–31, 144, 159, 174
Congress (US), 152
consequentialist, 26, 27–28, 46
Constitution (US), 10, 148, 149–50, 152, 155,
    159, 161, 162, 163–64, 172, 182–83
criminal law/codes, 46, 52–53, 92, 146–47, 151,
    155–56, 157–58, 164
criminal penalties, 88, 107, 146–47, 172

Crisis Intervention Team (CIT) training, 105–6
culpability, 9, 17, 46, 56–59, 61–62, 64, 67, 69,
        71, 73–82, 85–103, 108, 111, 125, 144. *See
        also* account
culture, 128

Dallas Police Department, 7–8, 167, 168*t*
decertification, 146, 147, 152
Declaration of Independence, 44
de-escalation, 7, 11, 36, 38, 54–55, 59, 99–100,
        101, 102–7, 109–10, 138, 140, 145, 152,
        166, 182, 183, 185
de Menezes, Jean Charles, 179–80
democracy, 2, 4, 12, 14, 110–11, 144–45, 147,
        151, 153, 185
Denmark, 89
deontological, 26–28, 46
Department of Justice (US), 89, 105–6,
        162, 167
depression. *See* mental illness
differential involvement hypothesis, 113–14,
        119–21, 122–23, 127
disability, 3, 65, 73, 75, 87–88, 89, 108–9, 110
disparate enforcement, 113, 118–23, 127, 129–
        30, 131
distributive justice, 6–9, 16–17, 75, 87–88, 89,
        108–9, 110
doctor, 66, 172
doing/allowing distinction, 156, 169–71, 180
drive-by shooting, 155
drugs, 75–76, 109, 118, 119, 121, 129–30,
        136, 140
Du Bois, W. E. B., 55–56
duty
    negative, 169–70
    positive, 44, 169–70
    to retreat, 9, 36, 54–55, 173

egalitarian, 8, 67, 68, 70, 80, 92–93, 97
equality before the law, 10, 156, 171–74, 180
error
    false-negative, 170–71, 179
    false-positive, 170–71, 179–80
Europe, 88
excuse, 15, 73, 75, 81, 87, 94–95, 97, 144

Fayetteville, NC, 130–31
Federal Bureau of Investigation (FBI), 102, 114,
        115, 167, 173–74
Ferguson, MO, 3
first-person shooter task (FPST), 116–17
fleeing felon rule, 147–48, 152, 153, 159, 161,
        163–64, 175–80, 182

Floyd, George, 3–4, 5, 112, 114, 124
forcible felony, 160, 161
Ford, Shannon Brandt, 176–77, 178
Fourth Amendment, 147–48, 161
France, 175
Fraternal Order of Police (FOP), 42–43,
        165, 182–83
Fullerton, CA, 89

Gallup, 3–4
Garmback, Frank, 138
Garner, Edward, 161, 174–75
Garner, Eric, 138–39
Geneva Conventions, 32, 35
Georgia, 168
Graham v. Connor, 148–49, 150–51, 183
Guardian, 114

harm
    collateral, 33, 130
    grave, 1–2, 5–6, 9, 15, 17, 22, 26–34, 41,
        47–62, 64, 66–67, 73, 78, 85, 90–102, 122,
        141–42, 156–79
    morally weighted, 26–28, 46, 47, 48,
        56, 101–3
Harmon, Rachel, 164, 165
Hispanic, 3, 114–15, 129–30
Holocaust, 12
homelessness, 11, 80, 152, 185
Hosein, Adam, 169–70
Houston Police Department, 167, 168*t*
Hutu, 74

Immigration and Customs Enforcement (ICE),
        184–85
imminence requirement, 17, 31, 156–81, 183
imminent threat, 17, 55–56, 135, 137–38, 139,
        142, 143, 155–80
Implicit Association Test (IAT), 116
International Association of Chiefs of Police
        (IACP), 42–43, 165, 182–83
international humanitarian law, 29–30, 32–33
Iowa, 144

Jewish, 12
Jim Crow, 53–54, 115
Johnson, Norman, 88–89
just aim, 16–17, 22, 24–28, 29–31, 37, 44, 48–49,
        75, 95–96
just war theory. *See* war
justice
    macro-level, 70–73, 76, 78–80, 81
    micro-level, 70–77, 78, 98

Kant, Immanuel, 43–44
King Jr., Martin Luther, 113–14, 124, 125, 131
Knight, Tom, 103–4
Krivo, Lauren, 125–26
Ku Klux Klan, 53–54, 115

lawyer, 172
Lazar, Seth, 77
legitimacy, 2, 39
Leider, Robert, 174–75
Leverick, Fiona, 158
lexical ordering, 57–58, 60, 61
liability, 32, 67, 75–77, 86, 92, 93, 94, 95, 96–97,
    98, 99, 100
libertarian, 8
Locke, Amir, 140
Loehmann, Timothy, 138
London, 178, 179–80
Los Angeles, 3, 149, 150
luck-egalitarian, 68

Mac Donald, Heather, 120, 122–23, 125, 127
Manhattan. *See* New York City, NY
Marcus, Nancy, 162
Maryland, 89, 119
Massachusetts, 166, 167
McMahan, Jeff, 32, 67, 68, 95, 96, 99
Medlock, Harold, 130–31
Memphis, TN, 112, 119, 128
mental health, 1–2, 3–4, 7–8, 17, 80, 85–88, 92,
    101, 102–11, 182, 185
mental illness, 1, 3, 7, 11, 17, 69–70, 73, 76–77,
    78, 85–111, 150, 152, 182, 185
    bipolar disorder, 87–88
    depression, 3–4, 87–88
    psychotic disorders, 87–88, 91
    schizophrenia, 1, 87–88, 89
Merzouk, Nahel, 175
Metropolitan Police Department (Washington,
    DC), 33, 34, 41
military, 22–25, 29–39, 95, 96
Miller, Seumas, 49–51, 53–54, 161–62
Minneapolis, MN, 3–4, 112, 140, 184–85
    Police Department, 105–6
Model Penal Code, 34–35, 47, 48, 92, 144, 158
Monaghan, Jake, 108
Montague, Phillip, 66–67, 69
moral consideration, 11, 16–17, 26, 39–40, 50,
    64, 71, 73, 95, 98, 170, 180
Mullenix v. Luna, 150

National Consensus Policy on Use of Force,
    42–43, 45, 48, 165–66, 167

National Vital Statistics System, 114
Native Americans, 3, 114–15
Nazi, 25
necessity, 2, 5–6, 15, 17, 27–31, 37–38, 41–55,
    66–77, 90–108, 121, 133–53, 155–67, 168*t*,
    170–80, 183
    narrow, 35–36
    wide, 35, 36–37
New York City, NY, 89, 130, 138–39
    Police Department, 58, 128, 130, 139, 141
Nichols, Tyre, 5, 112, 119, 128
Noble, Jeffrey, 162
no-knock raids/warrants, 6, 118, 136, 140, 142,
    150, 151
North Carolina, 130–31, 144

obligation
    individual, 17, 69, 71
    institutional, 9, 17, 37, 38–39, 122
O'Connor, Day Sandra, 148–49
Orellana-Peralta, Valentina, 33
Osagie, Osaze, 1–2, 182
Otsuka, Michael, 90–91

Pantaleo, Daniel, 138–39
Peace Officer Standards and Training (POST),
    152
Pearson v. Callahan, 149–50
Pennsylvania, 1, 52–53, 85, 155, 159, 160–61,
    163–64, 166, 181
Pennsylvania Legislative Black Caucus, 166
Peterson, Ruth, 125–26
Philadelphia, PA, 85, 102
Pittsburgh, PA, 155
pluralism, 8
police administrators/chiefs, 2, 17, 81, 103–6,
    110, 111, 115–16, 130–31, 134, 145–46, 151
Police Executive Research Forum (PERF),
    42–43, 182–83
police-generated killings, 17, 133–34, 137–42,
    143–47, 150–52
policymakers, 12–13, 17, 69, 82, 115–16, 131–
    32, 151, 156, 171, 180, 184, 185
Portland, OR, 89
Pretti, Alex, 184
prioritarian, 80, 92–93, 97, 99
proportionality, 16, 22–23, 24, 25, 26–28, 31, 44,
    46, 69, 73, 92, 101, 102–3, 159, 166–67
    narrow, 32–33, 34–35
    wide, 32–33, 34–35, 36–37
protection of life, 2, 5–6, 10, 16–17, 42–45, 48,
    56, 61, 62, 80, 134–37, 144–45, 154, 158,
    160, 175–80, 183, 184–85

psychotic disorders. *See* mental illness
punishment, 23–24, 92

qualified immunity, 10, 110, 149–50, 152, 175
Quong, Jonathan, 68, 69–70, 72

racial invariance thesis, 125–27
racism
    structural/systemic, 87, 114, 120, 122–27, 131
Rawls, John, 8, 57, 65
Reconstruction, 53–54, 131–32
reflective equilibrium, 12, 13
reform, 105, 111, 114, 127–32, 134, 149, 151–54,
    161, 182, 184, 185
retreat, 55–56, 62, 110. *See also* duty, to retreat
retribution, 23–24
Rice, Tamir, 133, 138, 139, 140, 145, 150–51
Richards v. Wisconsin, 136, 150
right to life, 4, 16–17, 29, 42, 44–45, 48–56
Rodin, David, 94
Rose II, Antwon, 155, 159, 166
Rosfeld, Michael, 155
Russia, 25
Rwanda, 74
Said, Hussein, 178
Saint Paul, MN, 63
San Francisco, CA, 110, 150
Sarasota, FL, 103–4, 104*f*, 106
schizophrenia. *See* mental illness
Scott v. Harris, 149, 150
Scott, Walter, 133, 147
Second World War. *See* war
self-defense, 9, 11, 16–17, 21–25, 29–40, 49–50,
    66–74, 134, 143–45, 157–58, 164
September 11th, 58
Sheehan, Teresa, 110–11, 150
Sherman, Lawrence, 145, 180–81
Slager, Michael, 133
Smith, Michael, 162
soldiers, 22–23, 24, 25, 29–30, 32, 33, 34, 35–
    36, 38–39
    child, 95–98, 99
South America, 14
South Carolina, 115, 133
State College, PA, 1
Stephenson, Adrean, 103–5, 104*f*, 106–
    7, 110–11
Stevenson, Bryan, 1, 79
Stonewall, 180

stop and frisk, 129–30, 136–37
Stoughton, Seth, 162
structural/systemic racism. *See* racism
Supreme Court (US), 30, 34–35, 53, 110,
    147–50, 152, 155, 159, 161, 164, 175,
    180, 182–83
Supreme Court of North Carolina, 144

Taylor, Breonna, 4
Tennessee, 162
Tennessee v. Garner, 30, 34–35, 53, 147–49, 155,
    156, 159, 182
terrorist, 21, 58, 179–80, 184
Thomas, Kelly, 89
Trump Administration, 184
Tutsi, 74

Ukraine, 25
uncertainty, 8, 11, 16–17, 34, 42, 56–62, 108,
    148–49, 158, 159, 177, 181
United Kingdom (UK), 102, 104–5, 109–10,
    140, 151
United Nations (UN), 42–43
Universal Declaration of Human Rights,
    44, 172
USS Cole, 21

Van Dorn, Richard, 88–89
Volavka, Jan, 88–89
vulnerability, 8–9, 17, 64, 75–76, 78–82, 86–100,
    105, 111, 122, 127, 185. *See also* account

Walker Jr., Ricky, 101–2
Wallace Jr., Walter, 85, 102–3, 107–8, 110–11
Walzer, Michael, 42–43
war
    just war theory, 25, 29–30, 32–33, 36–37, 39
    Second World, 25
warrior policing, 58–59, 60, 61, 62
Washington, DC. *See* Metropolitan Police
    Department
Washington Post, 5, 114, 178
White Americans, 112, 114–15, 117–18,
    119, 126–27
Wisconsin, 150, 157–58

Yanez, Jeronimo, 63
Yemen, 21
Young, Ta'Kiya, 141